VENTURI, RAUCH & SCOTT BROWN

John Rauch, Denise Scott Brown and Robert Venturi, 1985

Stanislaus von Moos

VENTURI, RAUCH & SCOTT BROWN

Buildings and Projects

RIZZOLI
NEW YORK

Front cover: Gordon Wu Hall, Butler College,
Princeton University (1980)
Back cover: House in Tuckers Town, Bermuda (1975)

Translation from the German by David Antal
German-language edition, *Venturi, Rauch & Scott Brown*
Copyright © 1987 by Office du Livre S.A., Fribourg, Switzerland

English translation:
Copyright © 1987 by Office du Livre S.A., Fribourg, Switzerland

First published in the United States of America in 1987 by:
Rizzoli International Publications, Inc.
597 Fifth Avenue/New York, NY 10017

Library of Congress Cataloging-in-Publication Data

Moos, Stanislaus von.
  Venturi, Rauch, and Scott Brown buildings and
projects

  Bibliography: p.
  Includes index.
  1. Venturi, Rauch, and Scott Brown—Criticism and
interpretation. 2. Architecture, Modern—20th
century—United States. 3. Architecture, Postmodern—
United States. I. Title.
NA 737.V45M6 1987   720'.92'2   86-42713
ISBN 0-8478-0743-6
ISBN 0-8478-0745-2 (pbk.)

Printed and bound in Japan

Contents

Foreword

In the early 1970s, showing sympathy for, or even siding with, the Venturis and their cause was tantamount to belonging to a forbidden sect, at least if one happened to belong, however marginally, to the architectural academe of the American East Coast. That time marked the appearance of *Learning from Las Vegas* (by Robert Venturi, Denise Scott Brown, and Steven Izenour), a book that taught me—and not a few of my students at the Department of Visual and Environmental Studies at Harvard, where I was an assistant professor from 1971 to 1975—to look afresh at the visual results of the "ersatz culture" typical of the American commercial strip. At any rate, it turned out to be an important milestone along the road of my own bittersweet discovery of America.

It was the Venturis who opened a generation's eyes to the reality of popular American everyday culture and to the echoes of the authentic visual traditions it contains, albeit in distorted form. Today, however, it seems to me that the merit of even that achievement is surpassed by their contribution as designers of extraordinarily relevant works of architecture. Thus, it is high time for the kind of preliminary survey attempted in the present book.

Of course, I regret that I cannot prevent this book from being misunderstood as a plea for postmodern architecture or being used as a mere treasure trove of superficial, formal borrowings.

Berlin, June 1986   Stanislaus von Moos

8

PART I:

THE CHALLENGE
OF THE STATUS QUO

5 Points on the Architecture of VRSB

1 History and "Common Sense"

The facade of a Palladian villa, the complicated spatial geometry of American country manors of the 1880s, marble encrustations of the cosmati, Le Corbusier's white villas, and the unrelieved monotony of a shopping center's parking lot after business hours—these are a few of the architectural images evoked in the buildings by Venturi, Rauch and Scott Brown, as if the intent were to recapture the totality of historical experience, not as an encyclopedic inventory of all there has ever been—much less as a reconstruction of it—but rather expressly as reminders, as consciously fictive tableaux.

It is the eye that takes in this visual inventory for us. The intent of this observation is not to relegate the work of the Venturis to the realm of a noncommittal aestheticism. The compelling appropriation of history and everyday reality in their work has been linked by the architects themselves to matters of social concern and cultural relevance, matters to be discussed in the following pages. The themes involved are deeply rooted in the intellectual discussion of the 1960s. At that time, architecture was again eagerly in search of a new cultural identity in a period of social and economic crisis, and it believed to have found that identity in disciplines such as history, psychology, sociology, and linguistics. Robert Venturi's first book, *Complexity and Contradiction in Architecture* (1966), remains one of the relevant outcomes of this reorientation, probably thanks not least to the precise formulation of his question and to the straightforward presentation of his arguments.

The book is an attempt to put criteria of literary theory to use in the aesthetic analysis of architecture. In the introduction, Vincent Scully wrote that it was "probably the most important architectural program since Le Corbusier's *Vers une architecture* of 1923."[1] Its sources included William Empson's *Seven Types of Ambiguity* and concepts drawn from T. S. Eliot, Kenneth Burke, Cleanth Brooks, and others.[2] The main objective was to set up a system of aesthetic principles that could be used to evaluate and to criticize the architect's own work while it was still on the drawing board. The decisive result of the endeavor, though, was that it broke a spell that Modernist ideological convention had cast over what was said and written about architecture, a spell that had threatened to tie down architects in their increasingly dubious role as social "visionaries," expert solvers of technical problems, and guarantors of permanent aesthetic innovation.

The Architect as Observer

From the literary aesthetics of complexity and contradiction that interested Venturi, new priorities did indeed emerge. The question was not so much how to "solve" (and thereby eliminate) complicated problems of a technical, social, or economic nature with the simplest means possible (in the way Le Corbusier wanted to "solve" the problems arising from the desperate living conditions in the center of Paris by simply building office towers there). Rather, the question was how to design while allowing for the existence of such problems. Such an outlook can be both artistically more promising for the designer and, in many cases, socially more responsible than modern architecture's classical problem-solving approach adopted from social engineering and the natural sciences. Thus it was that Venturi's "literary" approach almost inevitably converged in surprising ways with the empirical interests of American urban sociology as these were developed by authors like Melvin Webber and Herbert Gans in the 1960s.

This affinity was to become the foundation for the intellectual production of Venturi's office. Denise Scott Brown, the architect's wife and partner since 1967 and an architect and planner highly familiar with urban social issues and sociological methodologies, saw to it that their discourse, based as it was on the literary essay, came to be underpinned by the arguments of empirical sociology. This underpinning is evident in the second book, *Learning from*

Las Vegas, which appeared in 1972.[3] In terms of Wolf Lepenies's image of the "three cultures" among which the world of liberal arts is divided, the Venturis' thought has continuously moved away from the paradigms of the natural sciences to adopt those of literature and sociology.[4]

The result was an uproar, or, rather, a polarization of virtually the entire field of architecture (and not only in America) into opponents and sympathizers of the supposed or real "position" of the Venturis. To be sure, what a literary critic, a sociologist, or, say, an art historian was able to welcome as an astute analysis seemed to architects around 1970 to be less insightful than inciteful. It seemed tantamount to a desecration of professional integrity among those whose intellectual antennae were tuned to receiving idealistic, utopian recipes, but not to reacting sensitively to aesthetic messages conveyed by everyday visual reality. Among the architectural elite on the American East coast, whose idealistic self-image had, paradoxically, been reinforced more than it had been questioned by the student movement of the late 1960s, the reaction to *Learning from Las Vegas* was often no different from that of some people to pornography: moral outrage. All the big names of New Left criticism, from Adorno and Herbert Marcuse to Clement Greenberg, were cited by opponents to represent the Venturis' work as "cynical" and "reactionary."[5] In their zeal, these foes probably did not realize that they themselves were treading suspiciously close to conservative cultural criticism.[6]

Some of the problems addressed in this *querelle des anciens modernes et des post-modernes* (quarrel of the old Moderns and Postmoderns) will be discussed on pages 28 ff. of this essay. In the meantime the reader might expect a definition and a point of view on "postmodern architecture," whose list of founders and ideologues has always been led by Venturi (although he has more recently dissociated himself from specific aspects of the movement).[7] I consider it expedient, however, not even to approach this bottomless pit for now and prefer a strategy that deals with architectural issues rather than with ideological prejudice. In forming an idea of the architecture being documented here, it is probably helpful to find one's own way, undisturbed by the dogmatic bias of the opponents and the rapture of the admirers, to a certain degree remote even from the complex theoretical doctrine presented in the two previously cited books by the Venturis.

Perhaps the key to such an approach lies in the work itself. For that reason I shall select one project by Venturi and Rauch—the Guild House in Philadelphia (1961)—in order to explore some of the themes running through this firm's architecture and theory. However, thinking that works of art (including architecture) can be explained *exclusively* on the basis of their formal structure would be just as self-deceptive as thinking that it is sufficient to decipher their meaning from directly related historical sources or the declared intentions of the architects. (That cannot in any case be the purpose of a comprehensive study like this.) Two working hypotheses may therefore be suggested here as clues to the interests and issues documented in this book: one focusing on the aesthetic side of architecture, the other on its social role.

Perception and Analysis of Form

The "material" that Venturi treated in *Complexity and Contradiction* and that became the declared foundation for the work of his office is the history of architecture, with Italian Mannerism, French and German Rococo, and the Early Moderns receiving the most attention. From the very outset, this intellectual curiosity had inherent practical implications. It helped free the production of architecture from the economic *and* ideological fetters of industrial, assembly-line rationality and bring it back closer to the nature of a craft. That is what constitutes the topicality of Venturi's first book and of his and John Rauch's early architectural practice, especially since they coincided with a deep crisis in the industrial system.

On the other hand, hardly anyone will be surprised to learn that the catholicity of Venturi's aesthetic interests is precisely what bred the mistrust of many colleagues, including Colin Rowe:

> Venturi has, after all, not only the most elaborate recent pedigree—Sullivan, Wright, Le Corbusier, et al.—but we know that we only have to search a bit and we shall find both Aalto and Lutyens acting as sponsors; while we are well aware that, if we prolong our investigations, a whole host of more remote but equally important figures—Vanbrugh, Vittone, Soane, and almost any architect of the last four centuries who has displayed moderate sophistication—may safely be conscripted to decorate the lower branches of the genealogical tree.[8]

All the names cited here, however condescendingly, do indeed appear in Venturi's first book, as do many others. Both the selection and the size of the pictures (the first edition of the book contained no fewer than 350 plans and photographs, many of them dotting the margins of the text "like slides scattered on a light table," as William Jordy once noted) reinforce the impression of an agglutination of highly disparate but ultimately equally valid pieces of evidence for the ubiquity of "complex" and "contradictory" form in past and present (pl. 1). In this way the spectrum of historic reference can oscillate on a single page from the Palazzo Farnese in Rome and Michelangelo's Medici Chapel in Florence to Thomas Jefferson's university in Charlottesville, Vanbrugh's Eastbury in England, the American country manors of the Shingle Style, and a flag picture by Jasper Johns.

In terms of their own interests as historians, the critics who fault Venturi's reluctance to attempt explanation of the historical origins of and reasons for various forms of "complexity" illustrated in these examples are not wrong.[9] However, the reasons why visual "complexity" and "contradiction" came about in the examples shown in the book are not of much interest in the context of Venturi's thesis. These qualities may be the fruit of artistic intention, or they may have resulted from mere chronological sequence or from the chance overlap of functions or phases of construction: the effects may be intended or unintended. Understanding their genesis is obviously important to the overall task of writing architectural history, but what matters here is the visual impact that these phenomena have on the subjective perception of architectural form.

In that sense, then, "complexity and contradiction" are not historical but rather visual, perhaps symbolic and primarily subjective categories of architectural form. Venturi's early writings show that his interest in historical architecture is motivated by a search for aesthetic principles. An invaluable document in this context is the unpublished theoretical essay that the architect submitted with his Master's project in 1950 (pp. 23, 80). The opening words read:

> The intent of this thesis problem is to demonstrate the importance of and the effect of setting on a building. It considers the art of environment; *the problem of the whole environment as perceived by the eye.*[10] [Emphasis mine.]

The authenticity that interests Venturi in buildings is thus not primarily social, historical, or symbolic but rather the authenticity of their linkage to their respective environments, combined with which they constitute a "perceptual whole."

1 Page from *Complexity and Contradiction in Architecture* (1966) in original size

13

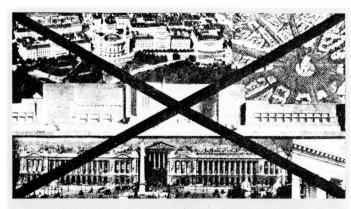

Komposition ist Starrheit — wir wollen das Lebensfähige, das Weiter-
schreitende: Jede Form ein Momentbild, bestimmt, zu verschwinden
und dem Folgenden Platz zu machen. Nur nicht für die Ewigkeit!
Ewig ist die Bewegung, die Vernichtung und das Neu-Entstehen.
Darum freuen wir uns an der Reklame, die ohne Hemmung ist, die
keine Rücksicht auf tote Fassaden nimmt, die auftaucht, wo die ge-
schäftliche Spannung am grössten ist, die verschwindet, sobald das
Zentrum sich verlegt.

2 "Komposition ist Starrheit," from *ABC* (1926)
[Composition is rigidity. We want what is viable, what keeps moving: every form a
snapshot destined to vanish and make way for what follows. Just not for eternity!
Movement, annihilation, and re-emergence are eternal. That is why we like advertizing
that has no scruples, that shows no consideration for dead facades, that turns up where
the work-a-day tension is greatest, that vanishes as soon as the center moves elsewhere.]

3 "La leçon de Rome," from Le Corbusier, *Vers une architecture* (1965)
[There are simple forms that trigger abiding sensations. The intervening modification
derived from and determining the primary sensations (ranging from major to minor
ones) with its entire scope of feasible combinations.]

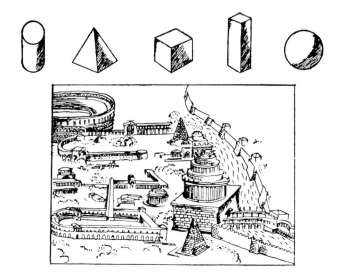

Il y a des formes simples déclancheuses de sensations
constantes.

Des modifications in-   jeur au mineur), avec
terviennent, dérivées, et   toute la gamme inter-
conduisent la sensation   médiaire des combinai-
première (de l'ordre ma-   sons. Exemples :

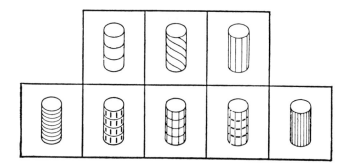

To the extent that Venturi thinks not as a historian but as a designer of urban spaces, he is an architect. To the extent that he allows himself to be guided by his eye—by subjective perception—he is part of a specifically modern tradition. Not coincidentally, one of Venturi's important points of reference at that time was the writings of Gyorgy Kepes on the nature of visual perception. That Venturi's theory of form is firmly rooted in the modern tradition may not occur to one at first, particularly in the light of the popular belief

that "Modernism" has ignored or even deliberately severed its links with "the past." This is known to be one of Postmodernism's myths of legitimation. Reality looks different, however, for Modernism presents itself in facets. In addition to the utilitarian extremism of the Swiss *ABC* Group, for example, which proclaimed around 1925 that "form" and "composition" in architecture—not to mention historical reference—were incompatible with the demands of building (pl. 2), there was the elaborate formalism of Le

14

Corbusier, who, speaking of architectural historicism, once remarked: "When I notice that I have dirty hands, I'd rather wash them than cut them off."[11]

Le Corbusier's essays in *Esprit Nouveau*, which appeared in 1923 as a book entitled *Vers une architecture*, present a spectrum of historical architecture whose scope ranks with that provided by Venturi in *Complexity and Contradiction*. To cite the Parthenon, the Hagia Sophia, St. Peter's in Rome, Santa Maria in Cosmedin, and the Petit Trianon in Versailles in one and the same volume as references of an architectural reform in the way that Le Corbusier did would have been inconceivable even during the nineteenth century's wildest period of architectural eclecticism. The nature of Le Corbusier's entire approach to historical architecture is aesthetic, too, however. The social, ideological, or economic factors shaping the buildings discussed—i. e., their "history"— is accorded as little space in Le Corbusier's writing (at least in *Vers une architecture*) as in Venturi's. Nevertheless, both architects use the past as a natural sphere of reference for design (pl. 3).

A book that Venturi always seems to have in mind for his own reflections is Sigfried Giedion's *Space, Time, and Architecture* (1941). Among other things, Giedion attempts in this book to anchor the "new tradition" of modern architecture in the spatial concepts of the Baroque, as shown by his famous comparison between Borromini's S. Carlo alle Quattro Fontane in Rome with the Crescents in Bath, England, and Le Corbusier's Plan Obus (pls. 4, 5). In the light of this book, at least, the reproach that "Modernism" was not interested in "history" collapses, for who was entitled to represent the point of view of the Modern Movement if not Giedion, the General Secretary of the International Congresses of Modern Architecture (CIAM)? As the Venturis see it, the main problem of the architecture propagated by the CIAM is not so much that it has replaced the awareness of past experience with the mythology of technocratic expediency (as it may actually have done in its early years around 1928), but that it has adopted historical models that seem to embody "simple" and "straightforward" solutions of complex problems, whereas the social and cultural reality of urban coexistence in general demands essentially "hybrid" and "complex" solutions.[12]

Which criteria did Modernism ultimately adopt to legitimize its extremely selective use of history?[13] This question would no doubt be more useful to consider than the current postmodern complaint that modern architecture on the whole had forgotten history (which history?).

Presumably, such a discussion would have to center on psychology, the theory of perception, and a practice of art history in which interest was focused primarily on "problems of form," as expressed by the well-known title of a book by Adolf von Hildebrandt, and in which basic concepts were developed according to formal criteria, as Heinrich Wölfflin had done in his *Kunstgeschichtliche Grundbegriffe* (Basic Concepts in Art History) of 1915.

It is worth noting that it was the psychologist Charles Henry who, along with Charles Blanc, the art theoretician and educator, provided Le Corbusier with the theory of *formes primaires* that was central to his thinking around 1920. The notion was that "primary forms" in art and architecture inevitably trigger "primary sensations" (pl. 3). Giedion, in turn, rooted his understanding of architecture's "space-time continuum" in the concepts that Wölfflin (his teacher) and A. E. Brinckmann developed in their attempts to explain the Baroque architecture of the seventeenth and eighteenth centuries, concepts that Giedion ingeniously related to the space-time concepts of modern physics.

Against this background, *Complexity and Contradiction in Architecture* does not appear as a break with the tradition of Modernism. Rather, it comes across as the continuation of a specifically modern obsession with *learning* from historical experiences in the light of relevant aesthetic issues. The issues discussed in the book revolve primarily around "form" and "space" in architecture, even though they address formal and spatial qualities quite different from those that interested the generation of Le Corbusier and Giedion: the hybrid (instead of the clear-cut), the both-and (instead of the either-or), the conventional (instead of the original), the presentation of contradictions (rather than their aesthetic leveling and neutralization). More specifically, the Hôtel de Matignon in Paris (pl. 6), with its circumstantial contradictions between interior and exterior composition, is more relevant to Venturi's search than are the elementary stereometry of grain silos or the "organic" continuum of space in Borromini's lantern of S. Ivo alla Sapienza in Rome, which Giedion compared to Tatlin's "Monument for the Third International" of 1922.

Lionello Venturi, one of the founders of modern art history, once wrote that Manet "introduced the principle of the autonomy of vision into art and all Modern art has used it as a basis and as a banner."[14] Perhaps it is not completely misleading to recall that, after all, the most influential aesthetic theory of Modernism—Impressionism—was based on an optical analysis of visual contrast between shadings and complementary colors and that, in this theory, the

4 Rome: San Carlo alle Quattro Fontane, from S. Giedion, *Space, Time and Architecture* (1941)

5 Le Corbusier: Plan Obus, Algiers (1931), from S. Giedion, *Space, Time and Architecture* (1965 edition)

reality of a work of art stems from a montage of corresponding contrasts. If Robert Venturi emphasized in his Master's thesis (1950) that context changes the meaning of form, he was not only reiterating a basic truth of any theory of signs, he was also representing the tradition of Eugène Chevreul. Chevreul's book, *De la loi des contrastes simultanés des couleurs* (1839), blazed the trail for the theory of Impressionism, especially where Chevreul stated that the quality of a color depends on that color's environment, the result being that a yellow can become an orange by virtue of its proximity to a blue.[15]

Interest in primary perceptual mechanism seems to play no role in *Learning from Las Vegas*. Or does it after all—under a different name? Apparently, the interest has shifted from an aesthetic and psychological perspective to a basically linguistic one. The authors are not concerned with the fundamentally timeless structure of architectural form but rather with its capacity to convey extremely temporal meanings and messages. But in neither case—neither the book of 1966 nor that of 1972—were historically determined

architectural phenomena subjected to social criticism or attributed to social dialectics. The obvious commercialism of Las Vegas may invite a violent critique of the gambling interests or, indeed, of the wider context of American capitalism that allows or even encourages their ostentatious visual display (see pp. 215ff.). As if wanting to provoke their more politically motivated critics, however, the Venturis restrict themselves to sober document of the formal and iconographic rules that underlie the Strip as a "system of communication." They keep to the visible, to that which can be visually perceived and photographically documented, and they stick to quantitative criteria that lend themselves to positivist description. In the end, they say as little or as much about the "morals" of Las Vegas as Pissarro had said about the social and economic background of Paris and fin-de-siècle leisure-time culture in his gorgeous paintings of the boulevard Montmartre or the boulevard des Italiens (pls. 7, 8). Their aim is to grasp reality as it is, not to uncover the social mechanisms that brought it about.

To that extent, even *Learning from Las Vegas* belongs to

a decidedly modern tradition that was ushered in by Impressionism in the fine arts. One needs only to be reminded of Fernand Léger's interest in the crass imagery of the Cirque Medrano, of Place Clichy or of Mondrian's *Broadway Boogie-Woogie* series (1941–1943) to realize that the unbiased visual assimilation of popular big-city everyday life—the fathers of the practice in literature were Baudelaire and Whitman—has been a central theme of modern art ever since.[16]

Functionalism and Social Concern

In the text of *Learning from Las Vegas*, the authors argue that isolating form and symbol for analysis does not imply indifference to architecture's social tasks. In the introduction they specify:

> Las Vegas is analyzed here only as a phenomenon of architectural communication. Just as an analysis of the structure of a Gothic cathedral need not include a debate on the morality of medieval religion, so Las Vegas' values are not questioned here. The morality of commercial advertising, gambling interests, and the competitive instinct is not at issue here, although, indeed, we believe it should be in the architect's broader, *synthetic* tasks of which an analysis such as this is but an aspect.[17]

In the book the authors contend that learning from the "messy vitality" of the Strip will help architects to sharpen their social sensibilities. Emerging from the turbulent 1960s, *Learning from Las Vegas* did in fact not lack in social comment. The comment and criticism, however, were not of Las Vegas but of architects, their view of architecture in society, and the social effects of that view.[18] At the same time the aesthetic pluralism of the Venturis was linked early on with social and political ideas relating to aspects that may be called "populism." Yet paradoxically, perhaps, within the circle of modern architecture's latter-day apologists, the Venturis' practice of invoking "the people" and "popular taste" may have prolonged their disrepute more than their unusual formal eclecticism had already done.

This may be so because the Modern Movement seems to have had great difficulty in imagining social involvement in any form other than that of climbing the barricades for freedom, that is, in terms of social and cultural leadership. In this view "grass roots" always means something that sagaciously emulates the "avantgarde."

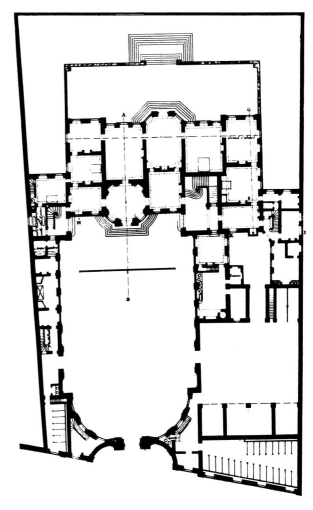

6 Paris: Hôtel de Matignon, plan (17th c.), from *Complexity and Contradiction in Architecture* (1966)

Now it could seem that the "populism" of the Venturis, while being rooted in the larger intellectual and aesthetic context of modern art and poetry, was also a polemic reaction to modern architecture's avantgarde syndrome described above. Although it is precisely that *as well*, its origins probably lie considerably deeper—in something that, for lack of a better term, one could call the "philosophy of common sense."

After all, one of its founders was David Hume (1711–1776), a leading spokesman of the Enlightenment. One of the axioms of philosophical "common sense" is that the "truth" of every statement is not established until it is

17

7   Las Vegas: "Upper Strip Looking North," from *Learning from Las Vegas* (1972)

8 Camille Pissarro: *Boulevard Montmartre, effet de nuit* (1897), National Gallery, London.

compared to the everyday experience of the "man in the street." Obviously, this viewpoint was bound to have a direct impact on the theory of taste and on the way the problem of "beauty" was dealt with in modern society. That is the subject of Archibald Alison's work, *Essays on the Nature and Principles of Taste*, which first appeared in 1790.

In the same vein as the axiom about the social relativity of philosophical truth, Alison stated that in order to discover what is "beautiful" one must first study the ideas that simple people have about beauty "in terms of both the picturesque and the sublime." Alison thus categorically denies the possibility of formulating a universal aesthetic judgment about an object. To him, considering an object to be "beautiful" or "ugly" is irrelevant as long as its exact *function* goes unrecognized. As far as architecture is concerned, the beauty of proportion is not a question of visual appearance at all. The only really interesting thing about architecture, and related issues like scale and composition, is whether a structure matches its function and whether it properly brings out that function.[19]

The following aesthetic axiom, which was also published in the *Essays*, shows that Alison in no way wanted to make the concept of function absolute or to divest it of affective associations. He was also interested in the aesthetic qualities of a building but was of the opinion that they had to be related to the sensibilities of the individual occupant. Something is beautiful if it evokes many novel and well-interrelated associations. The Alps, for example, may appear majestic to the eye, but only the person who knows that Hannibal led his troops over them is fully able to appreciate their majesty.

Thanks to J.C. Loudon, Alison's ideas found their way into the architectural literature of the nineteenth century. In his famous *Encyclopedia of Cottage, Farm and Villa Architecture* (1834), the "culminating anthology of the 'Picturesque'" (Hitchcock), Loudon expressly refers to Alison as his most important source. Loudon shares the opinion that objects evoke emotions in the beholder and that these feelings bring whole trains of associations into the conscious mind. He, too, thought that the longer and more interrelated these trains were, the more beautiful the object would be.[20]

It is interesting that hotels ("country public houses") have a significant place in Loudon's theory, and not only because of the especially rich and complex nature of the architectural "associations" to be found there. In a democracy, Loudon believes, hotels will play a role similar to the one that the palace and the cloister had previously had. One may certainly expect such a view to be shared by authors who, not quite a century and a half later, set out "to learn from Las Vegas."

But let us continue. For the construction of villas and private houses, Loudon stressed that their style should be inspired by the aesthetic habits of the future occupants. He thought that the Gothic or the Elizabethan style would be the obvious choice for a villa in England, for example, for the very reason that it triggered the richest series of associations in the English mind.[21]

He emphasized that the ornamental decoration of country manors would eventually yield to a plain and functional design but that until then the task would always be to satisfy the personal and temporal needs of individuals who for emotional reasons wish their house to remind them of very specific architectural traditions. For the *Encyclopedia*, Loudon drew a series of architectural "jackets" for "A Dwelling for a Man and his Wife without Children," presenting it, in turn, as a rustic country manor "with veranda and terrace," a small Gothic mansion with a castellated or monastic jacket, an Elizabethan country estate, or as a little house with either an Italian veranda or an Indian Gothic dome (pl. 9).[22]

16, 'A Dwelling for a Man and his Wife, without Children' from Loudon's Encyclopaedia . . .

. . . 20, with Castellated Gothic jacket . . .

. . . 18, with veranda and terrace . . .

. . . 21, with Monastic Gothic jacket . . .

. . . 19, with trellis . . .

. . . 22, with Elizabethan jacket.

9 J. C. Loudon: "A Dwelling for a Man and his Wife, with Children," in J. C. Loudon, *Encyclopedia* (1834), from *Learning from Las Vegas* (1972)

The early spokesmen of "common sense" in architecture thus not only helped to found functionalism. To a certain extent they also took the plurality of popular taste as a given and made this the starting point of their theoretical considerations. It is only of marginal interest here that philosophical "common sense" later acquired conservative overtones, especially in America, after it was propagated by the philosophical school led by Dugald Stewart and Thomas Brown, who established themselves after about 1830 at the College of New Jersey (later known as Princeton).[23] For Loudon and his theory of architecture, functionalism and

eclecticism are thus not the irreconcilable opposites that they have been since the 1920s for practically all theoreticians of the International Style; rather, they are complementary aspects of one and the same architectural system. It is thus no coincidence that the series of pictures in *Learning from Las Vegas* commences with the jackets of Loudon's cottage, which George L. Hersey published in his essay (1968). In fact, many places in this book seem to take off directly from Loudon, "that encyclopedist of the picturesque" (Hitchcock), particularly as far as the theory of the "decorated shed" is concerned.[24] Some time later, with Loudon in mind and tongue slightly in cheek, Robert Venturi even designed his own "Loudon" houses (p. 243).

The Iconography of "Marginal Man"

Loudon's *Encyclopedia* and other comparable works today survive in the commercialized images of American domestic life-styles, images that served as the raw material of the Venturis' studies on symbolism in the street and in the home (pl. 10). Certainly, Robert Venturi's background and experience as an Italian-American in a large city in the Eastern United States contains personal aspects that establish an affinity for the culture of diverse groups and of "simple folk." But these alone would hardly have been enough for the programmatic actualization of "common sense" in architecture that his firm's work demonstrates. To be able to catalogue (and interpret aesthetically) the images of the everyday culture of "ordinary people," it was necessary simultaneously to sense it from within *and* to study it from without. In short, drawing on this heritage to make the everyday reality of America the subject of architectural discourse required the background and sociological acumen of Denise Scott Brown.

She has speculated on "the marginal nature of [her] own relation to dominant cultures" and on the fact that much of her thinking draws on dual "colonial" heritages: "one American and the other African, both set in a European mold."[25] Accordingly, it is not by chance that the Venturis have focused their interests not on "Man" *per se,* that idealized abstraction postulated by modern architecture's implicit universalism, but on the cultures of social subgroups and marginal ethnic communities—on the "marginal man" who, as a cultural androgyne, relates to two cultures at once: that of his racial and ethnic heritage *and* that of middle-class America, into which he is partly assimilated. It is no coincidence that "marginal man," "the stranger," and "the wanderer" were the focus of the American urban studies conducted by the Chicago School of Sociology as early as 1920, studies that form the background of Herbert Gans's education and research and thereby also—indirectly— that of Denise Scott Brown.[26]

10 "Da Vinci." Type of family home from an American catalogue of prefabricated houses (VRSB archives)

2 Anatomy of a "Decorated Shed"

Few spokesmen of modern architecture would have been likely to recognize that the *vertu purgative, exorcisante du pastiche* (the purgative and exorcising virtue of pastiche) evoked by Proust in referring to Flaubert[27] might be taken seriously as a way to achieve quality in building as well. At an early stage, however, Venturi seems to have been familiar with classical rhetoric's recommendation to master a literary form by consciously emulating a model. He probably had heard this advice during his study at Princeton under two professors familiar with the architecture of the Ecole des Beaux-Arts, the architect Jean Labatut and the art historian. Donald Drew Egbert.[28]

It is interesting that Venturi's thesis project, written in 1950, was focused explicitly on compiling from history the formal models that inspired his design for a church set amidst a group of late nineteenth-century Victorian school buildings (pl. 11). Those models included the wide bands of brick wall in Mies van der Rohe's well-known villa project of 1924, then the mausoleum of Galla Placidia in Ravenna, the cross section of Salisbury Cathedral, the shed roofs of Albert Kahn's Chrysler Plant in Detroit with their characteristic "grooves" providing sidelight, and, finally, the skewed beams of Frank Lloyd Wright's winter residence in Taliesin West (1937; see also p. 147).

Venturi's explicit reference to models has continued throughout his career, and this makes his buildings fascinating subjects for a kind of analysis that peels away layers of historical allusion in order to label them and investigate their meaning.

The Guild House in Philadelphia– "Postmodernism's first large building," as Heinrich Klotz has called it–lends itself well to such a procedure. By concentrating on this building, I am for now merely following the path that the authors of *Learning from Las Vegas* took themselves. In that work the Guild House is presented in detail as a prime example of the theory of the "decorated shed" in architecture. It is imperative here to cite the entire definition of the architectural "duck" and the "decorated shed" from *Learning from Las Vegas* as well as the basic considerations leading to it.

We shall emphasize image—image over process or form—in asserting that architecture depends in its perception and creation on past experience and emotional association and that these symbolic and representational elements may often be contradictory to the form, structure, and program with which they combine in the same building. We shall survey this contradiction in its two main manifestations:

1. Where the architectural systems of space, structure, and program are submerged and distorted by an overall symbolic form. This kind of building-becoming-sculpture we call the *duck* in honor of the duck-shaped drive-in, "The Long Island Duckling," illustrated in *God's Own Junkyard* by Peter Blake (pl. 12).

2. Where systems of space and structure are directly at the service of program, and ornament is applied independently of them. This we call the *decorated shed* (pl. 13).

The duck is the special building that *is* a symbol; the decorated shed is the conventional shelter, that *applies* symbols. We maintain that both kinds of architecture are valid—Chartres is a duck (although it is a decorated shed as well), and the Palazzo Farnese is a decorated shed—but we think that the duck is seldom relevant today, although it pervades Modern architecture.[29]

11   Robert Venturi: "In It's Form," formal model from his Master's essay (Princeton University, 1950)

22

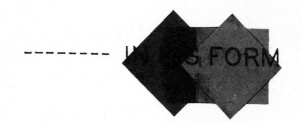

FORM

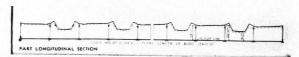

SALISBVRY.

PART LONGITUDINAL SECTION

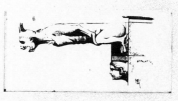

12 "The Duck," from *Learning from Las Vegas* (1972)

13 "The Duck and the Decorated Shed," from *Learning from Las Vegas* (1972)

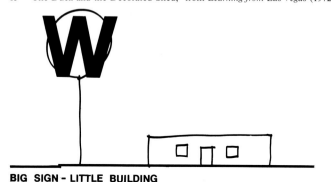

BIG SIGN - LITTLE BUILDING

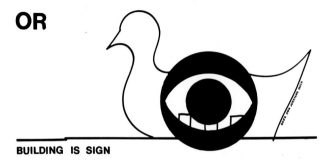

BUILDING IS SIGN

The Guild House

The most important facts about the Guild House, a senior citizens' home completed in 1963 on the edge of downtown Philadelphia, are given elsewhere in this book (pp. 282–86). The authors note that its six-story height was prescribed by the city's building code, but it is quite unusual for an architect to submit without complaint to a city zoning ordinance rather than attempt to circumvent it (while exploiting every square inch of the allowed volume). One would probably not go wrong in assuming that the point of this apparent surrender to the urban status quo is precisely to avoid breaking up the existing physiognomy of the street while at the same time adding a new element to it.

The plate on page 284 shows the floor plan. As a cursory first glance shows, the north side of the six-story building has a smooth facade, whereas the south side features a strongly articulated and broken outline. The small, one-room apartments face north, with the larger, two-room apartments being located on the corners, facing south at an angle that guarantees both good lighting and a variety of different views to or along Spring Garden Street. Clearly, one of the central ideas was to enable the elderly to participate visually in day-to-day urban life rather than to isolate them from it by immersing them in green gardens and fresh air.

The form and scale of the Guild House are not merely intended to be in keeping with the urban status quo, with Main Street being "almost all right"; the large windows literally absorb the city, soaking it up visually.

Architecturally, however, there is a contradiction in the fact that the highly articulated and broken southern facade faces Spring Garden Street. From the ground plan, one would expect to find the garden facade there, with the "street facade" to the north, where the building extends for the entire length of the property as a compact rectangular area (pl. 15).[30] On the other hand, the comparatively "pastoral" effect of the irregularly broken southern facade is neutralized somewhat by the palazzo-like, nearly square entry facade, which is attached to what would otherwise look rather like the rear side (but is, of course, actually the front). The effect is that of a central bay from which the body of the building is recessed symmetrically to the north in three successive parts.

By framing eight balconies, this facade embodies the duality—or the contradiction?—between representation (as demanded by the location on the street) and opening (as suggested by the orientation to the south). Furthermore,

24

within the six stories of the facade, a three-part division is suggested, through the use of white tile at the base and a higher level string course of the same tile, to represent the traditional divisions of, say, a Baroque palazzo. That kind of contradiction between a representative facade and a functional structure behind it is what is referred to in the passage quoted above, for according to the Venturis "symbolic and representational elements may often be contradictory to the form, structure, and program with which they combine in the same building."

That may sound like an architectural truism. Yet it is a truism that established modern architecture was scarcely able to accept, in this form at any rate. The modern doctrine implied that one of architecture's tasks was to translate symbolic, structural, and functional requirements into architectural form in such a way that the various elements coalesced into a "whole." Architectural meaning was supposed to result from the integration of these factors—and not from the subsequent addition of external signs as "conveyors of meaning."

Pastiche

The effect of "unity," of "formal integration," is clearly not sought here in the customary sense—quite unlike Paul Rudolph's Crawford Manor in New Haven, an old-age home that the authors of *Learning from Las Vegas*, in a witty analysis, hold up as a "heroic and original" counterpart to their own "ugly and ordinary" building (pl. 16).[31] What is sought is a hybrid type of unity, a unity that consists of varied formal and symbolic components beside, behind, and overlapping one another. Even so, this does not preclude the formal result from being organized hierarchically to meet an "obligation toward the difficult whole."[32] It consists of components in different registers: ceremonious (like the entrance facade) *and* common or everyday (like the "ordinary" apartment house facade behind it).

Let us look at the almost square entrance facade. It is intentionally thin and untectonic, not much more than the two-dimensional *image* of a facade. Still, it is an "image" that embodies an entire catalogue of overlapping architectural references. It is enough to make a complete circle out of the segmental arch of the lunettes in the upper story in order to discover the archetype of the circular hole in the rectangular box, so important in Louis Kahn's later work. One might

14   Philadelphia: Guild House (1961), general view of the street side

15   Guild House, rear side

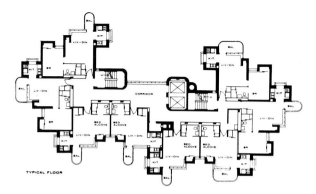

16   New Haven, Connecticut: Crawford Manor, typical plan (Architect: Paul Rudolph, 1966)

think of the monumental oculi that Louis Kahn introduced in his buildings in Ahmedabad or Dacca (pl. 17), and this is not surprising if one knows about the relationship between Kahn and Venturi in the early days of the Philadelphia School. For Venturi, as Denise Scott Brown wrote, Kahn was something of "an architectural mother."[33]

Yet the window is not circular, nor even semicircular; it is a segment of a circle that, by implication, suggests the scale of the large completed circle of which it is a part. The lunette motif itself has roots in the facade typology of colonial American houses of the seventeenth and eighteenth centuries, quite apart from the fact that the form points to the *finestra termale* (thermal windows) that Venturi knows from Palladian villas (pl. 18). Palladio's woodcut of the Villa Zeno in Cessalto from the *Quattro libri* was, after all, one of the pictures in *Complexity and Contradiction*. The tension between large and small windows, the fact that these windows are simultaneously part of various geometric configurations within one and the same facade, the definite hierarchical difference between the ceremonial dignity of the villa itself and the simplicity of the flanking colonnades and stables—the Palladian *barchesse* (see pl. 18)—all this reappears in the Guild House in a way that leaves no doubt as to the importance of the Cinquecento reference.

Venturi seems to want to pay his tribute not only to the new testament of architecture but to the old as well. Yet this facade's "sign language" consists not only of references to Kahn or Palladio and to Palladio's colonial offshoots in America. It emphatically refers to "lower" sources as well: the all-too-familiar imagery of the North American (and not only North American) apartment building. That is what prompted Serge Chermayeff to say about the Guild House: "It is like Colin, Ward, and Lucas again."[34] In fact, the overall concept—a concrete skeleton, a flat roof, and brick skin—deliberately draws on the imagery of public housing. The brick skin could hardly be more tautly stretched. This "mask" is precisely cut out so that not only the third, middle support of the reinforced concrete skeleton is exposed but half of the second and fourth as well. Moreover, the lunette in the upper story—like the thermal windows in Palladio's villas, it indicates the *salone*, the communal sphere—is cut to open a view into the concrete structure.

So behind a thin backdrop of historical references radiates the smiling face of everyday life, or, as far as the reinforced concrete skeleton is concerned, the once utopian hallmark of "modern architecture" (pl. 20) that has long since become a platitude. The proplike effect of the facade is further underscored by two slits to the left and right of the lunette

that faintly recall the crenellated stepped gables of traditional Dutch townhouses.

The first-floor level even displays an imagery reminiscent of the department store. The bold lettering and the white ceramic-tile cladding, which, in keeping with a neoclassical tradition, rises to the bank of windows on the second floor (and thus makes the first floor seem higher than it actually is) audaciously commercialize the facade (see pl. 21). Lastly, in front of the entrance stands a polished granite column, just as massive as the concrete frame above it is fragile, whose shape as well as awkward position on the median axis are a tribute to Frank Furness, the father of the Philadelphia School.[35]

17 Dacca: Ayub National Hospital, oculus (Architect: Louis I. Kahn, 1963–1965)

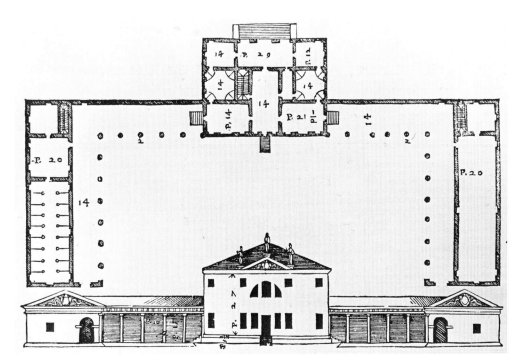

18 Villa Zeno in Cessalto, from Andrea Palladio, *Quattro Libri* (1570)

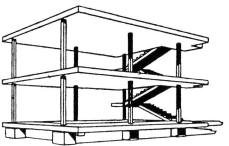

20 Le Corbusier: "Domino-Haus" (1914)

19 Guild House (1961), facade on street side

21   Faith, South Dakota: Main Street (ca. 1915)

22   Garches: Villa Stein-de Monzie (Architects: Le Corbusier and Pierre Jeanneret, 1927)

That is how the architects develop their catalogue of signs, drawing both from architecture's "high culture" and from the commercial imagery of Main Street America. As Vincent Scully put it at an early date: "So the whole mass steps up to the street, defines it with a flat and 'decorated' facade, identifies itself with lettering brasher than Roman, expansively Pop, and blooms generously upward to the large, arched opening of a common living room with a television aerial rising above it."[36]

"Transparency," Symbolism, and "Broken Form": Some Critical Reactions to the Guild House

In purely formal terms the facade itself, as indicated earlier, is not so much "architecture" as it is a two-dimensional screen recalling other buildings, often remote in space and time. Its flatness and the transparency of its overlapping layers recall Le Corbusier's white villas of the 1920s—specifically the Villa Stein in Garches, which, in its own tricky way, is Palladian and manneristic (1927; pl. 22). Speaking of

the Guild House, Heinrich Klotz said: "the structure of the walls has, in fact, remained that of modern architecture and the International Style."[37] The explicit formal references to other buildings, however, could hardly have been understood in terms of the moral and aesthetic standards of the Modern Movement. Writing about the kind of architectural symbolism to be found in this facade "screen," Kenneth Frampton noted:

> In contrast to a Scharoun or to an Aalto, Venturi's symbolism is neither anthropomorphic nor, in Jungian terms, archetypal. It restricts itself to detached empirical comment upon the inherent frailty of man and his institutional structures. It sustains itself through the construction of elaborate aesthetic metaphors and through the projection of paradoxes.... Unlike Kahn's heroic monumentality, to which it is related, Venturi's work does not gravitate towards the values of the archaic.[38]

The design for the Town Hall in North Canton, Ohio (pp. 154f.), perhaps illustrates this unarchaic yet solemn public symbolism even better than the Guild House does.

Leonardo Benevolo, too, emphasizes the empirical and experimental (rather than ideological) character of Venturi's "language of symbols," pointing out that Venturi had used stylistic elements from Kahn in his early houses and in the Medical Center of North Pennsylvania (see pp. 148 f.). Benevolo adds, though, that Venturi did so

> in an experimental way, as if to verify cold bloodedly the destructive effect of this experiment on the customary repertoire of the modern movement. Later, [Venturi] continued this experimental research in a coherent way.[39]

To another critic, William Curtis, the systematically multilayered and contradictory architectural statements come across quite simply as intellectually eccentric. Referring to the "Guild House," Curtis wrote of Venturi:

> ... his ideas were usually more convincing in writing than when built. The agonized self-consciousness betrayed the lack of an instinctive feeling for form, space or even proportion. Venturi set the tone for a literary conception of architecture in which more emphasis was put on imagery and quotation than on formal integration.[40]

It may be comforting to know that the American architect may share his existence on the fringes of "great" architecture with figures like Viollet-le-Duc (after all, Giedion, too, found Viollet's designs to be "hybrid"), Hector Guimard, Anatole de Baudot, and J. J. P. Oud. Each of them is charged by Curtis with lacking an instinct for form and stylistic coherence.

On the subject of "formal unity" and "proportion," Venturi admitted in his Master's thesis that he no longer felt able to do much with such words as "unity," which has lost precise meaning in criticism, and "proportion, which in its usual application Wright, for one, has amusingly succeeded in rendering useless."[41]

The criterion of "formal integration," basically a neoclassical paradigm, obviously has a long tradition—especially in American architectural criticism. It may suffice to recall Talbot Hamlin's judgment of Frank Furness (see pl. 23):

> Like so much American Victorian Gothic, the sense of scale is absolutely lacking: what should be small is big, and vice versa. Structural logic—the foundation of Gothic—is forgotten. Stumpy polished granite columns; arches, cusped, pointed, and segmental; offsets, brackets and meaningless gigantic moldings are piled together in astonishing ways. Such buildings are obvious proofs that the original is not always beautiful.[42]

It is no accident that Furness was rediscovered in the 1960s as the forerunner of the Philadelphia School of architecture,

23 Philadelphia: National Bank of the Republic (Architect: Frank Furness, 1884; destroyed)

whose "masters" were Kahn, Giurgola, and Venturi. Furness is repeatedly referred to in various veins in *Complexity and Contradiction in Architecture*. A passage about the National Bank of the Republic (1884; pl. 23), which was torn down long ago, reads: "The half-segmental arch, blocked by the submerged tower which, in turn, bisects the facade into a near duality, and the violent adjacencies of rectangles, squares, lunettes, and diagonals of contrasting sizes, compose a building seemingly held up by the building next door: it is an almost insane short story of a castle on a city street."[43]

29

Bruno Taut's Hufeisen Siedlung, Berlin, 1926 (top) and Robert Venturi's Guild House, Philadelphia, 1963. It took us thirty-seven years to get this far.

24   Page from Tom Wolfe, *From Bauhaus to Our House* (1981)

James O'Gorman has rightly stressed that Venturi's description differs from Hamlin's only in that Venturi likes the mannerisms that Hamlin finds unbearable.[44] It is, then, a matter of aesthetic preferences; neoclassical taste here, mannerist taste there. But there is something else. An architect who is capable of interpreting a bank building as the "short story of a castle on a city street" evidently takes it for granted that it is one of the inherent possibilities of architecture to tell "stories" about other, spatially or temporally more or less remote, examples of architecture. For that architect, the nature of a building is not shaped solely by its formal, structural, and spatial features but also by the possibilities of its implied narrative structure.

"Bauhaus" or "Our House"?

There are reasons to believe that for most people "architectural form" is something that is appreciated first for its capacity to evoke associations rather than for its abstract spatial or aesthetic "quality." In the light of the linguistic model of architectural communication so favored by postmodern theory, the Guild House thus appears to be above all an attempt to make architecture readable and familiar again for its users as well as for a larger public. The way this is achieved, with the help of an "ordinary" architecture that explicitly uses everyday images in order to be understood by "the man on the street," deliberately diverges from the Bauhaus approach—or, more generally, from the Modern Movement's exclusive emphasis on function and pure form.

Yet the inherent populism—the "social concern"—that underlies the aesthetic program of the Guild House (and much of the Venturi's work) is not altogether dissimilar to the social utopias of the Modern Movement, while on the other hand modern architecture has by no means been as aseptically abstract and formalist as postmodern rumor would have it. At least that is what one seems to gather indirectly from the reaction of Tom Wolfe. In his tract *From Bauhaus to Our House* (1981), he tries to demonstrate that modern architecture, ostensibly so unloved in the United States, is the fruit of a European gospel heralded by an academic elite in Cambridge, Chicago, and New York. Some of the protagonists of the "plot" reconstructed by Wolfe are "The Silver Prince" (Walter Gropius) and "Utopia Limited" (the Museum of Modern Art in New York). In the order of their appearance, there come "The Apostates" (E. Durrell Stone, Eero Saarinen, Philip Johnson, and other early partisans of the "International Style" who went over to historicism) and the "scholastics."

Wolfe places Venturi in the latter group (the coauthors of Venturi's books and projects do not seem to be worthy of mention). Convinced that American architecture has languished too long under the yoke of Modernist purism and that it is in need of a rebel who will finally liberate it from European guardianship, Wolfe relishes quoting Venturi's puns with approval—above all, "Less is a bore" (playing on Mies van der Rohe's "Less is More") and "Main Street is almost all right." Anyone who knows Wolfe's earlier diatribes against modern art and its "high priests"[45] will not be surprised that Wolfe is fascinated with those aspects of

Venturi that are so unbearable to the latter-day trustees of modern architecture: his playfully disrespectful way of dealing with the "pioneers" of the movement and his sympathy for American everyday life.

But Wolfe praises Venturi's theory—only to turn around and mock his architecture. How far it lags behind the architect's populist ideas is supposed to be shown in a comparison between the Guild House and Bruno Taut's Britz Hufeisensiedlung (Horseshoe Housing Development) in Berlin (1926; pl. 24). Wolfe seemed to be shocked. Concerning the Guild House, he wrote: "It took us thirty-seven years to get *this* far."[46]

According to Wolfe, one should not be surprised that Venturi is closer to the elitism of the Modern Movement than he might wish to be, given his alleged populist theories. After all, says Wolfe, Venturi's first book, *Complexity and Contradiction in Architecture*, appeared with "Utopia Limited."

The Venturis have consistently pleaded for an architecture that takes the Modern Movement further instead of resisting it, and it is amusing that Wolfe's criticism should come to support this claim, if only involuntarily. Indeed, one must go beyond that and admit that the idea of comparing Venturi to Bruno Taut and the Guild House to the Horseshoe Housing Development (instead of to the buildings by Gropius, Häring, or Mies van der Rohe—just to stick to the Berlin of the 1920s) shows more understanding of architecture than do many of the professional critics so obsessed with Venturi's supposedly unconditional sympathy for Las Vegas or his generational conflict with Kahn. Actually, Taut had never forgotten the possibilities of architectural language that the Venturis had to rediscover in the 1960. In that sense, and despite all the differences in social milieu and scale, the Guild House of 1961 is, paradoxically, indeed more closely related to the Horseshoe Housing Development of 1926 than may seem to be the case at first glance.

3 Themes and Variations

What distinguishes the buildings by Venturi, Rauch and Scott Brown from the postmodern picturesqueness that is currently in vogue? Or, more generally, what kind of formal identity can be characteristic of an architecture that is programmatically "Both-And," that stands for ironic accommodation, articulated inconsistencies, and ambiguity? And what about the "style" of an architecture that presents itself as a medley of styles?

The theoretical essays of the Venturis do not answer such questions completely. Their intention seems to be to undermine the validity of universal rules in architecture. Since Alberti, Filarete, or Francesco di Giorgio, that is, since the rediscovery of Vitruvius in the fifteenth century, architectural theory had been essentially normative. The main concern was the establishment and the polemical spread of a formal language and of systematic rules that were supposed to guarantee "correct" building. The Venturis, however, view stylistic "purity" with suspicion. With them it does not seem at all to be a matter of substituting new forms of architectural language for old ones but rather of introducing the aesthetic principle of complexity in order to avoid the uncritical application of allegedly universal forms and rules.[47]

It would be naive, however, to interpret the architectural practice of the Venturis as a mere illustration of their ideas. Whatever the architectural complexity and the pluralistic syncretism of styles argued for in *Complexity and Contradiction in Architecture* and in *Learning from Las Vegas,* the Venturis have ultimately done what architects have always done when opening up new avenues in a period of transition: They have developed elements of an architectural language. It is enough here to recall just a few of Robert Venturi's formal inventions that have become part of the vocabulary of international architecture over the past two decades:

The wedge-shaped, "bowlike" building or building element. Prototype: The North Penn Visiting Nurses' Association Headquarters (1961; pl. pp. 148 f.). Famous "variation" on

25 Bremen: Hochhaus "Neue Vahr" (Architect: Alvar Aalto, 1959–1962)

26 "Neue Vahr," plan

27 Helsinki: Nordic Bank (Architect: Alvar Aalto, 1962)

28 New Haven, Connecticut: Yale Mathematics Building (Venturi and Rauch: competition project, 1969; drawing: W. G. Clark)

this theme: I.M. Pei's East Building of the National Gallery of Art in Washington, D.C. (1968–1978).

The apparent "enlargement" of windows by adding extra "symbolic" frames. Prototype: The North Penn Visiting Nurses' Association Headquarters (1961). One of many modifications of this theme: the Westchester House in Armouk, New York, by Robert Stern and John Hagmann (1974–1976).

"Splitting" the traditional gabled housefront by separating the parts and recessing the middle section. Prototype: Vanna Venturi House (1961; pl. pp. 244–48). Variation on the theme in the AT & T building by Philip Johnson and John Burgee in New York (1978–1984). The Vanna Venturi House serves almost worldwide as an aedicule on the roofs of tall buildings and is even sanctified in the zoning regulations of San Francisco and Seattle.

The use of the square window with symmetrical sash bars in apartment buildings. Prototypes: Vanna Venturi House and Guild House (1961; pl. pp. 283–86). Adopted by Aldo Rossi, for example, in the Gallaratese apartment building in Milan (1968; see p. 61) and by Charles Moore (Moore, Lyndon, Turnbull, and Whitaker) in Whitman Village in Huntington, Long Island, New York (1974). Now an established cliché of the postmodern architectural vocabulary.

The vertical integration of entrance and openings in the stories above to form a "giant order." Prototype: Guild House;

unlimited variations in international postmodern architecture, "for better or worse."

The use of monumental facade "screens" behind which "functional" and conventionally built spaces are arranged. Prototype: Competition design for the Town Hall in North Canton, Ohio (1965; pl. pp. 154 f.); immeasurable impact.

Ghost architecture: Architecture as a symbolic representation of architecture that no longer exists. Prototype: Franklin Court, Philadelphia (1972; pl. pp. 104–9); now an internationally accepted formula for competition projects on the frontiers of urban design and preservation of monuments.

Decorative facade patterning with colored, glazed brick tiles or marble panels. Prototype: House in Greenwich, Connecticut (1970; pl. 53); Allen Art Museum, Oberlin, Ohio (1973; pl. 54); immeasurable impact.

Has there been a competition anywhere in the Western world since 1976 at which variations on any one of these themes has not been entered?

Aalto's Impact

A critical survey might suggest that the work of Venturi, Rauch and Scott Brown is developing along a relatively limited number of architectural themes. Indeed, the

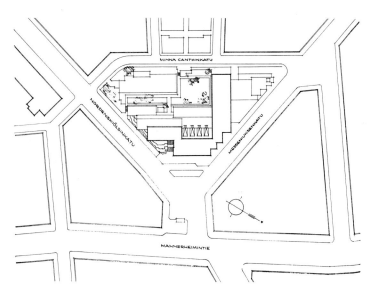

29 Helsinki: senior citizens' home, site plan (Architect: Alvar Aalto, 1952–1956)

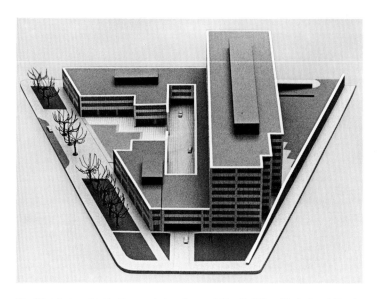

30 Washington, D. C.: Transportation Square Office Building (Venturi and Rauch: competition project, 1967)

characteristic features of the Guild House mentioned in the previous chapter betray certain architectural interests, and these interests are not necessarily limited to the types of buildings examined here—apartment buildings. They surface in houses, villas, shops, and office buildings as well. The "irregular" floor plan of the Guild House, for instance, reminds one of Aalto, whereas the entrance facade recalls Kahn and Palladio; the entrance itself, an A & P store, and so on. If my assumption is correct, then one should be able to find these interests mirrored in other buildings designed by Venturi, Rauch and Scott Brown, regardless of their respective function. That is indeed the case. The Guild House is neither the starting point nor the goal of this formal evolution, but it is an early and formally very complex major work. In that sense it embodies a wide variety of architectural perspectives that can be followed right down to the firm's most recent production.

Referring to Alvar Aalto's apartment tower in Bremen, Venturi wrote in *Complexity and Contradiction* that "the inherently rectangular order of structure and space of Aalto's apartment house in Bremen yields to the inner needs for light and space toward the south like the growth of a flower toward the sun"[48] (pls. 25, 26). As we have seen, that is the case with the Guild House, too, at least in principle, although the location at the side of the road seems to prohibit an "organic" fan-shaped organization of the plan. In the project for two apartment towers in Brooklyn (1967), the

matter was easier in that the street actually did run to the north (pl. pp. 288 f.). It is hardly surprising that Venturi and Rauch fell back on the fan-shaped plan (or rather the curved architectural volume) for buildings whose urban situation made this possible. This was particularly true of the Yale Mathematics Building in New Haven (pl. 28), which probably would have been an early masterpiece had it been built, and in the Carol W. Newman Library of the Virginia Polytechnic Institute in Blacksburg, Virginia, also designed in 1970 but built some years later.

In both cases, the analogy to one of Aalto's characteristic motifs is only the external symptom of a deeper, fundamental affinity.

Alvar Aalto's work has meant the most to me of all the work of Modern masters. It is for me the most moving, the most relevant, the richest source to learn from in terms of its art and technique.[49]

What interests Venturi about Aalto, this "Andrea Palladio of the Modern Movement," as he puts it, is the precarious balance between order and disorder, common and elevated language, the juxtaposition of modesty and monumentality. Those are qualities that one actually does find in the Yale Mathematics Building, and it is no wonder that some of Aalto's own solutions, like that of the SAS Building in Helsinki (see pl. 27), are directly recalled in the way this

34

31 Frankfurt am Main: exhibition hall (competition project, 1979; drawing: James H. Timberlake)

32 Guild House (1961), side view

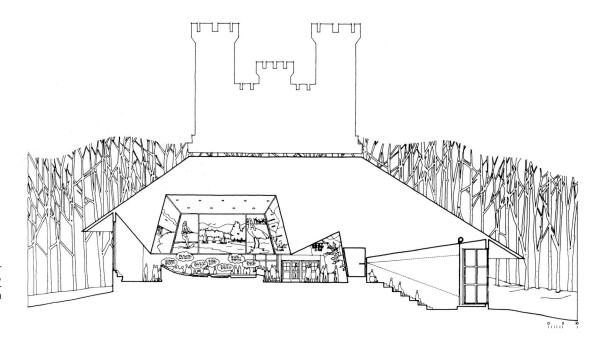

33 Hartwell Lake, Georgia: Hartwell Lake Regional Visitors' Center, section (Venturi and Rauch: competition project, 1978; drawing: Steven Izenour and Frederic Schwartz)

project inserts itself into the existing street by picking up the roofline of the beautiful Victorian buildings nearby.

The side view of the Guild House (pl. 32) reveals the articulation of the building's mass in terms of setbacks to be an ingenious formal means of taking a deliberately "boring" architecture and transforming it into a dynamic whole. A more recent project for an exhibition hall in Frankfurt am Main exhibits a similar solution (pl. 31). The streamlined envelope of this building is organized in a way that recalls both the body of a Chevrolet from the 1940s and the facade of Aalto's cultural center in Wolfsburg (1958). Here once again, the rhythm of the setbacks unifies the gigantic volume. Much earlier, the architects had proceeded in a similar vein with the design of the Transportation Building in Washington, D.C., a project whose urbanistic *parti* is clearly based on Aalto's solution for the Social Security Office in Helsinki (pls. 29, 30). In both cases, the difficult situation of a building that is virtually squeezed between the two axes of a bifurcation is neither ignored nor merely reflected in the architectural volumes. The "encroachments" made upon the structures by the diagonal traffic arteries actually seem to enhance them. On the other hand, Aalto's brilliance in using residual spaces for unforeseen functions and making them a factor of architectural meaning surfaces in the Venturis' work time and time again. Think only of Aalto's outdoor concert stage of 1929 and the impact it

had on the rear side of the "Football Hall of Fame" (pl. pp. 160-62) and, more recently, on the *parti* of the Laguna Gloria Art Museum in Austin, with its "residual spaces" serving as an outdoor café or children's playground on either side of the bay (pl. pp. 212-14).

Poché

Giedion admired Aalto's "combination of standardization with irrationality." Referring to Giedion, Venturi adds, however: "I prefer to think of Aalto's art as contradictory rather than irrational—an artful recognition of the circumstantial and the contextual and of the inevitable limits of the order of standardization."[50] The habit of considering Aalto as an "irrational" antipode of architectural rationalism and the "New Objectivity" says nothing about his real position as an architect, as has recently been demonstrated by Demetri Porphyrios. Basically, Porphyrios argues that Aalto cannot be understood in terms of the "Modern Movement." His deviations from the idea of formal "coherence" that was inherent in the work of the International Style, his predilection for loose "agglutinations" of building parts that are independent in structure, form, and spatial configuration, and his pleasure in hybrid compositions are rooted

36

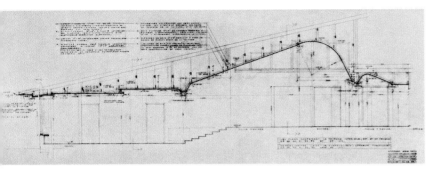

34 Bazoches: Villa Carré, section (Architect: Alvar Aalto, 1956)

35 Purchase, New York: State University of New York, Humanities Building (1968), entrance hall

historically in the culture of northern architecture around 1900 and in the conventions of the Ecole des Beaux-Arts. In this sense, Aalto's work embodies a "modern eclecticism."[51]

Combining very dissimilar parts into complex spatial sequences, a practice characteristic of Aalto's architecture from his free-standing houses to his monumental public buildings, is partly based, as Porphyrios has shown, on the ground plans for country manors around 1900, which at first glance seem unintelligible.[52] It is no coincidence, of course, that Venturi is fascinated in his own way by the country manors of the Shingle Style and the way that various domestic functions and flows of movement are dealt with in them (see p. 241). What Lindqvist, Gesellius, Lindgren, and Saarinen were for Aalto as the masters of northern national romanticism, McKim, Mead, and White; Furness; Richardson; and many others are for Venturi. Both architects seem to have adopted the formal principle of heterotopy from their masters. (It should be noted, in passing, that Richardson exerted a great influence on Scandinavia around 1900.)[53]

One of the axioms of Aalto's architecture is that the limits of an interior space must be defined by its function and character, not by the volume of the exterior or by the way its envelope is made up. In other words, interior space is an entity independent of both external appearance and structure. That is why Aalto often tolerates a certain amount of no-man's land between the shell of an interior room and the building's external skin, both in plan and in elevation. Two typical examples are the ground plan of the Institute of International Education in New York (1963) and the elevation of the Villa Carré in Bazoches-sur-Guyonne (1956; pl. 34) with its acoustical ceiling.[54]

The Ecole des Beaux-Arts named such interstices *pochés*. The mastery with which Aalto used this formal technique is a measure of his independence from the theories of orthodox Modernism and its belief that structure, space, and form in architecture must be identical.[55] It is not surprising that Venturi, too, playfully introduce "sectional" *pochés* as an architectural theme, as is most beautifully illustrated in the saillike vault of the corridor in the Humanities Faculty in Purchase, New York (1968; pl. 35). One might argue, in turn, that the line between architectural quotation, parody, and "American bastardy" (in G.L. Hersey's sense of the term) appears to be deliberately blurred in some later projects like the Hartwell Regional Visitors' Center (pl. 33) or a Jazz Club in Houston (pl. p. 222).

37

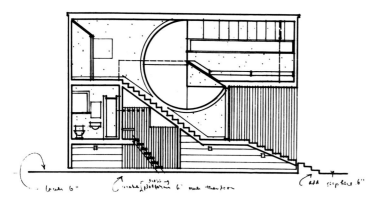

36   Loveladies, New Jersey: Lieb House, section (1967)

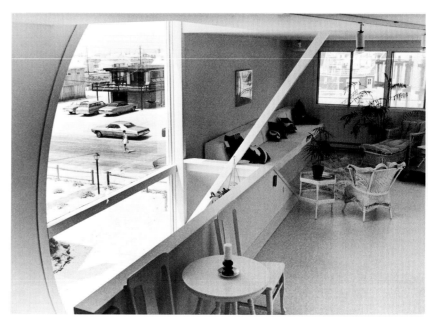

38   Loveladies, New Jersey: Lieb House, view from residential floor (1967)

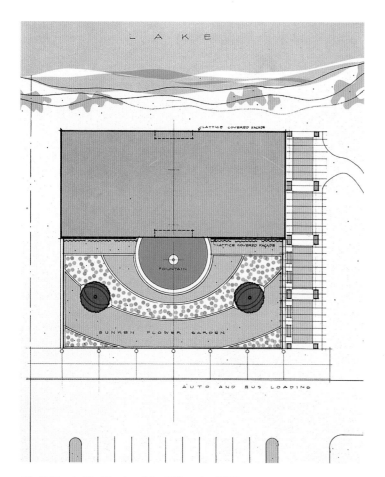

37   California City Planning, Sales Office, plan (1970)

39   Philadelphia: Guild House, community room with lunette window (1961)

"Inside" Is Not "Outside": The Dialectics of Frontality

In *Complexity and Contradiction* Venturi maintains that "contrast between the inside and the outside can be a major manifestation of contradiction in architecture. However, one of the powerful twentieth-century orthodoxies has been the necessity for continuity between them: the inside should be expressed on the outside."[56]

As is well known, Kahn had broken with this "orthodoxy" long before. His "asymmetrical architecture of 'almost nothing' depended no longer on the manifestation of structure as frame but rather on the manipulation of surface as the ultimate agent for the revelation of light, space and support."[57] Evidently, one of the functions of the lunette that integrates the facade of the Guild House is to demonstrate the "contradiction" mentioned earlier. As we have seen, the form of the segmental arch itself points to Kahn, for the archetype of the rectangular box with an inscribed circular "hole" is obviously implied as an architectural figure in the facade of the Guild House. In somewhat later projects like the Lieb House in Loveladies (1967; pls. 36, 38) or in the design for a vacation home for the art historian G. L. Hersey (1968), the same formula reappears even more explicitly— and suggests monumental scale for a small building. The project for the Sales Office in California City or the Humanities Building in Purchase show how such (Kahnian?) circles can be transferred from the elevation to the ground plan and brought into play there against the immaculate rectangularity of the ordinary American "box" and its constraints on scale (pls. 36–38).

The circle, suggested by the segmental arch, lends the facade of the Guild House its almost ceremonial identity. Moreover, it shows (and simultaneously veils) the fact that "a building can include things within things and spaces within spaces."[58] The facade is set onto the interior, as it were. Far from simply "expressing" the interior on the outside, it seems to want to take on some of the interior's spatial complexity while impressing some of its formal identity and scale upon the much smaller and far less formal rooms behind.

But the inside and the outside remain "autonomous." The outline of the opening as it cuts into the facade does not match the boundaries of the room to which it belongs. This opening (or the pieces of wall that frame it) serves as a means of both confining and directing the field of vision, as

40 Taplow: Nashdom (Architect: Sir Edwin Lutyens, 1905–1906)

41 Poissy near Paris: Villa Savoye (Architect: Le Corbusier, 1931)

42 Newton Square, Devon, Pennsylvania: Wike House, model (Venturi and Rauch, 1968)

43   Atlantic City, New Jersey: Marlborough Blenheim Hotel, renovation (Venturi and Rauch: project, 1977)

44   Paris: Ecole des Beaux-Arts on the Quai Malaquais (Architect: Félix Duban, 1860–1862)

45   Tuckers Town, Bermuda: House, view of interior (1975)

in the lounge of the Guild House or in the living room of the Lieb House, where one almost has the feeling of being trapped inside a camera the very moment the shutter snaps (pls. 38, 39). Elsewhere, in the lobby of the Humanities Building in Purchase, New York (pl. 35), the huge window in the flat brick façade is bigger than the actual opening behind. Seen from the inside, the vault of the lobby hangs below the glass and seems to be suspended from the sky.

Such exhilarating spatial tensions are an important theme in Venturi's early designs of villas and attain a virtuosolike quality in the unexecuted Wike House of 1968, where a curved, screenlike facade is placed upon the front like the mask of a tragic actor (pl. 42). In keeping with its residential function, the house is asymmetrical. References to the Villa Savoye and its "crowded intricacies within a rigid frame"[59] are combined with references to the Nashdom country manor in Taplow by Sir Edwin Lutyens (pls. 40, 41). An impressive set of preliminary studies by Venturi documents the quest for the "difficult whole" of the overall composition that would balance symmetry and asymmetry.

This architectural *parti* is realized at last in the house in Greenwich, Connecticut (see pp. 260–65) and was taken up again on quite a different scale in the competition for the government center in Canberra (pp. 195–97). In retrospect, the villa designs appear to have been, in part, laboratory experiments for solutions aiming at the monumental.

In this context, however, any drawings or plans chosen from the corpus of the firm's work can illustrate some of these themes. The geometric figure of the segmental arch, for example, meanders from the rear of the Vanna Venturi House to the upper story of the Guild House and onto commercial architecture, where it survives as the flat arch opening of the "Sales Office," as the portal sign above a group of stores in California City, or in the design of a hotel for Atlantic City, where it becomes the beaconlike sign rising above a hotel tower that is, in turn, bisected in a way that reminds one of the Guild House's giant order. Used in a more classical way as a genuine thermal window, the arch reappears in Gordon Wu Hall, where it terminates a vista and gives light to the library (p. 207).

This is how form can lead an autonomous life in architecture. "High windows" other than the lunette form discussed here are a favorite motif, too. There is a curious analogy between the oculus windows in the wing of the Ecole des Beaux-Arts built by Duban on the Quai Malaquais in Paris (1860–1862; pl. 44) and the Penn State Faculty Club and even the house in Westchester County and the house in Tuckers Town, Bermuda (pls. 44, 45; see pp. 266 f.).

Portal and Proscenium

Standing in front of the North Penn Visiting Nurses' Association Headquarters in Ambler, where Venturi had "symbolic" frames placed directly on the wall around small cellar windows in order to make them appear more important on the outside than they were on the inside (pl. 46), a friend and colleague put his arm around Venturi's shoulder and said: "Never put a frame around a window!" That was in 1960, when such things still caused uproar. Later, in *Complexity and Contradiction*, Venturi brought together a few historical examples from Baroque and Egyptian architecture to demonstrate that the use of symbolic frames to lend monumentality to small window openings (pls. 47, 48) was in fact a classical means of architectural accentuation.[60]

The resources for creating architectural fiction were exploited in the Guild House only on the entrance side—massively so in the portal. Compared to later works, however, the solution was restrained. Take the fire station (1966) in Columbus, Indiana, and its partly real, partly "ghost" facade. In addition to the actual wall that is twice the height of the building behind it, the architects suggested a "conceptual" wall, indicated merely by a surface of white brick that seems to form a large rectangle that is not physically there (pp. 158f.). Memories of the "shop-front" of the Midwest merge with those of cathedrals in northern Italy.

Although reminiscent of a shop-front, the white portal of the Guild House resembles rather the entrance to a wind tunnel—an effect underscored by the ominous, truncated column. At the same time, this recess seems to have taken the segmental arch that rounds off the facade and transferred it to the ground plan. The building's considerable depth, which is manifested in the successive recession of the three sections on either side of the center block, is thereby hinted at in the entrance facade as well.

In essence it is a proscenium, and in the middle of it stands a truncated column—a kind of architectural *Ubu Roi*. The allusion to a stage set seems to be confirmed by a comparison with the magnificent project for the Transportation Building in Washington, D.C. (1967; pl. 30), which the local Fine Arts Commission rejected as "ugly and ordinary."[61] Whereas the Guild House seems to want to thrust its volume onto the street bit by bit, the office building planned for Washington retreats from the curb, leaving the "cour d'honneur" framed by two-story com-

46 Ambler, Pennsylvania: North Pennsylvania Visiting Nurses' Association Headquarters (1961)

47 Karnak: symbolic gate, from *Complexity and Contradiction in Architecture* (1966)

48 Rome: Collegio di Propaganda Fide (Francesco Borromini, 17th c.), from *Complexity and Contradiction in Architecture* (1966)

mercial wings to stand, so to speak, as the empty shell of the Guild House's recessed mass. Thus an urban square emerges as a stage. The perspective drawing accentuates the "proscenium" and the "stage sets" that subdivide the space behind, give it rhythm, and emphasize the portal, which

49   Guild House, perspective view (1961; drawing: RV)

50   Greenwich, Connecticut: House (1970), rear with dining room extension

rises three stories high in the center of the building (pl. p. 217). In the same year the "scenographic" theme became completely explicit in the outdoor theater at the Humanities Building in Purchase (1968; p. 164). The small annex that gathers indirect light on the rear side of the house in Greenwich, Connecticut, brings it back into the sphere of the private country house (pl. 50). Recently, the theme has been both flattened and apotheosized in the facade of the Laguna Gloria Art Museum.

"Impressionist Architecture?"

As we have seen, simultaneously examining the facades of the Guild House and the photographs in *Complexity and Contradiction* can give one insights into the kind of architecture that has been part of the Venturis' reservoir of experience since 1960. The same is true, of course, for other projects completed by the firm: the Vanna Venturi House in Chestnut Hill, for example (1961).

The street facade, with its two separate yet connected triangular flanks, adopts the "duality" of the facade of Luigi Moretti's apartment house on Via Parioli in Rome (about 1950). The overall outline recalls the form of the William Low House by McKim, Mead, and White (1887). The frontality and symmetry of the overall form; the asymmetry

of the windows, which is derived from their domestic functions; the flatness of the facade; and, last but not least, the motif of the *fenêtre en longeur* recall Le Corbusier, particularly the Villa Stein in Garches (1927; pl. 22). On the other hand, references to Rome and Vicenza are embodied in these analogies, too. One is reminded of the rear wall of the nympheum of Villa Barbaro in Maser by Palladio and Alessandro Vittoria, whose arches, gracefully ornamented by a garland, simultaneously separate and join the two wings of the rear wall. Inevitably, Michelangelo's Porta Pia in Rome comes to mind as well (see p. 244).

Clearly, the two facades of the Guild House and of the Venturi residence are not meant to be replicas of their historical sources but rather ephemeral "symbols" that do nothing more than call to mind the physical contours and visual complexity of earlier historical buildings. As Venturi writes: "We cannot construct Classical buildings, but we can *represent* them, via *appliqué* upon the substance of the building."[62]

It may not be altogether inappropriate to apply the term "impression" to the type of visual references embodied in the Guild House or the home for Vanna Venturi. The concept of "Impressionist architecture" is in fact not new. It had been used by Hendrik Petrus Berlage, the father of modern architecture in Holland (1856–1934). "Impressionism in general," as Berlage defined the term, "means the reproduction of the image as it is perceived not objectively,

51 Guild House (1961)

52 Philadelphia: ISI Building (1978), detail of facade

53 Greenwich, Connecticut: House (1970), study for facade

54 Oberlin, Ohio: Allen Memorial Art Museum (1973), galleries

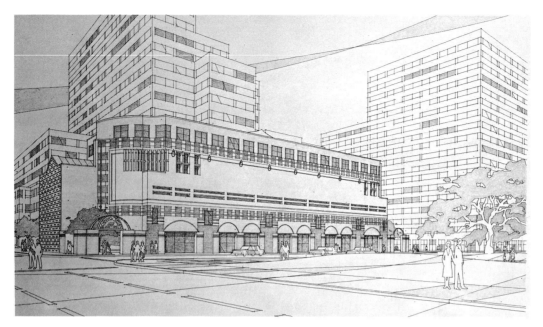

55 Austin, Texas: Laguna Gloria Art Museum (1985), entrance facade (VRSB: project, 1985; drawing: Richard Mohler)

56 "De Luxe Bulletins," from Wilmot Lippincott, *Outdoor Advertising* (1923)

but subjectively…. [It] treats the detail as subordinate to the whole and this, in turn, as subordinate to the great general impression."[63] Wessel Reinink has pointed out the paradox that Berlage's theory combined the emphasis on perception characteristic of Impressionist painting with the stress on form demonstrated in the work of a Symbolist painter like Jan Toorop, in which the rituals of industrial life seem to be

consecrated through art.[64] In a way, this may be comparable to what characterizes the two buildings mentioned above. They are impressionistic in their relationship to history while embodying an architectural "symbolism" that relates the everyday to the sacred.

It may have something to do with the Venturis' growing interest in the architecture and decorative arts of Art

44

Nouveau, specifically, their interest in Vienna (and particularly the late work of Otto Wagner), that iridescent facades divided into variegated surface patterns have become an increasingly important architectural theme in the firm's work since the early 1970s. The topic is broached for the first time—in what one might call a still brutalist "let-it-all-hang-out" manner—in the "oversized" holes punched in the metal balcony balustrades of the Guild House (pl. 51). In the pattern of the glazed bricks of the house in Greenwich, Connecticut (1970), it is spread over the entire facade, which, when the light is right, flashes like a Fata Morgana out of the greenery (pl. 53; see pp. 260–61). Occasionally, as with the gallery added to the Allen Art Museum of Oberlin (1973) or with the ISI Building in Philadelphia (pls. 52, 54), the architecture as a whole even seems to be set aflutter like the screen of a poorly tuned-in television set (or the flower-strewn lawn of a landscape by Gustav Klimt).

The facade of the Laguna Gloria Art Museum (pl. 55) embodies not only references to Le Corbusier's Villa Schwob but to Aalto's Enso Gutzeit Administration Building in Helsinki and to American billboards (pls. 56–59) as well. The archetype that incorporated and anticipated all the elements of this architectural "pastiche" (in the literary and musical sense) is the seventeenth-century Aqua Paola near S. Pietro in Montorio on the Gianicolo hill in Rome—not far from the American Academy.

It is a building whose colossal inscription could prove that even that all-American institution, the billboard, is rooted in the high architecture of Europe. So what the Venturis repeatedly stress seems indeed to be true: that the road from Las Vegas does lead back to Rome (pl. 58).

Yet the building in Austin is a museum, and not only for James Stirling is it *de rigueur* in the context of this genre to go back to Schinkel's Altes Museum in Berlin. Venturi does not pick up any single element of the classical language, say, the motif of the colonnade as such (or, as with Stirling's National Gallery in Stuttgart, the rotunda). Rather, he responds to the pulsating visual mixture of the wall panels that appear behind the classical colonnade and subvert its austere order with syncopation (pl. 59).[65]

57 La Chaux-de-Fonds: Villa Schwob (Architect: Ch. E. Jeanneret, 1915)

58 Rome: Acqua Paola (Architect: Flaminio Ponzio, 1610–1614)

59 Berlin: Altes Museum (Architect: Karl Friedrich Schinkel, 1822–1830)

These are effects traditionally sought and achieved less in the medium of architecture than in that of craft trades involving textiles or marquetry. That is why "tabernacle" is the key word most likely to come to mind when one views this facade. In the light of Venturi's affinity to decorative art and handicrafts, it is not surprising that, through impressionism (for lack of a better term here), Venturi and his team found an almost disarmingly direct—or indeed naive—way of responding to the architecture of Islam.

In their design for the Iraqi State Mosque in Baghdad, these architects did not plan to produce a literal copy of any one style but rather to integrate a broad spectrum of traditional Islamic shrines. References to Isfahan, Samarkand, Córdoba, and Samarra are combined with elements of the Ibn Tulun mosque in Cairo and the great mosque in Kairuan and woven into a gigantic architectural fairy tale (pl. 60; pp. 198 f.).

The historical premises for this kind of architectural orientalism are clearly to be found in eighteenth-century chinoiseries and, even more directly, in the works of Sir Edwin Lutyens. For what is true of the design for Baghdad is also true of Lutyens's magnificent capitol buildings of New Delhi, which have always intrigued Venturi (just as they had Le Corbusier). The very way they integrate historical motifs—in Lutyens's case, those of Indian architecture—places them within a profoundly European and Anglo-Saxon tradition. Their style may look postmodern; the culture that underlies them is all the more thoroughly modern.[66]

60 Baghdad: State Mosque, view of interior (VRSB: competition project, 1982-1983)

4 Language Games and Mass Media

A trademark of the Guild House is the systematic use of square windows. The motif, which has its roots in "ordinary" Philadelphia row housing and recalls Bruno Taut's work as well (see pl. 24), keeps reappearing in the designs of Aldo Rossi, Charles Moore, Oswald M. Ungers, Giorgio Grassi, Michael Graves, and Alvaro Siza, to name a few protagonists of the postmodern academe. Yet it is the way in which the architects of the Guild House dealt with this motif that is exciting–or unnerving–but in any case unmistakably Venturian.

Ostensibly, the size of the windows varies according to the needs of the interior spaces they serve. The more limited the field of vision, the smaller the opening cut into the facade. It is only logical, therefore, that the windows looking directly onto the opposite side of the street are comparatively tiny, whereas those in the recessed, already somewhat more distant, parts of the building are "normal" in size, and those opening on the side and affording a view along the street are large, extending almost from floor to ceiling (pl. 62). Yet this variation serves a formal purpose. As Venturi explains, "The change in scale of these almost banal elements contributes an expression of tension and a quality to these facades, which now read as both conventional and unconventional forms at the same time."[67]

If we replace the term "facades" in this passage with the word "flags," we have an exact description of the effect that Jasper Johns must have intended with his *Three Flags* (pl. 61). The picture was painted in 1958, and since a photograph of it appears in *Complexity and Contradiction*, it is obviously part of the immediate artistic context of the Guild House.[68] The theme is the paradox of a categorically unaesthetic and exclusively symbolic motif that is presented

61   Jasper Johns: "Three Flags" (1958), New York, Whitney Museum of American Art (50th Anniversary Gift of the Gillman Foundation, Inc., the Lauder Foundation, A. Alfred Taubman, an anonymous donor and purchase, Acq. No. 80.32)

62   Philadelphia: Guild House (1961), side view

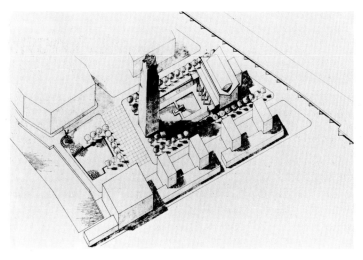

63 Rotterdam: reconstruction design of the Late Gothic Sint Laurens Kerk, badly damaged in World War II, with the tower restored and a model replica in front (Architect: J. J. P. Oud, 1950)

64 Philadelphia: Welcome Park with miniature replica of the house of William Penn (1982)

by the artist in a way that forces the observer to perceive it aesthetically—as pure form. In both the painting and the building, the motif is hammered into our minds, as it were, by triple repetition; by its gradation into foreground, middle ground, and background: and, finally, by a shift of scale that almost hurts by contradicting and neutralizing the foreshortening, implied by the gradation in the painting and through the setbacks in plan in the building.

"Meaning" and "Symbolism"

In *Complexity and Contradiction* Venturi writes: "Familiar things seen in an unfamiliar context become perceptually new as well as old."[69] This says two things. First, that in order to be seen and appreciated as "art," the everyday object has to be transferred to a place that switches off its conventional meaning as a functional appliance.[70] Basically, this is the "decontextualization" that Marcel Duchamp undertook when he put a toilet bowl into a museum, thereby declaring it to be an object worthy of aesthetic appreciation. On a more literal level, Venturi's phrase says that "meaning" in architecture is something that changes according to the context in which an architectural form appears. This had been the key idea in his Master's project of 1950.[71]

Big and little. On one hand, Venturi's design features the detail that is "too big," beginning with the holes in the metal balustrades of the Guild House, developed further in the facade patterns of the gallery wing in the Allen Art Museum (pl. 54), playfully carried to an extreme in the "book" marking the entrance to the art library there (pl. 78). On the other hand, there are the miniature replicas of historical buildings. Reminiscent of the *presepio* or the doll house, such architectural representations are frequently located on the site of the buildings to which they refer—or rather, next to them—one purpose being to present these buildings on a smaller scale because they are either too large or too inaccessible for passers-by to behold easily. The intent is no different than that behind the architectural representations ornamenting the entrance lobbies of New York's old skyscrapers, whose architecture cannot be seen as long as one is standing right in front of them (see pl. 66).[72] Thus, Richardson's Trinity Church is duplicated as a toy in the middle of Copley Square in a 1966 project for Boston, and in Galveston, Texas, a miniature replica of the Strand street front was designed to adorn a children's playground. Then

65 Exhibition panel for *Signs of Life* (1976) ▶

WELCOME, FREE ASPRIN, ASK US ANYTHING, STYLISH STOUTS, SURF, CITY HALL, ONE WAY, STOP.

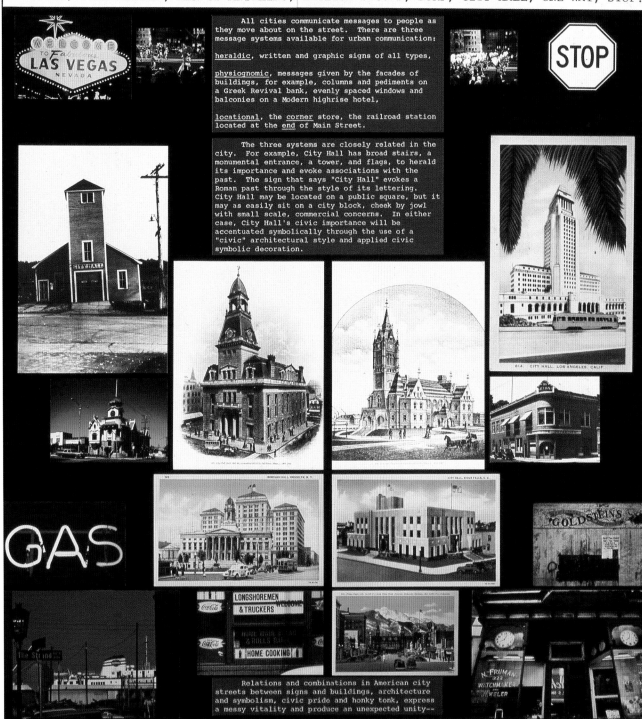

All cities communicate messages to people as they move about on the street. There are three message systems available for urban communication:

heraldic, written and graphic signs of all types,

physiognomic, messages given by the facades of buildings, for example, columns and pediments on a Greek Revival bank, evenly spaced windows and balconies on a Modern highrise hotel,

locational, the corner store, the railroad station located at the end of Main Street.

The three systems are closely related in the city. For example, City Hall has broad stairs, a monumental entrance, a tower, and flags, to herald its importance and evoke associations with the past. The sign that says "City Hall" evokes a Roman past through the style of its lettering. City Hall may be located on a public square, but it may as easily sit on a city block, cheek by jowl with small scale, commercial concerns. In either case, City Hall's civic importance will be accentuated symbolically through the use of a "civic" architectural style and applied civic symbolic decoration.

Relations and combinations in American city streets between signs and buildings, architecture and symbolism, civic pride and honky tonk, express a messy vitality and produce an unexpected unity—

not an obvious or easy unity, but one derived from the complexity of city life, a unity that "maintains, but only just maintains, a control over the clashing elements that compose it." (August Heckscher, 1962)

66 New York: Fuller Building, entrance hall with "representation" by Elie Nadelman (1931) (Architects: Walker & Gaillette, 1928-1929)

there are the models of the Capitol Building and the White House in Washington, D.C. (p. 119), the wood mock-ups of which, unfortunately, were never realized in stone after all. Lastly, there are the bronze maquette of the William Penn sculpture that stands atop Philadelphia's City Hall and the bronze model of Penn's House, both erected in VRSB's charming "Welcome Park" on the edge of Philadelphia's old town (pl. 64). Curiously enough, J.J.P. Oud had proposed a similar idea thirty-five years earlier in his scheme for a new Sint Laurens Kerk in Rotterdam (pl. 63).[73]

These miniature replicas represent a type of architectural "meaning" somewhat different from that symbolic ambiguity and formal tension that Venturi postulated in his early writings and designs. Their meaning is based on mimetic "representation" of models, although combined with miniaturization. Their "symbolism" is direct, unambiguous, and denotative in nature. One can trace how, under the impact of the crass iconographies of Las Vegas, the concern for the "forgotten symbolism" of conventional architectural signs has become increasingly important in the work of this office since about 1970. In her study on "the city as a communication system" (1976), Denise Scott Brown brought together the results of her years of research on the forms of verbal and iconographic denotation and connotation that make the traditional American city function as a communication system (pl. 65). These studies parallel and relate to the theoretical research that was conducted during the 1960s by the sociologist Melvin Webber, among others.[74]

On the other hand, the work of Venturi, Rauch and Scott Brown reflects issues that were formulated in the realm of art history decades ago by authors like Sedlmayr, Krautheimer, Baldwin Smith, Bandmann, Reinle, and Wittkower. Indeed, the Venturis' interest in "symbolism" relates to the "meaningless formalism"[75] of the predominantly late modern architecture of the 1960s in much the same way that the interest in architectural iconography documented in the work of the authors cited above relates to traditional art history's primary (and one-sided) preoccupation with the structural, formal, and stylistic make-up of architecture. The authors of *Learning from Las Vegas* know only too well that the theoretical foundations of modern architecture are closely linked with the questions of modern art history, particularly with the aesthetics of "pure visibility."[76] This is all the more so because their own theoretical interests—at least Venturi's—focused originally on *gestalt* psychology and the mechanisms of visual perception. To that extent, their more recent embrace of the crass, popular realism of the Strip and the malicious pleasure with which they declare gigantic mock-up animals, a sailing ship, and even a red apple the size of a circus tent to be motifs of a contemporary monumental art (pl. 95) are both a critique of their earlier and much more abstract imagery of urban design and a low blow against the aesthetic convictions of established Modernism.

In 1982 Venturi stressed that the historicism practiced by his firm had nothing to do with the "battle of styles" of the nineteenth century, when the choice between one or the other idiom of Gothic architecture—perpendicular or decorated—was a theological question of faith: "Our historicism should involve less a rivalry and more a medley of styles; like the free eclecticism of late eighteenth-century garden pavilions."[77] The reason given for this is social. The Venturis believe that historicism used in this way provides a spectrum of architectural forms capable of responding to the plurality of tastes in our society. Yet they are well aware that knowledge of the symbolic conventions underlying popular everyday life—whether in Las Vegas or in Levittown—is not enough to produce architectural works to which a "symbolic" quality in a higher sense is peculiar. What a difference there is between the representational "symbolism" of any neocolonial ranch house—or indeed of Gropius's replica of Independence Hall at the New York World's Fair of 1939[78]—and the evocative rather than denotative symbolism of Venturi's ghost architecture of Franklin Court.

Language Games and Theory of Signs

Many of the buildings documented in this book have inscriptions that seem to be too big and that must be as puzzling to the uninformed passer-by as they may be informative to the insider. The Strip's system of communication seems to have become an aesthetic theme on such facades. But it would be inadequate to see in this nothing but a pop theme. As Denise Scott Brown wrote on one of the didactic panels in the 1976 exhibition entitled "Signs of Life":

> Nineteenth and early twentieth-century architects made more use of signs on buildings than do architects today.... For important buildings, mottos and hortatory texts might be extended across facades in the classical Roman manner, as for example on the Pantheon. These inscriptions were considered by architects as part of the decoration of buildings... [whereas] in today's climate of revulsion against the vulgar, building signs are often reduced in size until they are almost imperceptible and sometimes appear to have been an afterthought.[79]

It is not difficult to detect behind this historical overview a concern that has occupied Venturi and Rauch since the early 1960s, for the lettering above the portal of the Guild House is also, in fact, primarily "decoration."[80]

In *Learning from Las Vegas*, the Venturis have taken a close-up description of the facade of the Guild House as a vehicle for expounding an architectural theory of signs, however fragmentary. Some of its passages read like the empirical checklist of criteria that Umberto Eco presented in his famous essay on architectural semiology.[81] Reading the Venturi text, one is led to believe that their architecture serves as a complex system of denotations and connotations, informing the occupant and the visitor about the function of the building in question. The Guild House thereby appears to be a demonstration of the semantic "multivalence" postulated by Charles Jencks[82] as an antidote to the reductionist definitions of architecture in terms of structural logic or spatial flow. Yet the fragments of information and signs that make up this facade ultimately underlie a logic different from that of simple denotation and information. They constitute a closed system of artistic meaning.

Therefore, the "signs" constituting this facade, even the bold characters of the inscription above the portal, do not primarily convey information to the "naive" user. To the

67   Robert Rauschenberg: *Trophy I* (1959), Zurich, Kunsthaus

extent that this facade represents a piece of architectural Pop Art, these signs are elements of an artistic discourse. What Denise Scott Brown said of the inscription above the portal of the Allen Memorial Museum in Oberlin applies to that of the Guild House, too: "The design effect of the text was more important to the architect than its content."[83] Seen in

51

68 Philadelphia: Grand's Restaurant (1961), interior

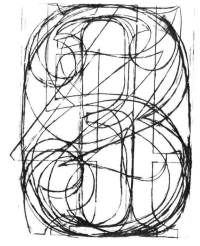

69 Jasper Johns: *O Through 9* (1960)

the Guild House, which has an inscription like a department store, a "Palladian" lunette, and the replica of a television antenna, pulls off a similar aesthetic and semantic balancing act. It is not just "language" used as a means of communication; it is essentially a "language game," to use the term John Russell proposed in his discussion of Pop Art in general.[84]

In the present context this may suffice to indicate the purpose of "commercial" signs and associations in the Guild House. In view of the home's function for senior citizens, the question of appropriateness remains. Such thoughts are idle when they involve buildings having a commercial character from the outset. In the remodeling of Grand's Restaurant in Philadelphia in the same year (1961), the owner's name ("GRAND'S") was spread across the entire width of the two connected row houses. The letters were made correspondingly large. It is clear that the function of this inscription is more ornamental in nature than informative, for in the middle the monogram is interrupted by a large, three-dimensional replica of a coffee cup. Moreover, the panel that carries the lettering is blue on the left, yellow on the right. The two halves of the one-syllable monogram do not make sense; the passer-by reads either "GRA" or "ND'S," depending on the angle of vision. The information that comes across is the "sign quality" of the bold characters as decoration—not the name of the establishment (p. 299). In this way, the sign *does* ultimately follow the advertising principle of making a sign difficult to read to ensure that it will be read, as in the reversed "R" in the toy store sign and the "XX" in Exxon.

Venturi describes the interior as follows:

> The patterns of the letters spelling the proprietor's name, which extend almost the whole length of the room, have the character of conventional stencils. On the facing wall a direct reflection is juxtaposed against the "windows" to the open kitchen. These illogicalities emphasize the more ornamental function of the typography."[85] (pl. 68)

In this context the next obvious step is to refer to Jasper Johns again, for it was he who introduced this type of stenciling in the iconography of Pop Art.[86] Typography as ornament, or more precisely, the use of lettering in such a way as to have a general, aesthetic quality that takes precedence over any informational content. That is the theme of John's charcoal drawing *0 Through 9* (pl. 69) executed shortly before, in 1960.[87] What one "reads" in that drawing is obviously not one or other of the numerals superimposed upon each other but rather the flickering that

such a way the lettering on the Guild House can be compared with the dented and rusted "WATCH YOUR STEP" sign that Robert Rauschenberg inserted into his 1959 picture entitled *Trophy I* (pl. 67).

Evidently, Rauschenberg was aiming here to create a precarious balance between ready-mades that belong to various levels of reality and yet entertain ironic interrelationships. The sign "WATCH YOUR STEP" is a comment on the delicate balancing act that Merce Cunningham is performing on the press photo in the upper right corner. The facade of

their combination produces, like a digital clock running too quickly.

Compared to later Venturian solutions, the attempt to use this small student restaurant *à tout prix* as a laboratory for transferring Pop-Art "language games" to architecture may seem a bit forced. In the Dixwell Fire Station in New Haven, Connecticut (1967), the relationship between script and building is resolved in a classical way. Not without reason does Venturi like to speak of this firehouse as a kind of Palladian *barchessa*. The names of the individual fire brigades—"Rescue Truck Co. 4, Engine Co. 6, and Engine Co. 3"—are arranged to form a frieze spanning the entire width of the facade and beyond. The letters themselves, placed above the garage door, have a symbolic and stylistic affinity with the subdivisions of the windows set in the large doors, which recall industrial architecture of the 1930s. To the right of the building, the curved facade peels slightly away from the mass of the structure like a billboard, as if to provide the extra length needed for the letters of the sign. The irony that this inscription conveys information unlikely to be of vital interest to anyone does not occur to one until the second glance. Its real message is evidently not in the cumbersome identification of three fire brigades that happen to be quartered there, but rather: writing = ornament (see p. 177).

In this way, via strip and shopping mall, architecture once again ties into the tradition of classicism. Yet above all else, it is a comment on the visual reality of the Strip, where architectural language, reduced to a minimum, is compensated for by an excess of verbal messages that are perceived as only so much visual "noise." When the Dixwell Fire Station was commissioned, the Venturis were busy analyzing the images that they had brought back from their study trips to Las Vegas. It was at this time that they drew the diagram (pl. 71) recording the interaction between space, scale, speed, and type of commercial symbolism in traditional and modern urban situations, from the medieval market to the North American Strip. A few years later, the architects were offered the opportunity to pick the most radical type of "decorated shed" documented in the study and to realize it: a facade consisting only of letters that are twice as high as the neutral and unornamented hall behind them (pl. 70).

Indeed: "What do you do with a building that is 16 feet high and 1,100 feet long, with only two doors and no windows?" The response indicates what kind of effect was to be achieved by the row of five, bright red letters: "The vast space of the parking lot coupled with the unrelieved banality

70   Bristol Township, Pennsylvania: BASCO Showroom (1971)

DIRECTIONAL SPACE

	SPACE · SCALE section 1in.:50 ft.	SPEED	SYMBOL sign-symbol · bldg. ratio
EASTERN BAZAAR		3 M.P.H.	▲
MEDIEVAL STREET		3 M.P.H.	● ▲
MAIN STREET		3 M.P.H. 20 M.P.H.	w ▲
COMMERCIAL STRIP		35 M.P.H.	● W ▲
THE STRIP		35 M.P.H.	●W ▲
SHOPPING CENTER		3 M.P.H. 50 M.P.H.	● w ▲

SPACE · SCALE · SPEED · SYMBOL

71   Space-Scale-Speed symbol, from *Learning from Las Vegas* (1972)

53

73 Boston: City Hall (Architects: Kallmann, McKinnell and Knowles, 1963–1968)

72 Robert Venturi: ironical counter-project for Boston City Hall

74 Philadelphia: PSFS Building (Architects: G. Howe and W. Lescaze, 1932)

of the architecture suggested a design of bold communication rather than one of subtle expression."[88] Evidently, the BASCO solution represents an extreme. From there, the road continues, or leads back, to the ceremonial inscriptions of Gordon Wu Hall at Princeton, the Laguna Gloria Art Museum at Austin, and the extension to the National Gallery in London, which once again recall Renaissance and neoclassical models (pp. 203, 212f.).

Ceci tuera cela

Let us remain for a moment with this firm's early involvement in the dialectics of "writing and building," a problem that is evidently central in the work of architects who are engaged not only in the business of design but also in writing about their designs. At first glance their juxtapositions of "writing" and "building" may strike one as playful. Yet despite the sometimes polemical and paradoxical nature of their discourse, more basic matters are

concerned—indeed, the development of a new definition of architecture. This was shown by 1972, when Venturi published a sketch for an office building that was topped by a blinking sign reading, "I am a monument" (pl. 72).[89]

It was a "counterproposal" for the new City Hall in Boston, which, together with the surrounding complex, was to represent, as the authors of *Learning from Las Vegas* put it, "the archetype of enlightened urban renewal." Writing about the city hall itself (pl. 73), Venturi, Scott Brown, and Steven Izenour stated:

Its profusion of symbolic forms that recall the extravagances of the General Grant period and the revival of the medieval piazza and its palazzo pubblico is, in the end, a bore. It is too architectural. A conventional loft would accommodate a bureaucracy better, perhaps with a blinking sign on top saying "I AM A MONUMENT."[90]

Is this statement merely a joke? A paradoxical declaration of architecture's bankruptcy? Or both?

Or is the sketch to be interpreted as an apology by the "International Style" for the formalism of late modern

76 "Bern Anno 1950," from Eduard von Rodt, *Das alte Bern* (1880)

75 A. and V. Vesnin: offices of the *Leningradskaya pravda*, Leningrad (cover of the journal *Sovremennaya arkhitektura*, 1926)

architecture? Even this interpretation would not be entirely wrong, for it is worth remembering that giant signboards and illuminated letters, combined with steel and glass architecture, played a considerable role in the language of the "New Architecture" of the 1920s and 1930s. It is enough to think of the magnificent PSFS building by Howe and Lescaze in Philadelphia (pl. 74).[91]

One of the modern prototypes of a programmatic combination of writing and glass architecture might be the project by the Vesnin brothers for the *Leningradskaya pravda* building in Leningrad (1926). The architecture involved is little more than a kind of architectural scanner, an information terminal with a "viewing screen" on which the latest dispatches appear (pl. 75).[92]

Overcoming architecture, or its murder by the written word, is a topic of the nineteenth century. Not a few do-gooders at that time loved to evoke the future of architecture and of the city in pictures of eerily monotonous rows of houses whose only "decoration" were the huge signs identifying the function of their parts. An example is the title page of a book on "Old Berne" from 1880.[93] One sees the

writing on the wall: "Berne in the year 1950." Instead of depicting the medieval town's picturesque streets, the drawing presents monotonous blocks of houses with factory smokestacks (pl. 76). Only the inscriptions make it clear that the buildings themselves serve various functions: "Neighborhood Heating," "9% Interest," "Public Kitchen," "Painting Factory," "Darwinianum" (presumably as a substitute for Berne's Gothic cathedral).

It would be nonsensical to draw too close a relationship between the content of these three examples of "writing and building." Venturi's ironic proposal of 1966, Vesnin's utopian project of 1926, and Eduard von Rodt's conservative, frightening vision of 1880 serve in this context only to document the existence of an extensive background to the interests of the Venturis. After all, of course, it was Victor Hugo who saw the relationship between word and building as *the* critical issue of architecture in modern times: "Why should we be surprised that human intelligence has left architecture for the printer's shop?"

In the Renaissance, according to Hugo, the printed book, that "woodworm of the edifice," had already begun to suck

77   Paris: Bibliothèque Ste.Geneviève (Architect: Henri Labrouste, 1838–1850)

78   Oberlin, Ohio: Allen Memorial Art Museum (1973), entrance to library

dry and consume architecture, which, during the period of the Gothic cathedral, had once spoken in its own language:

> L'architecture va se ternissant, se décolorant, s'effaçant de plus en plus. Le livre imprimé, ce ver rongeur de l'édifice, la suce et la dévore. Elle se dépouille, elle s'effeuille, elle maigrit à vue d'œil. Elle est mesquine, elle est pauvre, elle est nulle.
>
> [Architecture is becoming duller, losing color, fading more and more. The printed book, that woodworm of the ediface, is sucking and devouring it. It is being denuded, it is being defoliated, it is being emaciated before our very eyes. It is shabby; it is poor; it is nil.][94]

After the invention of the printing press, said Hugo, architecture relinquished its hereditary role as the "grande écriture du genre humain" [great literature of the human race] having to yield it to the book. As he saw it, architecture since the Renaissance had come to be condemned to a wretched existence in the background of contemporary culture. "Ceci tuera cela. Le livre tuera l'édifice." [This will kill that. The book will kill the edifice.][95]

One should at least note in passing that this thought was translated almost literally into architectural reality during Hugo's own lifetime in the magnificent Bibliothèque Ste. Geneviève in Paris (1838-1850; pl. 77).[96] The architect, Henri Labrouste, who was one of Hugo's friends, took the

opportunity afforded by this commission—a library, after all—to elaborate on the theme of architecture being superseded by the printed word. He did this on one hand by reducing the architectural articulation—base, door frame, entablature, and pilasters—to a thin relief and, on the other hand, by ornamenting the fields between the pilasters in the upper story with the names of the authors whose works were preserved behind them in the library's reading room.[97]

Speaking on what he believes to be "The Right Lessons from the Beaux-Arts" during a symposium on Beaux-Arts architecture at the Architectural Association in London (1978), Venturi showed his competition project of 1967, the "Football Hall of Fame" (pp. 160–62), and compared it to the Bibliothèque Ste. Geneviève, which Neil Levine had analyzed in a previous session. The project could be seen, he said, as "a later evolution of architecture as book, described by Neil Levine in his analysis of the Bibliothèque Ste. Geneviève, referring especially to its facade."[98] However, he added, this "Bill-Ding-Board" was not situated next to the Place du Panthéon but on the edge of a giant parking lot, a fact that explains the choice of architectural imagery inspired by commercial equipment. The project itself, a design for a kind of national football memorial with a huge bulletin board on which current sporting events could be announced (as was to be the case, *mutatis mutandis*, with the Vesnins' *Leningradskaya pravda* building!), is described elsewhere in this book.

56

But there are even more direct connections between Labrouste and the firm of Venturi, Rauch and Scott Brown. Labrouste gave the facade of his library's upper story the shape of a gigantic bookshelf on which the enlarged stone spines of books, bearing the great names of world literature, are lined up. At Oberlin College, the entrance to the art history library is flanked by a 5'10" replica of a book. Although the book's primary function is to conceal an electronic security system, it could almost have been taken from Labrouste's shelf and transplanted to the Allen art history library (pl. 78). Be that as it may, during his lecture Venturi stated: "I see [this book] as a symbol of Victor Hugo's 'Ceci tuera cela.'" And in connection with Franklin Court (pp. 104–9), he asked: "Might not this ghost also symbolize the death of architecture as predicted by Hugo?"[99]

79   Philadelphia, Guild House (1961), view from street side

Architecture's Abdication?

As early as 1966, Venturi wrote in *Complexity and Contradiction in Architecture*:

> The architect who would accept his role as combiner of significant old clichés—valid banalities—in new contexts as his condition within a society that directs its best efforts, its big money, and its elegant technologies elsewhere, can ironically express in this indirect way a true concern for society's inverted scale of values.[100]

If architecture wants to survive as a discipline, he argues, it must accept its place on the sidelines and learn to live with the fact that the medium of architecture plays only a subsidiary role in the culture of industrial society.

Venturi's affinity to Hugo is thus no coincidence; nor is it the result of an "influence."[101] Basically, the "death of architecture" for this architect is not a matter of philosophical speculation; it is a *fait accompli*.

Yet above all, it is an artistic *theme*. It is symptomatic enough that the passage cited above does not make a plea, say, to use architecture to correct "society's inverted scale of values" but rather to use it as a means "to express concern for [those] values." The early buildings by Venturi and Rauch could, in the end, *also* be interpreted as attempts "to express" the intricate and complicated situation of the modern city and, especially, of architecture in it.

This seems to be particularly true of the Guild House and its facade, which may be interpreted as a latter-day stylization of Hugo's view of architecture being "denuded," "defoliated," and "emaciated": an embodiment of a bodiless architecture wasted away so much that from behind the superimposed brick facade, which just barely manages to evoke Palladio and Kahn, even the building's wretched skeleton peeks through.

Electronics and Architecture

The media, which in the Venturis' opinion consign architecture to the background in our society, are allowed to make a rather indecently overt showing in the Guild House. The commercial nature of the lettering over the entrance has already been mentioned. Originally, the central axis of the entrance facade was crowned by a shimmering, gold-colored aluminum replica of a large television antenna—introduced here both as the symbol for the preferred leisure-time activity of senior citizens and as an ironic variation on the theme of classical facade sculpture.

The motif is not new in the history of modern architecture. Antennae and broadcast wires stylized into symbols, often supported by illuminated letters and bulletin boards for information and slogans (as exemplified by the Vesnin brothers) were used by the Soviet avantgarde in the early 1920s as emblems of the forced industrial development

80 Historic buildings with radio tower and antenna (anonymous drawing, USSR, about 1923)

81 Cambridge, Massachusetts: "The Tree of the World," metal sculpture by Richard Lippold in the courtyard of Harkness Commons, 1949 (with photo of Walter Gropius and associates)

prompted by the new elite (pl. 80). But what the Constructivist avantgarde in the Soviet Union around 1925 idealized as the anticipation of a socialist future (ironically with reference to industrially advanced America) is acknowledged by the American architect around 1960 primarily as a sign of the times. When it comes to media theory, it is no longer the time of Tretyakov but that of Webber and McLuhan—whose seminal book, *The Gutenberg Galaxy*, appeared in 1962 while the Guild House was under construction. The theme of Venturi's architecture is not the future but the present, and as for electronics and the modification it has caused in the cultural status of architecture, the present has long since caught up with yesterday's dreams of the future.[102]

Let us return to Victor Hugo. This antenna documents a situation in which it is not actually the printed word that has killed the building but rather the television screen that has killed the book. In purely formal terms the antenna resembles a kind of monstrance made of a concave wire frame with a circular contour. Perpendicular "arms" stretch out above it. In its two-dimensionality, the whole is like a visual abbreviation of the Guild House facade itself: an architectural replica reduced to a graphic cipher (pl. 82). The architects seem to have been thinking of Richard Lippold's metal sculptures as well—perhaps of the "Tree of the World" at Harvard (pl. 81)?[103] But they maliciously alienated this reference through the overtly "old fashioned" placement of the sculpture *atop* the facade (instead of on the ground next to it, as was sacrosanct practice in classical modern architecture).

The antenna, then, is both a diadem *and* a "ready-made." As a visual shorthand for an architectural theory, it is to Venturi's concept of architecture being consumed by modern mass media what the proverbial bidet in *L'Esprit Nouveau* is to Le Corbusier's idea of architecture as applied hygiene. Of course, both Venturi's antenna and Le Corbusier's bidet have an ancestor in Marcel Duchamp's "fountain" (1917), mentioned earlier in this chapter.

Rauschenberg and Johns should once again be noted as being among the American artists who have mixed levels of reality in a comparable way—the level of art and the level of everyday life. Venturi is fascinated by the way Rauschenberg takes raw material of everyday life, say, a chair placed in front of a canvas (in a work that is illustrated in *Complexity and Contradiction*) and in this way articulates a contradiction between various levels of function and meaning of the work of art and its milieu. (In other cases, Rauschenberg uses a tire, a stuffed hen, or a blaring radio.)[104]

Like Rauschenberg's pictures or, even more directly comparable, Jasper Johns's "Painted Bronze" (1960; "still life" consisting of a beer can and a bronze cast of a beer can), the antenna of the Guild House is an antenna and yet not an antenna; it is a multifaceted symbol "in the gap between life and art" (Claes Oldenburg)—and at the same time a kind of negative status symbol of the occupants. (I shall return to this aspect.)

It may seem exaggerated to interpret a motif like this in terms of iconography in the first place and to infer from it the existence of a "media theory" that allows one to think of Victor Hugo. But there are also other clues to the Venturis'

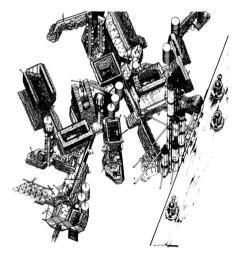

82 Guild House (1961), antenna

83 Archigram: "Plug-In City, Medium Pressure Area" (design: Peter Cook, 1964)

interests in media theory. In direct analogy to the architecture of classic Modernism, the early work of Gropius, Mies, and Le Corbusier, the authors of *Learning from Las Vegas* proclaim that, to stay relevant, architecture must reflect the technological reality of its time. Of course, they do not mean steel and glass construction or the Purist stereometry of the industrial architecture of 1910. "The relevant revolution today is the current electronic one."[105]

They wish not to be misunderstood, however. Nothing, they emphasize, is further from their minds than a glorification of the aesthetics of electronic installations as conveyed in the "Plug-In City" by Archigram, for example (1964; pl. 83).

Architecturally, the symbol systems that electronics purveys so well are more important than its engineering content.[106]

Of course, the production of Venturi, Rauch and Scott Brown is not completely uninfluenced by engineering "installations." The "technology" of conveying commercial information along the "Strip" has certainly not stopped shaping their world of forms. Part of their work—from Fire Station No. 4 (pp. 158f.) to the "Football Hall of Fame" and the Dixwell Fire Station (pp. 177f.) to the Museum of Austin (pp. 212f.)—is composed of variations on the theme of the American billboard. In that sense, the "Football Hall of Fame" and the Museum of Austin are to Las Vegas what Gropius's Fagus works are to the Ford Plant in Detroit. In both cases the theme is the "aesthetic filtration of American directness."[107]

If the idea that architecture must find its means of expression in the electronic media's "symbolic systems" (instead of in its engineering infrastructure) were to be taken to its logical conclusion, there would, in fact, be nothing left for architecture other than a noncommittal eclecticism. On the other hand, is not such an eclecticism appropriate for many of the day-to-day tasks that architects are called upon to perform? In that sense, perhaps a vacuum is filled when traditional, nineteenth-century architectural concepts of historical reference return in more recent Venturi projects.

5 The City as a Stage

In a famous passage of his architectural treatise, completed in about 1452, Alberti wrote that a palace is a small city, whereas a city is a large palace. Around 1960, Aldo van Eyck came back to this thought when he said: "A house must be like a small city, or it is not a proper house; and a city must be like a large house, or it is not a proper city."[108] It is no coincidence that Denise Scott Brown should explicitly refer to van Eyck's ideas, which have probably been more important to her and to Venturi's thinking than might appear at first glance. In an essay that appeared in 1967, five years after completion of the Guild House, she quoted the following maxim of her Dutch colleague: "What you should try to accomplish is built meaning. So get close to the meaning and build!" But he asks, "If society has no form—how can architects build the counterform?"[109]

The orphanage of Amsterdam (1958-1960, pl. 84), a building that is representative of a whole generation's architectural outlook, deeply rooted as it is in the experience of Black African folk architecture, can demonstrate how the Dutch architect answered his own question. According to him, if society has no form, then it is the architect's job to use his skills to suggest possibilities for more humane ways to coexist. It is therefore not merely a question of formal organization if the orphanage is structured as an open network of cells grouped around the core, with the number of cells being small enough to prevent the whole from disintegrating into an endless pattern of individual units, yet large enough for the orientation to a center to make sense. Architecture here is not merely the place where a community of human beings may form; it actually functions as the physical matrix, the spatial symbol of "community," in a way similar to that of the architecture of the North American pueblos, whose symbolism van Eyck has studied intensively.

Like the orphanage in Amsterdam, the Guild House is programmatically "built meaning," and, like its Dutch counterpart, it tries to give the idea of "community" an architectural form. Yet the Venturis' architecture is not a direct reflection of any "social form." Today, such a form is utopian. The Venturis' architecture therefore operates simultaneously on a more abstract *and* on a more obvious level. Although it uses architectural signs (instead of spaces), those signs tie into the historical and familiar models of "the house." To the extent that the Guild House interprets the city as it is (and not the romantic utopia of an urban community), the building—at least its imagery—is more "matter of fact" and therefore no doubt closer to the everyday experience of the "man in the street" than is the case with van Eyck's orphanage, built only about two years earlier.

84   Amsterdam: municipal orphanage (Architect: Aldo van Eyck, 1958-1960)

85 Milan: Gallaratese residential building (Architect: Aldo Rossi, 1968)

86 Montpellier: Antigone housing estate (Architect: Ricardo Bofill, 1980)

The Guild House, too, can be understood as a "little city." Insofar as its facade embodies the entire spectrum of the typical American city's imagery, from the commercial shopfront to the ordinary brownstone walk-up, it relates to its location in a way that is once again reminiscent of one of van Eyck's well-known maxims: "Whatever space and time may mean, place and opportunity mean more."[110] As a kind of architectural laboratory experiment, the Guild House offers a survey of the American city and its domestic and commercial iconographies, documented and studied by Robert Venturi and Denise Scott Brown since the late 1950s (see pp. 49, 84, 85, 281, 305).

"Realism" versus "Pop"

In its relation to the city, the Guild House is "representational architecture." The keyword here is "realism." Yet quite paradoxically the term implies something that hardly exists in the work of the Venturis, and even then only in the disguise of irony: reverence for the "ideal." "Realism" has been an important issue in the European architectural discussion, especially since World War II. More recently, however, architectural "rationalists," unlike American "pragmatists," seem to consider "reality" not as something that must be found but rather as something that must be postulated. It is, therefore, not sociological and anthro-

pological observation but rather the fiction of a "collective will" extending over vast periods of time that serves Giorgio Grassi, for example, as the axis of architectural realism.[111] Aldo Rossi, on the other hand, decides for himself which kind of architecture is "real" enough to be evoked as a historical reference for his own housing projects, such as the apartment building in the Gallaratese quarter in Milan (pl. 85), the cloisters of the Certosa di Pavia, the portico of Salvatierra, and an anonymous hay shed.[112] The choice of images that can illustrate the continuity of history and that are at the same time "popular" is made in the name of a preconceived idea of architecture. In such a perspective, nothing appears to be less relevant for architecture than the images and symbols that correspond to the *actual* everyday experience of Italian workers *today*.

In other words, European architects prefer to define "realism" in terms of humanistic "ideality." The procedure is not new. In the 1930s socialist realism as a politico-cultural program postulated humanism as idea and classicism as style. Ricardo Bofill picks this up again today by exaggerating the monumentality of Soviet and East European People's Palaces from the Stalin era in the bombastically orchestrated royal palaces he builds for the workers and clerks of Paris suburbs or some industrial centers of southern France (pl. 86).

Measured against such a realism of swagger, the work of the Venturis would have to be referred to as architectural "verism." Instead of flattering their clients by providing

87 Sugden, England: home (Architects: Alison and Peter Smithson, 1956)

88 Advertisement, about 1955, from A. and P. Smithson, *Ordinariness and Light* (1970)

them with tangible signs of social ascendancy, the Venturis seem to hold a mirror before them in the hope that they will recognize themselves in it.

Seen in this context, the aesthetic program of the Venturis, as realized in the Guild House, has its immediate roots both in the International Style and in Pop Art. With its department-store inscription and its ill-reputed antenna, it can be understood as the anticipated counterpart to Claes Oldenburg's definition of painting that "is asked to go for a swim, is given a cigarette, a bottle of beer…, is taught to laugh, is given clothes of all kinds, goes for a ride on a bike."[113] In 1965, the date of Oldenburg's incitement, architecture, especially American architecture, had by no means overcome the condition that he had diagnosed. It

went on slumbering "in its golden crypts," as the painter put it, referring to the abstract expressionism of the 1950s. Kahn celebrated his "Orphic words" (Vogt) while plush, marble, chandeliers, fountains, and symmetrical axes popped up again in the Lincoln Center for the Performing Arts in New York.

"New Brutalism" and the Aesthetics of Ugliness

In the pointed way in which it is found in the Guild House, "ordinariness" as an architectural means of expression, as an aesthetic theme, seems to have few, if any, precedents in American architecture. The situation is somewhat different in England. "Ordinariness" as a positive quality was introduced into Britain's architectural discussion by the Smithsons.[114] As early as 1954–1955 they had studied advertisements as documents of contemporary taste that were relevant to their own work as architects (pl. 88):

> Gropius wrote a book on grain silos,
> Le Corbusier one on aeroplanes,
> And Charlotte Perriand brought a new object to the office every morning;
> But today we collect ads.[115]

In the same year that this aphorism was published (1956), they helped to prepare the exhibition "This is Tomorrow" in London's Whitechapel Gallery. It was an event that focused on America—not on her high culture (not to speak of her high architecture) but rather on the throwaway aesthetics of her canned foods and household appliances and on the glamour of Hollywood. Out of this interest in the quality of the ordinary came the Smithsons' design for the intriguingly paradigmatic single-family house in Sugden, England (1956; pl. 87).

For the organizers of the famous exhibition in the Whitechapel Gallery, "Pop" was not only the art that should emerge from contact with modern mass culture. "Pop" at that time was modern mass culture itself. As Lawrence Alloway, one of the organizers, later put it:

> In the postwar years, there developed an uncoordinated but consistent perspective on art that had more to do with history and sociology than with traditional art criticism and aesthetics.… Parallel to this anti-idealistic perspective on art a throw-away aesthetic developed in England during

the 1950s that was to get a grip on the ephemeral folk arts. These were, so it was said, no longer basically different from high art.[116]

At this time, Denise Scott Brown made contact with the Smithsons while she was studying at the Architectural Association in London.[117] In her aforementioned essay entitled "Team 10, Perspecta 10, and the Present State of Architectural Theory" (1967), she wrote of the "Aesthetics of Ugliness" cultivated by the "New Brutalists":

> The Brutalists' liking of the ugly—liking what they did not like—was an attempt to keep fresh eyes and to stay out of aesthetic ruts. A commonly used adjective at this time (the early 1950s) to describe a "good ugliness" or a shocking directness in the solving of a problem was "terrific."[118]

The call for an architecture that was to be deliberately "ugly and ordinary," as the Venturis later put it in *Learning from Las Vegas*,[119] was therefore not without its European premises. In the essay cited earlier, Scott Brown also went into detail about Venturi's ideas. In many ways, they seemed in fact to be related with those of the "New Brutalists":

> Although it does not come out here [in *Complexity and Contradiction*], Venturi shares with the Brutalists their early enjoyment of Pop and perversity and of the uncomfortably direct solution which breaks the architectural rules and makes other architects exclaim "But you can't do that!"[120]

Scott Brown brought part of her interest in everyday architecture with her from England (and from earlier experiences in Africa). However, she questions the claim made by some English and European architects to have played an initiatory role in the aesthetic evaluation of "strip" and "sprawl." As she points out, the idea that Cedric Price "discovered" Los Angeles in 1961 and that Reyner Banham "discovered" the Santa Monica Pier[121] only proves how unfamiliar today's critics are with the writings of American sociologists and cultural or art historians like Melvin Webber, John B. Jackson, or Esther McCoy.

One could go even further. Taking *Learning from Las Vegas*, in which these Pop interests culminate, for what it *also* is—a picture book and a collection of photographs—one sees that it is indeed part of an American tradition: that of the photo albums compiled by the Californian artist Edward Ruscha in the 1960s, for example (pp. 82–83).[122] The Venturis explicitly refer to him in their book. Moreover,

89 Walker Evans: "Gas Station, Reedsville, West Virginia" (1936)

there is the earlier work of American photographers like Walter Evans, Dorothea Lange, or Ben Shan, who were commissioned by the Farm Security Administration under the New Deal to document the everyday life of American migrant workers and the poor in small Midwestern towns and along forgotten highways in order to bring it out of the social and cultural shadows to which it had been banned by the conscience and good taste of elite culture (pl. 89).[123]

The City as a Stage

Be that as it may, the central theme of *Learning from Las Vegas* is the American city, not so much as it should be but *as it is*. The basic thesis of the book had already been clearly formulated in *Complexity and Contradiction*. The last two pictures in the essay part of that book show Thomas

Jefferson's University of Charlottesville juxtaposed with "typical Main Street USA." The pair of pictures, taken from a book by Peter Blake (*God's Own Junkyard*, 1964), document in a nutshell what the work is about (pls. 90, 91). Venturi wrote:

> In *God's Own Junkyard* Peter Blake has compared the chaos of commercial Main Street with the orderliness of the University of Virginia. Besides the irrelevancy of the comparison [why should a town look like a university campus?], is not Main Street almost all right? Indeed, is not the commercial strip of a Route 66 almost all right?... The seemingly chaotic juxtapositions of honky-tonk elements express an intriguing kind of vitality and validity, and they produce an unexpected approach to unity as well.[124]

Quite apart from the "unexpected formal unity" offered by the picture of the American "chaos"—the formal whole of the impressionist painting as it were (see pp. 16 ff.)—are not the two pictures that conclude Venturi's argument and serve as an emblem of his viewpoint to be seen as a coded variation of the contrast between *scena tragica* and *scena comica* in Sebastiano Serlio's *Primo libro di architettura* of 1551 (pls. 92, 93)? In both cases there is a confrontation between the daily environment of the "prince" and that of the "common people." In both cases middle-class and aristocratic respectability is contrasted with vulgar unmannerliness. More specifically, a classical "modern" architecture of palaces studded with ancient ruins (in the *scena tragica*) is contrasted with the shabby medieval shops and houses of "ordinary people" (in the *scena comica*).

If one had to relate the position of the Venturis to any one of the three genres of classical theater—tragedy, comedy, and satyr play—the choice would have to be different for each individual project designed by them. Yet Venturi's comparison of 1966 seems to suggest a special affinity with comedy. Describing the architectural features of comedy and tragedy, Vitruvius wrote:

> Comic decoration portrays private homes, oriels, and projections with windows in the style of ordinary houses.... Tragic decorations consist of columns, pediments, ornamented columns, and the other objects belonging to a royal palace.[125]

The Venturis do seek formal and iconographic raw material for their work in the social milieu that is today's equivalent of the classical theater's stage for the comic and burlesque: the ethnic row house, Levittown, and Las Vegas.

64

90 "Typical Main Street USA," from *Complexity and Contradiction in Architecture* (1966)

91 Charlottesville, Virginia: University of Virginia (Architect: Thomas Jefferson), from *Complexity and Contradiction in Architecture* (1966)

92 Sebastiano Serlio: "Comic Scene," woodcut from *Primo libro di architettura* (1551)

93 Sebastiano Serlio: "Tragic Scene," woodcut from *Primo libro di architettura* (1551)

Yet that is not all. On many occasions the Venturis themselves seem to slip into the role of the Harlequin in the stage set. When they speak of the architectural "duck," Walt Disney comes to mind, and when they say "Less is a Bore," they seem to be paying a tribute—oblique and ironic though it may be—both to Mies van der Rohe and to James Joyce. In the words of Ada Louise Huxtable, the 1976 exhibition "Signs of Life" studied "the Pop World of the Strip and the Sprawl,"[126] with speech balloons decoding the stylistic mishmash that constitutes the decoration of these typical American middle-class homes (pl. 94)—all to the delight and edification of a public recruited mainly from upper-middle-class culture.

It would be difficult to draw a precise line between those of the Venturis' statements (and forms) that are frankly funny (while at the same time being dead serious as art) and those that are tantamount to satire. Scott Brown has said that the role of "jester," with its use of irony and its paradoxical function as mediator between groups, is more suitable for today's architect than that of the norm-setting cultural "leader." The bold "Big Apple" on Times Square may stand as an emblem of this antiutopian utopia. It is superfluous to insist that this hilarious (and tragic) landmark owes much to both Magritte and Oldenburg. Paradoxically, it compromises any chance for realization by subverting the "seriousness" of Philip Johnson's monumental group of towers with its "commercial" (meaning fun) iconography that denotes irony even as it symbolizes fun (pl. 95).

The jester's pose, the irony and wit in the way that the Venturis deal with the taboos of architecture (the nonchalance with which they characterize the Cathedral of Amiens as a "decorated shed," for example) is not suited to currying popular favor, but at least it is capable of dispersing the mist of academic affectations and thereby of laying bare some of the *précieuses ridicules* of architectural theory—and of architecture. At another level, it is the stance of artists who confront a flawed society: They "laugh in order not to cry."[127]

The fact that Venturi should have ferreted out Serlio's archetypal comparison between the "tragic" and the "comic" scene in the two pictures from *God's Own Junkyard*, instead of looking it up in the history books, speaks for itself. It is worth adding that the comparison does indeed belong to the stereotypes of recent architectural history. Not long ago Joseph Rykwert introduced his book, *The First Moderns* (note: not "The First Post-Moderns"!), with precisely those famous two plates from Serlio.[128] Colin Rowe and Fred Koetter are even more straightforward in their book, *Collage*

65

94 Washington, D. C.: interior from the exhibition *Signs of Life* (1976)

95 New York: "Big Apple," project for the reconstruction of Times Square, New York (VRSB with Philip Johnson, 1985; drawing: Frederic Schwartz)

City (1979). They, too, show Serlio's tragic and comic scene, but, interestingly enough, reverse the order, making the "comic" (i.e., medieval) precede the "tragic" (i.e., classical) city. Moreover, they regretfully comment on the belated combination of utopia and ideal city, "of Filarete and Castiglione, Thomas Moore and Machiavelli" that had "acted to substitute the formula of Serlio's tragic scene for that of the comic" as early as the Renaissance. This combination, they continue, has done its part to transform a "world of random and medieval happenings into a more highly integrated situation of dignified and serious deportment." But, they added, "the metaphysical aloofness of the classical utopia was not to be sustained."[129] That was true in a certain sense of Blake's picture of the University of Virginia—and in that sense Colin Rowe's critique of the "classical" city does in fact head in the same direction as Venturi's.

In connection with architecture, "theater" is known to be a loaded word, and because the architecture of the Venturis spontaneously strikes most people as "theatrical," it is also a word that their opponents have used (and will continue to use) against them.[130] In the rhetoric of modern architecture, terms like "scenography," "masquerade," "Hollywood," or "Cinecittà" have for decades been synonymous with betrayal of almost everything that was sacrosanct: function, form, space, and social responsibility. Modern architecture seems to have forgotten that the theater—or, more precisely, the art of scenography—was not only an important branch of architectural practice from at least the fifteenth century right into the nineteenth, but was, to put it briefly, in a certain sense the medium through which the European city came to develop an aesthetic awareness of its form. Palladio and Scamozzi were part of this process just as much as Piranesi and Galli-Bibiena or, later, Schinkel and Wagner. The development of perspective space in the Renaissance suffices in itself to indicate how closely both perception and the production of urban space have for centuries been linked to the conventions of the visual arts and the theater.[131]

Populism and Popularity

However, it should not be overlooked that the playful quality of the work by Venturi, Rauch and Scott Brown, its programmatic irony and its delight in the "ordinary," also makes for problems. By flirting with the notion that many of their buildings are "ugly and ordinary," they exploit

rhetorical conventions of the theater. Indeed, Shakespeare was not the first to seek and achieve effects with the "ordinary" and the "vulgar."[132] This is a difficult aesthetic strategy to pursue in architecture, for whereas satire and irony need an instructed audience to play to—the public—the primary function of buildings remains to serve their users. And the laughter of the public can reflect on the users as mockery.

Let us return to the Guild House. More than twenty years have passed since it was opened, and if it is still completely intact and if it is still fulfilling its purpose satisfactorily, that is probably not because of its explicit social "imagery" but rather in large part in spite of it. It is quite simply a well-conceived senior citizens' home with sensible floor plans, pleasant views, and details designed with love. The aluminum antenna, by contrast, was not replaced after it corroded a few years after the building was opened.[133]

Nothing would be less pertinent than to judge the Venturian "populism" as a shrewd marketing strategy to land fat contracts. Many projects of these architects remain unexecuted precisely *because* they draw on the images of everyday life rather than swim against the current, as did the urban-renewal projects and the "interesting" and "daring" concrete citadels of the 1960s.

It is enough to recall the "Bill-Ding-Board" that the architects proposed in 1967 as a national memorial for the heroes of American football: a combination of drive-in movie and fun palace (pp. 160–62). The clients had spoken of "an Ideological Center, serving our social and educational structure and our competitive economy," and of their conviction that "honoring [football heroes]… brings into focus at a time of the long hair, beard, beatnik revolt on the campus… that the disciplines of football make it the biggest and best classroom in the nation for teaching leadership."[134] Given their ideals, the authors of a program like that were *bound* to interpret the Pop proposal submitted by the Venturis as outright mockery.

There was also the charming project for a small bank branch in Fairfield, Connecticut. The problem was how to make a bank out of a little building at a fork in the road. The architects intended to keep the existing structure and place a golden dome on top of it, quoting directly from classical New England architecture of the eighteenth century (p. 227). The project was rejected because the city planning agency ruled that the design would contribute to the "visual pollution" of the suburban landscape. Evidently, as this body saw it, an architectural sign saying a "little white house with a golden dome flanked by obelisks" fatally signaled "fast

96 Philadelphia: restoration of the
St. Francis de Sales church (1968),
neon lighting in choir

97 Siena: Madonna altar in San Francesco,
neon lighting (photo 1984)

food." The members must have felt that the proposed design suggested the kind of place where one eats fried chicken, ice cream, or hamburgers; it did not make the building look like a serious bank. No doubt the architects would have had an easier time had they proposed a "modern" structure, preferably of steel, glass, and concrete.[135]

One more example of a symbolic blur in the work of these architects is the renovation of St. Francis de Sales, a beautiful neo-Byzantine church in Philadelphia. The Venturis had used a white neon tube to illuminate the choir. Yet, inevitably, some members of the congregation protested, so the tube was taken down after just a few weeks, although the architects insisted that the tube's intended symbolic function had by no means been to debase the sacred but to ennoble the profane. Interestingly enough, Italian parishes do not seem to have such scruples, for from Milan southwards electric candlelight and neon halos are commonplace in churches (pls. 96, 97).[136]

If it can be said that one of the roles of architecture is to help private or public clients to establish public identity, then it is also true that clients in general do not expect architecture to show who they really *are* but rather who they would *like to be*. And certainly it is precisely the idealistic disguises that broadcast the instincts of the parvenu most blatantly. That applies ultimately even to the city of Frankfurt am Main and its new Museum of Arts and Crafts. Frankfurt wanted to present itself on the Museumsufer as the city of Goethe, as a park with elegant villas. This desire seemed to call for nothing less than the quiet grandeur and chaste "ideality" of Richard Meier's architecture, which had the additional advantage of belatedly exculpating twenty years of most brutal urban growth on the other bank of the river by ritually evoking the great masters of classical

modern architecture—Le Corbusier, Stam, and Gropius (pl. 98).

Not so with the project by Venturi, Rauch and Scott Brown (pl. 99), and given this situation, it perhaps never really had a chance from the outset. The idea was to pick up on the architectural imagery of the housing along the Schaumainkai and to continue working on the city as a system of unbroken facades along the streets and quays, as had been done in the early days of postwar reconstruction. But 1979 was still too early in Frankfurt for a rediscovery, much less a rehabilitation, of the 1950s. Instead of a museum that was intended to link the tradition of classical modern architecture carefully with historical detail (in a way somehow reminiscent of certain postwar works by J.J.P. Oud in Holland), and thereby to represent the building's function as a shrine for the preservation of works of pottery, furniture, and silverware, a rationalist bravura was built.

The "image" of everyday life, the "symbolism of the ordinary" as evoked in many of the projects by Venturi, Rauch and Scott Brown, does not seem to want to square with everyday life itself. On one hand, as we have seen, the Venturis had shown an early interest in the role of popular symbolism and convention in architecture; on the other hand the practical application of their studies in their work as designers often seems to fall outside the symbolic conventions of popular taste. In a superficial way it may appear as if they stumble over their own intention to get close to the popular idiom. In cases where the Venturis employ an explicitly "ordinary" language, many people seem to expect an "elevated" one; where the Venturis choose an "elevated" mode (as was the case with the bank in Fairfield), some people seem to misunderstand it as trivial and commercial.

That the "populism" of the Venturis is not necessarily "popular" should not come as a surprise. The lack of broad, popular effect is the paradox of "popular" attitudes and forms in elite art. Even in the case of a "revolutionary" artist like Courbet, a subject of debate was the question as to whether his realism was a realism as style (and as such not popular, but elitist) or whether it was a realism of morals (and as such artistically irrelevant). In other words, it was argued whether the way he used popular subjects was more successful at invigorating museum art or, on the contrary, at ennobling the ordinary, everyday life of the people.[137]

In terms of Herbert Gans's taxonomy of taste cultures,[138] the Venturis define their role as high-culture architects who, like the composer Beethoven, derive themes from folk and popular culture and who ultimately strive to create an

98 Frankfurt am Main: Museum of Arts and Crafts (Architect: Richard Meier, 1979–1985)

99 Museum of Arts and Crafts, view from Schaumainkai (VRSB: competition project, 1979)

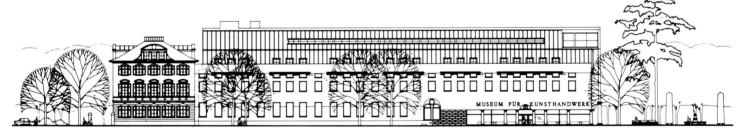

architecture that, like Verdi's music, will be broadly evocative in different ways to many groups. Their interest in the rhetorical possibilities of the theater and the opera, even of jokes and irony, as a means of architectural communication thus relate to their view of the architect's social responsibility.

Yet irony is a serious matter, and comedy as a dramatic genre exists only in relation to tragedy. True, Serlio's comic scene seems to have been a point of reference for the Venturis at the time they studied Las Vegas and Levittown, but even then they were implicitly concerned with the classical aura of Serlio's *scena tragica*. In the "City Room" of the 1976 "Signs of Life" exhibition, an early attempt was made to relate the imageries found in Las Vegas to the public symbolism of the late nineteenth-century city (p. 49).

In the recent work of the Venturis, aspiring to the classical has become an explicit theme. The sources of popular culture, so important in their projects of the 1960s, have been subsumed into a broader array of influences: The journey from Rome to Las Vegas has led back again to Rome.

Looking at the Guild House with Gordon Wu Hall or the Austin Museum in mind, one sees the 1961 "palazzo" for the elderly—the Guild House—even more clearly reveal its Palladian and classical provenance, while its Pop-symbolism of the "ugly" and the "ordinary" no longer appears in retrospect as satire or social mockery but as a necessary ingredient of great art, whose purpose has always been to come to grips with a reality that is too frightening and too new to be the subject of mere prettification.

Notes

1 See the introduction to Robert Venturi, *Complexity and Contradiction in Architecture,* 2nd ed. (New York: The Museum of Modern Art, 1977), p. 9.

2 The most important references cited in *Complexity and Contradiction* (see note 1) are Cleanth Brooks, *The Well Wrought Urn* (New York: Harcourt, Brace & World, 1947); Kenneth Burke, *Permanence and Change* (Los Altos: Hermes Publications, 1954); T. S. Eliot, *Selected Essays 1917-1932* (New York: Harcourt, Brace & Co., 1932); *idem, Use of Poetry and Use of Criticism* (Cambridge, Mass.: Harvard University Press, 1933); and William Empson, *Seven Types of Ambiguity* (New York: Meridian Books, 1955) (see R. Venturi, *Complexity and Contradiction,* pp. 20 ff., and *passim*).

3 Robert Venturi, Denise Scott Brown, and Steven Izenour, *Learning from Las Vegas* (Cambridge, Mass.: MIT Press, 1972).

4 Wolf Lepenies, *Die drei Kulturen. Soziologie zwischen Literatur und Wissenschaft* (Munich and Vienna: Hanser, 1985).

5 See in particular Kenneth Frampton, "America 1960-1970: Notes on Urban Imagery and Theory," *Casabella* 389/390 (May-June, 1971): 24-38. See also Denise Scott Brown, "Reply to Frampton," *Casabella* 389/390 (May-June, 1971): 36-46; reprinted in Robert Venturi and Denise Scott Brown, *A View from the Campidoglio: Selected Essays 1953-1984,* ed. P. Arnell, T. Bickford, and C. Bergart (New York: Harper & Row, 1984), pp. 34-37. Disputes with other critics are in *Learning from Las Vegas,* pp. 104, 108, and *passim.* (Unless otherwise stated, all references are to the first edition.)

What makes much leftist criticism of the Venturis suspect in my eyes is not the intention of subjecting the market economy to ideological critique but rather the tendency to view popular culture as celebrated in the mass media and the consumer world as the exclusive theater of all the evils of capitalist society. Many critics seem to feel that mere adherence to a position critical of "mass culture" places them outside the deeper logic of consumerism. In reality, though, American society and its virtues and vices are as authentically represented in the Seagram Building as they are in the Las Vegas Strip.

The critical reception of the Venturis' ideas, especially in Germany, will be discussed in another context. I am thinking, for example, of the interesting pamphlet by Michael Müller, *Architektur und Avantgarde* (Frankfurt am Main: Syndikat, 1984). For the time being, see Stanislaus von Moos, "Über Venturi und Rauch, die Konsumwelt und den doppelten Boden der Architektur," *Bauwelt,* 23 (May 1980), pp. 842-43.

6 The fact that the arguments of conservative and neo-Marxist critics of mass culture are largely interchangeable has already been demonstrated by Umberto Eco in "Massenkultur und 'Kultur-Niveaus,'" in *idem, Apokalyptiker und Integrierte: Zur kritischen Kritik der Massenkultur* (Frankfurt am Main: S. Fischer, 1984; original Italian edition, 1964), pp. 38-58. See also Herbert Gans, *Popular Culture and High Culture: An Analysis and Evaluation of Taste* (New York: Basic Books, 1974), pp. 17-64. The latter book is the starting point for Denise Scott Brown's important essay, "Architectural Taste in a Pluralistic Society," *Harvard Architecture Review,* Spring 1980, pp. 41-51.

In the history of art and architecture, the subject of kitsch and trivial art has attracted a good deal of attention in recent years. See, among others, Renato De Fusco, *Architettura come Mass Medium* (Bari: Dedalo, 1967); Maurizio Calvesi, *Le due avanguardie,* 2 vols. (Bari: Laterza, 1971); Werner Hofmann, "Kitsch und Trivialkunst als Gebrauchskünste," in *idem, Bruchlinien: Aufsätze zur Kunst des 19. Jahrhunderts* (Munich: Prestel, 1979), pp. 166-79; and Jean-Pierre Keller, *Pop Art et évidence du quotidien* (Lausanne: Age d'homme, 1979).

7 See Robert Venturi, "The RIBA Annual Discourse," in *Transactions* 1, 1981-1982, pp. 47-56; reprinted in R. Venturi, *A View from the Campidoglio* (see note 5), pp. 104-7; and *idem,* "Diversity, Relevance and Representation in Historicism, Or Plus ça Change... plus a plea for Pattern All Over Architecture with a Postscript on My Mother's House," *Architectural Record,* June 1982, pp. 114-19; reprinted in R. Venturi, *A View from the Campidoglio* (see note 5), pp. 108-19.

8 Colin Rowe, "Robert Venturi and the Yale Mathematics Building," *Oppositions* 6 (1976): 11-19, especially page 11.

9 This has been the thrust of the critique by Manfredo Tafuri, *Teorie e storia dell'architettura* (Bari: Laterza, 1970), p. 257; and Alan Colquhoun, "Sign and Substance: Reflections on Complexity, Las Vegas and Oberlin," in *idem, Essays in Architectural Criticism: Modern Architecture and Historical Change* (Cambridge, Mass.: MIT Press, 1981), pp. 139-51, especially pp. 139-40.

10 Robert Venturi, "Context in Architectural Composition," unpublished manuscript, 1950, p. 1. A chapter of Venturi's Master's thesis appeared as "The Campidoglio: A Case Study," *Architectural Review,* May 1953, pp. 333-34; reprinted in Venturi, *A View from the Campidoglio* (see note 5), pp. 12-13.

11 Le Corbusier, *Œuvres complètes 1910-1929* (Zurich: Girsberger, 1935), p. 8.

12 The Venturis repeatedly juxtapose their position and Giedion's. See, for example, R. Venturi, *Complexity and Contradiction* (see note 1), p. 55 and *passim* as well as R. Venturi *et al.,* Learning from Las Vegas (see note 3), pp. 8, 104, 107, 114, 134 (rev. ed., 1977). More recently, see Robert Venturi, "Learning the Right Lessons from the Beaux-Arts," in *A View from the Campidoglio* (see note 5), pp. 70-95, especially p. 70.

13 As far as this question is concerned, Manfredo Tafuri's book, *Teorie e storia dell'architettura* (see note 9) is still in a class by itself, although several of the judgments therein would probably need to be updated.

14 Lionello Venturi, *Impressionists and Symbolists,* trans. F. Steegmuller (New York: Scribner, 1950), pp. 6-7. The Italian art historian and the Philadelphian architect are not related.

15 Eugène Chevreul, *De la loi des contrastes simultanés des couleurs* (Paris: Charles Martel, 1839).

16 For a much more thorough discussion of the issues brought up here, see especially Thomas Crow, "Modernism and Mass Culture in the Visual Arts," in *Modernism and Modernity: The Vancouver Conference Papers,* ed. Benjamin H. D. Buchloh, Serge Guilbaut, and David Solkin (Halifax: The Press of the Nova Scotia College of Art and Design, 1983), pp. 215-64, and Andreas Haus, "Impressionismus - Industrialisierung des Sehens," in *Forma et subtilitas. Festschrift für Wolfgang Schöne zum 75. Geburtstag,* eds. W. Schlink and Martin Sperlich (Berlin: De Gruyter, 1986), pp. 254-68.

17 *Learning from Las Vegas* (see note 3), p. xviii.

18 On this point see Denise Scott Brown, "On Architectural Formation and Social Concern: A Discourse for Radical Chic Architects and Social Planners," *Oppositions* 5, (Summer 1976): 99-112, and "Architectural Taste in a Pluralistic Society" (see note 6).

19 Archibald Alison, *Essays on the Nature and Principles of Taste,* 2 vols. (London: J. J. G. and G. Robinson, 1790), 2:126. My comments are based on George L. Hersey, "J. C. Loudon and Architectural Associationism," *Architectural Review,* August 1968, pp. 88-92.

20 See G. Hersey, "Loudon and Architectural Associationism" (see note 19). The Henry-Russell Hitchcock quotation is from *Architecture, Nineteenth and Twentieth Centuries* (Harmondsworth: Pelican History of Art, 1958; reprint ed., Hammondsworth: Penguin Books, 1971), p. 600, note 12.

21 G. Hersey, "Loudon and Architectural Associationism" (see note 19), p. 91.

22 J. C. Loudon, *An Encyclopaedia of Cottage, Farm and Villa Architecture and Furniture,* ed. J. W. Loudon (London: Longman, Brown, Green and Longmans,

1846); reprinted with slight changes in Hersey (see note 19) and later also reproduced in *Learning from Las Vegas* (see note 3), p. 1.

23 On this point see Herbert W. Schneider, *A History of American Philosophy* (New York: Columbia University Press, 1946), pp. 246–50; *Geschichte der amerikanischen Philosophie,* trans. Peter Krausser (Hamburg: Felix Meiner, 1957), pp. 151–55. I am grateful to Dr. Werner Sewing for having pointed out this source to me. Theodor W. Adorno, in his *Minima Moralia* (Frankfurt am Main: Suhrkamp, 1951), pp. 87–88, describes "Common Sense" as "the evaluation of the just relations, the cosmopolitan view, exercised at the marketplace, that shares with dialectics the freedom of dogma, limitation, and obstination." And he adds: "The generality of the opinion, directly taken over from society as it is, necessarily has accordance as its immediate content" (translation by S. v. Moos).

24 In *Learning from Las Vegas* (see note 3), for example, the expression of a building's function via association or via style is described as "a symbolic manifestation of functionalism" that preceded the "substantive" functionalism of the twentieth century (p. 114, 1977 edition); with reference to Donald Drew Egbert.

25 Denise Scott Brown, "Invention and Tradition in the Making of American Place," in David G. De Long, Helen Searing, and Robert A. M. Stern (eds.), *American Architecture: Innovative and Tradition* (New York: Rizzoli, 1986), pp. 158–70, especially 168.

26 Concerning the figure of "marginal man" or the "wanderer," see, for example, Donald N. Levine, Ellwood B. Carter, and Eleanor Miller Gorman, "Simmels Einfluß auf die amerikanische Soziologie," in *Geschichte der Soziologie,* 4 vols., ed. Wolf Lepenies (Frankfurt am Main: Suhrkamp, 1981), 4:32–81, especially p. 56.

27 Marcel Proust, "A propos du 'style' de Flaubert," in *Contre Sainte-Beuve. Procédé de pastiches et mélanges et suivi d'essais et articles* (Paris: Pleiade, 1971), p. 594. In this context see also Fernando Ferrara *et al., Le lettere rubate. Studi sul pastiche letterario* (Naples: Instituto Universitario Orientale, 1983). (Reference kindly supplied by Professor Luciano Zagari.) On the relevance of the term "pasticcio" in music, especially in eighteenth-century Italian theory of opera, see, for example, the corresponding entry in the *New Grove Dictionary of Music and Musicians,* vol. 14 (London: Macmillan, 1980).
    "Pastiche" still seems to be charged with exclusively negative connotations in architectural discussion. See, for example, William Curtis, "Principle versus Pastiche," *Architectural Review* 8 (August, 1984): 10–21, 39–47. In an essay that is especially relevant in the present context, George L. Hersey argues, in turn, that the distorting and alienating adaptation of historical models is an intrinsic hallmark of American architecture. See "Replication Replicated: Notes on American Bastardy," *Perspecta* 10 (1965): 211ff.

28 Donald Drew Egbert, *The Beaux-Arts Tradition in French Architecture* (Princeton: Princeton University Press, 1980). See R. Venturi, "Donald Drew Egbert—A Tribute," *ibid,* pp. xiii–xiv; for reference to J. Labatut in particular, see R. Venturi, "Learning the Right Lessons from the Beaux-Arts," *Architectural Design,* 1979, pp 23–31.

29 R. Venturi *et al.,* Learning from Las Vegas (see note 3), p. 64. The concept of the "decorated shed" itself would deserve a discussion more detailed than the one attempted here, especially as far as its roots in nineteenth-century architectural theory (and in Giedion) are concerned. I shall return to this in a separate study.

30 Stuart Cohen, too, has justifiably stressed this contradiction. See "Physical Context/Cultural Context: Including It All," *Oppositions* 2 (1974): 1–39, especially page 21.

31 R. Venturi *et al., Learning from Las Vegas* (see note 3), pp. 66ff.

32 R. Venturi, *Complexity and Contradiction* (see note 1), pp. 88ff.

33 "A Worm's Eye View of Recent Architectural History," *Architectural Record,* February 1984, p. 72. After returning from Rome, Venturi worked for nine months (1956–1957) with Kahn, whom he had met in 1947. Later, both architects taught side by side in the School of Architecture at the University of Pennsylvania. In her essay, Scott Brown tries to show how this intensive contact left its traces in the work of both architects.
    A comparative study on the architecture of Kahn and Venturi would be promising. For the time being, see the rather preliminary essay by John Lobell, "Kahn and Venturi: An Architecture of Being in Context," *Art Forum,* February 1979, pp. 46–52.

34 As reported to the author by Denise Scott Brown.

35 The best study of the work of Frank Furness is James O'Gorman, *The Architecture of Frank Furness* (Philadelphia: Philadelphia Museum of Art, 1973).

36 Vincent J. Scully. *American Architecture and Urbanism* (New York: Praeger, 1969; reprint ed., New York: Praeger, 1975), p. 236.

37 Heinrich Klotz, *Moderne und postmoderne Architektur der Gegenwart, 1960–1980* (Brunswick/Wiesbaden: Vieweg, 1984), p. 156. Colin Rowe was the first to analyze the "mannerist" quality of Le Corbusier's architecture of the 1920s and the way that architect achieved effects of "literal and phenomenal" transparency in his buildings; see Rowe's article, "Mannerism and Modern Architecture," *Architectural Review,* May 1950, 289–99; and Heinrich Klotz and Robert Slutzky, "Transparency: Literal and Phenomenal," *Perspecta* 8 (1963): 45–54.

38 K. Frampton, "America 1960–1980" (see note 5). In this context I am not concerned with the fact that Frampton is able to understand these qualities only as an expression of alleged conservative "cynicism," nor with the fact that, presumably for this reason, Venturi's architectural work is not documented in Frampton's new book, *Modern Architecture: A Critical History* (London: Thames and Hudson, 1980).

39 Leonardo Benevolo, *L'ultimo capitolo dell'architettura moderna* (Bari: Laterza, 1985), p. 108.

40 William J. R. Curtis, *Modern Architecture since 1900* (Oxford: Phaidon, 1982), pp. 351ff.

41 R. Venturi, "Context in Architectural Composition" (see note 10), p. 3. Venturi's relationship to Wright, and to "organic architecture" in general, would need separate treatment (see below, p. 240). In 1950 Venturi assisted with the preparation of the important Wright exhibition, which was shown in America and Europe.

42 Talbot Hamlin, *The American Spirit in Architecture* (New Haven: Yale University Press, 1926), p. 160.

43 R. Venturi, *Complexity and Contradiction* (see note 1), p. 57.

44 O'Gorman, *The Architecture of Frank Furness* (see note 35), p. 71.

45 The most important being *The Painted Word* (New York: Farrar, Straus, & Giroux, 1975).

46 Tom Wolfe, *From Bauhaus to Our House* (New York: Farrar, Straus, & Giroux, 1981), p. 105.

47 This point of view was recently stressed by Alan Chimacoff and Alan Plattus in "Learning from Venturi," *Architectural Record,* September 1983, II, pp. 86–97.

48 R. Venturi, *Complexity and Contradiction* (see note 1), p. 82. See also Venturi's beautiful homage, "Alvar Aalto," *Arkkitehti* 7–8 (1976): 66–67; reprinted in R. Venturi and D. Scott Brown, *A View from the Campidoglio* (see note 5), pp. 60–61.

49 R. Venturi, "Alvar Aalto" (see note 48), p. 60. On Aalto's influence on the architecture of Venturi and Rauch, see especially Robert Maxwell, "The Venturi Effect," *Venturi and Rauch: Architectural Monographs* I (1977): 7–28, especially pp. 25–28.

50 R. Venturi, *Complexity and Contradiction* (see note 1), p. 44. The corresponding passage by Giedion is in *Space, Time, and Architecture* (Cambridge, Mass.: Harvard University Press, 1941; reprinted Cambridge, Mass.: Harvard University Press, 1963), p. 565.

51 Demetri Porphyrios, *Sources of Modern Eclecticism: Studies on Alvar Aalto* (London: Academy Editions, 1982).

52 *Ibid.,* pp. 5–10, 22ff., and *passim.*

53 On this point see Leonard K. Eaton, *American Architecture Comes of Age* (Cambridge, Mass.: MIT Press, 1972), pp. 143–75.

54 The latter example is also included in R. Venturi, *Complexity and Contradiction* (see note 1), p. 73 (pl. 153). On the ground plan for the Institute of International Education, see Porphyrios, *Modern Eclecticism* (see note 51), pp. 22–23.

55 *Ibid.,* pp. 22–23.

56 R. Venturi, *Complexity and Contradiction* (see note 1), p. 70. George L. Hersey emphasizes that the "incoherence" between inside and outside has been a hallmark of American architecture since the eighteenth century. See "Replication Replicated," pp. 214–15 (see note 27) and elsewhere ("unintegrated formalism").

57 Frampton, *Modern Architecture* (see note 38), p. 242.

58 R. Venturi, *Complexity and Contradiction* (see note 1), p. 71.

59 *Ibid.,* p. 72.

60 *Ibid.,* pp. 39 (pl. 55), 75 (pl. 162), and elsewhere.

61 "Under the suasion of Gordon Bunshaft," as D. Scott Brown remembers; see *Learning from Las Vegas* (see note 3), pp. 138–41.

62 R. Venturi, "The RIBA Annual Discourse" (see note 7), p. 105.

63 As quoted in Manfred Bock, *Anfänge einer neuen Architektur, Berlages Beitrag zur architektonischen Kultur der Niederlande im ausgehenden 19. Jahrhundert* (The Hague and Wiesbaden: Staatsuitgeverij s'Gravenhage and Franz Steiner Verlag, 1983), p. 230. See also Bock's interesting discussions on the concept of architectural Impressionism, pp. 229–67.

64 A. W. Reinink, *Amsterdam en de beurs van Berlage* (The Hague: Rijksdienst voor de monumentenzorg, 1975), p. 120; Bock, *Anfänge einer neuen Architektur* (see note 63), p. 231.

65 See below, pp. 212–14. On the influence of Schinkel's Altes Museum on James Stirling's National Gallery in Stuttgart, see Thorsten Rodiek, *James Stirling. Die neue Staatsgalerie Stuttgart* (Stuttgart: Hatje, 1984), pp. 32–33 and elsewhere.

66 It is interesting that the Capitol buildings of New Delhi should have sparked a sharp controversy between Alison and Peter Smithson on one hand and Robert Venturi and Denise D. Scott Brown on the other. See R. Venturi and D. Scott Brown, "Learning from Lutyens: Reply to Alison and Peter Smithson," *RIBA Journal*, April 1969, pp. 146–54; reprinted in *A View from the Campidoglio* (see note 5), p. 223. In this context see also the important study by Allan Greenberg, "Lutyens' Architecture Restudied," *Perspecta* 12 (1969): 129–52.

67 R. Venturi, *Complexity and Contradiction* (see note 1), p. 116.

68 *Ibid.*, p. 59 (pl. 100). Venturi refers to the 1964 exhibition catalogue of Jasper Johns's work (edited by Alan R. Solomon) in the Jewish Museum in New York. A more recent source is Richard Francis, *Jasper Johns* (New York: Abbeville Press, 1984; Lucerne: Bucher, 1985), pp. 19–28.

69 R. Venturi, *Complexity and Contradiction* (see note 1), p. 43.

70 On this point see, for example, Jean-Pierre Keller, *Pop Art ou évidence du quotidien* (Lausanne: Age d'homme, 1979), especially pp. 43–50.

71 "Context in Architectural Composition" (see note 10). As we have seen, the thought played an important role in *Complexity and Contradiction* as well (p. 43); see also pp. 15f. in this book.

72 Rosemarie Haag-Bletter, "Métropolis réduite," *archithese* 18 (1976): 22–27.

73 This analogy has been suggested to me by Ed Taverne; an early source is *Bouw*, October 7, 1950, pp. 658ff.

74 See, for example, Melvin Webber, "The Urban Place and the Nonplace Urban Realm," in *idem, Explorations into Urban Structure* (Philadelphia: University of Pennsylvania Press, 1964), pp. 79–153. See particularly the section entitled "The City as a Communication System," pp. 84–87. An early work by Denise Scott Brown, "The Meaningful City" (*Journal of the American Institute of Architects,* January 1965, pp. 27–32) is indebted to the thought of David A. Crane.

75 H. Klotz, *Moderne und postmoderne Architektur* (see note 37), p. 15.

76 In this context, see the critical discussion of Giedion's "concept of symbolism" in architecture in R. Venturi *et al., Learning from Las Vegas* (see note 3), p. 73; rev. edition (1977), p. 104. That R. Wittkower's seminal book, *Architectural Principles in the Age of Humanism* (New York; Norton, 1971), has played an important role for Venturi was pointed out by D. Scott Brown, "A Worm's Eye View..." (see note 33), p. 77. The question if the Venturis' interests are based on issues of art history in the first place would be worth exploring at another time. For the time being, see Stanislaus von Moos, "Rund um die Fernsehantenne des Guild House. Anmerkungen zum Thema Architektur, Zeichensprache und Massenkultur," in *Grenzbereiche der Architektur. Festschrift Adolf Reinle*, ed. Thomas Bolt, Karl Grunder, Pietro Maggi, Benno Schubiger, Peter Wegmann, and Caspar Zollikofer (Basle, Boston, and Stuttgart: Birkhäuser, 1985), pp. 221–41.

77 R. Venturi, "The RIBA Annual Discourse" (see note 7), p. 109.

78 On this point see Winfried Nerdinger, *Walter Gropius* (Berlin: Gebrüder Mann Verlag, 1985), pp. 200–201. A photograph of Gropius's replica is in the catalogue of the New York World's Fair of 1939.

79 Denise Scott Brown, "Learning from Levittown." (Unpublished manuscript.) See below, pp. 304–7.

80 R. Venturi *et al., Learning from Las Vegas* (see note 3), plates 11, 12, 14, and others.

81 *Ibid.*, pp. 64ff.; Umberto Eco, "La funzione e il segno. Semiologia dell'architettura," in *La struttura assente. Introduzione alla ricerca semiologica*, ed. Eco Umberto (Milan: Bompiani, 1968), pp. 189–249. The Venturis do not base their views on Eco, however, but rather, they say, on their own "empirically derived categories augmented by fragmentary reading of literary criticism and a

scanning of some works of Roman Jakobsen." Although an essay by Charles Jencks, "Semiology and Architecture," and one by George Baird, "'La Dimension Amoureuse' in Architecture," (in *Meaning in Architecture*, ed. George Baird and Charles Jencks [London, Barrie, and Rockliff: Cresset Press, 1969], pp. 11–25 and 79–99, respectively) influenced some early directions of their research, they attribute much greater weight to an article by Alan Colquhoun, "Typology and Design Method," *Arena*, June 1976, pp. 11–14 (also reprinted in the previously cited anthology), which they quote at length in *Learning from Las Vegas* (see note 3) (oral communication by Denise Scott Brown).

82 Charles Jencks, *The Language of Postmodern Architecture* (London: Academy Editions, 1977), *passim*.

83 D. Scott Brown, "Learning from Levittown" (see note 79).

84 John Russell, *The Meanings of Modern Art* (New York: Museum of Modern Art, 1974), p. 354.

85 R. Venturi, *Complexity and Contradiction* (see note 1), p. 112.

86 *Ibid.*, p. 59 (pl. 100). As far as this type of lettering is concerned, Heinrich Klotz erroneously refers to Robert Indiana in *Moderne and postmoderne Architektur* (see note 37), p. 166. See also note 69, above.

87 The theme is treated in numerous oil paintings. See R. Francis, *Jasper Johns* (see note 68), pp. 44–45, 63.

88 See below, pp. 232f.

89 R. Venturi *et al., Learning from Las Vegas* (see note 3), p. 100.

90 *Ibid.*, p. 99.

91 R. Venturi, *Complexity and Contradiction* (see note 1), p. 33 (pl. 41).

92 See, for instance, the recent discussion of the project in Adolf M. Vogt, *Russische und französische Revolutionsarchitektur 1917/1789* (Cologne: DuMont Schauberg, 1974), pp. 158ff. Within the Modernist movement, Oscar Nitzchke has brought the theme of "words attached to buildings" to a rare culmination in his beautiful project for a "Palais de la Publicité" in Paris (1934–1936). On this see Joseph Abram, "The Dividing Line: The French Itinerary of Oscar Nitzchke, 1920–1938" in *Oscar Nitzchke*, exhibition catalogue (New York: Cooper Union School of Architecture, 1985), pp. 40–47.

93 Paul Hofer, "Bern im Jahre 1950. Eine satirische Zukunftsvision vor achtzig Jahren," in *idem., Fundplätze, Bauplätze* (Basle and Stuttgart: Birkhäuser, 1970), pp. 82–85.

94 Victor Hugo, *Notre-Dame de Paris* (Paris: Gallimard, 1842), pp. 206–7.

95 *Ibid.*, p. 198.

96 Neil Levine, "The Book and the Building: Hugo's Theory of Architecture and Labrouste's Bibliothèque Ste. Geneviève," in *The Beaux-Arts and Nineteenth-Century French Architecture,* ed. Robin Middleton (London: Thames and Hudson, 1982), pp. 139–73.

97 When Heinrich Klotz says that "conventional decorum" has lost its "representational weight" in the Guild House and that in this building "the weight of manifested power ... has deserted the representative forms taken from architectural history" (*Moderne und postmoderne Architektur* [see note 37], p. 159), the statement applies equally well to Labrouste and the other architects of nineteenth-century historicism.

98 Robert Venturi, "Learning the Right Lessons from the Beaux-Arts," *Architectural Design* 1 (1979): 21–31; reprinted in R. Venturi and D. Scott Brown, *A View from the Campidoglio* (see note 5), p. 71.

99 *Ibid.*, p. 72.

100 R. Venturi, *Complexity and Contradiction* (see note 1), p. 44.

101 It is quite likely that it was Neil Levine's studies on Labrouste's architecture that drew Venturi's attention to Hugo's famous statement. Neither *Complexity and Contradiction* nor *Learning from Las Vegas* make any reference to Hugo or to the architect of the Bibliothèque Ste. Geneviève.

102 On the role of Constructivism's "multimedia" architecture and its revivals in the projects of the Archigram Group in England, see Charles Jencks, *Modern Movements in Architecture* (Harmondsworth: Penguin Books, 1973), pp. 371–80.

103 R. Venturi, *Complexity and Contradiction* (see note 1), 1977 ed., p. 116.

104 *Ibid.*, pp. 34–35.

105 R. Venturi *et al., Learning from Las Vegas* (see note 3), p. 102.

106 *Ibid.*

107 Adolf Behne, *Der moderne Zweckbau* (Munich: Drei Masken Verlag, 1926), p. 32. Cited by Nerdinger, *Walter Gropius* (see note 78), p. 10.

108 As quoted in Adolf M. Vogt, Ulrike Jehle-Schulte Strathaus, and Bruno Reichlin, *Architektur 1940-1980* (Frankfurt, Vienna, and Berlin: Propyläen, 1980), p. 254.

109 Denise Scott Brown, "Team 10, Perspecta 10, and the Present State of Architectural Theory," *Journal of the American Institute of Planners,* January 1967, pp. 42-50, especially 44. See also *idem.,* "Little Magazines in Architecture and Urbanism," *Journal of the American Institute of Planners,* July 1968, pp. 223-32. Among the sources specifically referred to by Scott Brown in her work is Alison Smithson (ed.), *Team 10 Primer, Architectural Design,* 32 (December, 1963) and the Dutch magazine *Forum* between 1959 and 1963 (at the time Aldo van Eyck was one of the editors). In *Learning from Las Vegas* van Eyck is highlighted as one of the few architects interested in "symbolism" (p. 103).

110 As quoted in Vogt *et al., Architektur 1940-1980* (see note 108), p. 61.

111 On architectural *razionalismo* see Aldo Rossi, *Architettura razionale* (Milan: Triennale di Milano, 1973) and Hanno-Walter Kruft, "Rationalismus in der Architektur – eine Begriffsklärung," *Architectura* 9 (1979): 45-57. On *realismo* see Giorgio Grassi, "Architekturprobleme und Realismus," *archithese* 19 (1976): 18-24; S. von Moos, "Zweierlei Realismus," *werk. archithese* 7-8 (1977): 58-62. See also the important essay by Manfredo Tafuri, "Architettura e realismo," in *L'avventura delle idee nell'architettura 1750-1980,* ed. Vittorio Magnago Lampugnani (Milan: Electa, 1985). Amazingly, Tafuri does not include the history and theory of socialist realism in this essay, and he states that rural forms and populist attitudes since 1950 have been able to survive "only on the level of snobby games, as shown by some more recent experiences of American architects acclaimed by chauvinist critique" (p. 136).

112 Aldo Rossi, "An Analogical Architecture," *a + u* (5) 1976. Interestingly, Rossi rejects dogmatic fixation on the concept of realism for architecture. See A. Rossi, "Une éducation réaliste," *archithese* 19 (1976): 25-28.

113 Claes Oldenburg in "The Artists Say," *Art Voices,* Summer 1965, p. 62, as quoted in *Pop Art,* ed. Lucy Lippard (London: Thames and Hudson, 1966), p. 180.

114 Alison and Peter Smithson, *Ordinariness and Light, Urban Theories 1952-60, and Their Application in a Building Project 1963-70* (London: Faber and Faber, 1970). The concept of "ordinariness" is not made explicit in the book, however. What the reader was to make of it did not become clear until the appearance of their later work, *Without Rhetoric* (London: Latimer New Dimensions, 1973). On the aesthetic of the ugly in general, see the classical work by Karl Rosenkranz, *Ästhetik des Hässlichen* (Königsberg: Gebrüder Bornträger, 1853; new edition, Darmstadt: Wissenschaftliche Buchgesellschaft, 1979).

115 As quoted in C. Jencks, *Modern Movements in Architecture* (see note 102), p. 277.

116 Lawrence Alloway, "Popular Culture and Pop Art," *Studio International,* July-August 1969, pp. 17-21. This author's article, later reprinted in Lucy Lippard's anthology (see note 113), suggests that the sociological thrust of the Venturian "Pop"-aesthetics has more to do with the concerns of English—as opposed to American—Pop Art. See in this context also the wonderful book by Richard Hamilton, *Collected Words* (London: Thames and Hudson, 1982).

117 Although Denise Scott Brown did not study directly under Peter Smithson nor see the exhibition "This is Tomorrow," she was a member of a group of students who sought out Smithson for "crits" before he joined the AA faculty. Her thesis project (p. 63) was considered a Brutalist design. ("Worm's Eye View" [see note 33], p. 70). It was Smithson who recommended that she study under Kahn at the University of Pennsylvania.

118 D. Scott Brown, "Team 10, Perspecta 10" (see note 109), p. 44. See Scott Brown's equally insightful observations about Brutalism in "Worm's Eye View" (see note 33), p. 70 and about Pop Art in "Learning from Pop," *Casabella,* December 1971, pp. 15-23 and in "On Pop Art, Permissiveness, and Planning," *Journal of the American Institute of Planners,* May 1969, pp. 184-86.

119 R. Venturi *et al., Learning from Las Vegas* (see note 3), pp. 70, 86, and *passim.*

120 D. Scott Brown, "Team 10, Perspecta 10" (see note 109), p. 46.

121 D. Scott Brown, "A Worm's Eye View . . ." (see note 33) p. 69. Reyner Banham's beautiful book, *Los Angeles: The Architecture of Four Ecologies* (New York: Harper and Row, 1971), appeared one year before *Learning from Las Vegas.* However, the American discovery of "ordinary" architecture had started much earlier—in the journal *Landscape,* edited by John B. Jackson, for example (see below, pp. 80ff.). See also D. Scott Brown, "Invention and Tradition in the Making of American Place" (see note 25).

122 Edward Ruscha, *Twenty-six Gasoline Stations* (Los Angeles: Edward Ruscha, 1962); *Every Building on the Sunset Strip* (Los Angeles: Edward Ruscha, 1966); and *Nine Swimming Pools and a Broken Glass* (Los Angeles: Edward Ruscha, 1968). On the significance of photography for the Venturis' concept of architecture, see S. von Moos, "Architektur als Bilderbogen," in *Jahrbuch für Architektur, 1980-1981* (Brunswick: Vieweg, 1980), pp. 95-111.

123 See the magnificent picture book by Hank O'Neal, *A Vision Shared: A Classic Portrait of America and Its People, 1935-1943* (New York: St. Martin's Press, 1976) and R. J. Doherty, *Sozialdokumentarische Fotographie in den USA* (Lucerne and Frankfurt am Main: Bucher, 1974).

124 R. Venturi, *Complexity and Contradiction* (see note 1), p. 104.

125 The quotation in English is based on Curt Fensterbusch's German translation of Vitruvius' *Ten Books on Architecture* (Darmstadt: Wissenschaftliche Buchgesellschaft, 1964).

126 Ada Louise Huxtable, *The New York Times,* 21 March 1976; see list of references for further information.

127 In this context see S. von Moos, "Lachen, um nicht zu weinen" (interview with Robert Venturi and Denise Scott Brown), *archithese,* 13 (1975): 17-26. More recently, Denise Scott Brown has rightly emphasized that, while "the ironic (*not* the satiric) is an important theme for people who need to laugh about what they value most, there was always a difference of degree in the jokes." And, speaking of the firm's architecture, she adds: "Real projects were treated less ironically than hypothetical projects. The more a project is developed, the more the "play" settles into a role as augmentor of the serious, demonstrator of the tragic, or supporter of the monumental, by contrast" (communication of June 18, 1986). According to Adolf M. Vogt, Venturi repeatedly performs "those gestures of the Harlequin that make precise that which people themselves feel in an imprecise way" (*Architektur 1940-1980* [see note 108], p. 47). Hanno-Walter Kruft, in turn, is not wrong in his perception that "fun" appears to be "taken more or less seriously" by the Venturis as a criterion for architectural quality (Hanno-Walter Kruft, *Geschichte der Architekturtheorie von der Antike bis zur Gegenwart* (Munich: Beck, 1985), p. 512.

128 Joseph Rykwert, *The First Moderns* (Cambridge, Mass.: MIT Press, 1980), p. 4.

129 Colin Rowe and Fred Koetter, *Collage City* (Cambridge, Mass.: MIT Press, n.d. [1979?]), pp. 14-15. In this context, see also Charles Jencks, "Free Style Classicism," *AD Profile* 1/2: 1-120 (in book form), in which the Temple facade that Venturi designed for the "Strada Novissima" (Venice Biennale 1980) is inserted into Serlio's view of the "scena tragica" (introduction).

130 As when, for example, M. Tafuri asks "Pourquoi associer le plaisir à un bal masqué?" in "Les cendres de Jefferson," *Architecture d'aujourd'hui,* August-September 1976, pp. 53-58. Equally symptomatic in this context is Kenneth Frampton's inflationary use of terms like "reactionary," "cynical," and "ideological" when he comes to blame the organizers of the 1980 Biennale in Venice for having reproduced Scamozzi's false perspective of the Teatro Olympico in the catalogue. See "Towards a Critical Regionalism: Six Points for an Architecture of Resistance," in *The Anti-Aesthetic; Essays on Postmodern Culture,* ed. Hal Foster (Port Townsend: Bay Press, 1983), pp. 23-38.

131 It is no coincidence that Richard Krautheimer was able to interpret two of the most famous surviving Italian Renaissance paintings of ideal cities as recreations of scenographic designs for tragedies or comedies. See Richard Krautheimer, "The Tragic and Comic Scene of the Renaissance: The Baltimore and Urbino Panels," *Gazette des Beaux-Art,* 1948, pp. 327-46.

132 The three categories of the "ugly" are taken from K. Rosenkranz, *Ästhetik des Hässlichen* (see note 114).

133 Scully, *American Architecture and Urbanism* (see note 36), p. 236; Wolfe, *From Bauhaus to Our House* (see note 46), pp. 97-98; and S. von Moos, "Rund um die Fernsehantenne des Guild House" (see note 76). In this context, Heinrich Klotz is probably right in saying that the architects had "not taken into consideration that in general social symbolism articulates idealizing aspirations, whereas pinpointing unadmitted weaknesses is evidently not deemed to be worthy of immortalization" (*Moderne und postmoderne Architektur* [see note 37], p. 157).

134 See p. 160 in this book.

135 See H. Klotz, *Moderne und postmoderne Architektur* (see note 37), pp. 159-60.

136 See pp. 301 f. in this book.

137 See Meyer Schapiro, "Courbet and Popular Imagery," *Journal of the Warburg and Courtauld Institutes* 4 (1940-1941): 164-91.

138 See H. Gans, *Popular Culture and High Culture* (see note 6).

PART II:

VRSB

Buildings and Projects, 1960–1985

Abbreviations

AA	Architectural Association (London)
AA	*L'Architecture d'aujourd'hui*
AD	*Architectural Design*
Arch. Forum	*Architectural Forum*
Arch. Rec.	*Architectural Record*
a + u	*architecture + urbanism*
AVC	*Robert Venturi and Denise Scott Brown, A View from the Campidoglio, Selected Essays 1953 – 1984,* edited by P. Arnell, T. Bickford, and C. Bergart (New York: Harper and Row, 1984).
CCA	Robert Venturi, *Complexity and Contradiction in Architecture* (New York: Museum of Modern Art, 1966). (1977 edition.)
DSB	Denise Scott Brown
LLV	Robert Venturi, Denise Scott Brown, and Steven Izenour, *Learning from Las Vegas* (Cambridge, MA.: MIT Press, 1972).
Moderne und Postmoderne	Heinrich Klotz, *Moderne und Postmoderne Architektur der Gegenwart, 1960 – 1980* (Brunswick/Wiesbaden: Vieweg, 1984).
New Directions	Robert Stern, *New Directions in American Architecture* (New York: Braziller, 1969).
NYT	*The New York Times*
PA	*Progressive Architecture*
PM	*Philadelphia Magazine*
Revision der Moderne	Heinrich Klotz (ed.), *Die Revision der Moderne. Postmoderne Architektur, 1960 – 1980* (Munich: Prestel, 1984).
RV	Robert Venturi
SI	Steven Izenour
VRSB	Venturi, Rauch and Scott Brown
WP	*Washington Post*

Most projects and buildings done prior to 1979 are documented in a more summary way in the Zurich exhibition catalogue (Stanislaus von Moos and Margit Weinberg-Staber, *Venturi und Rauch. Architektur im Alltag Amerikas* [Zurich: Kunstgewerbemuseum der Stadt Zürich, 1979]).

1 Urban Design

It is intriguing that one of the earliest urban design projects by Venturi, Rauch and Scott Brown was for a fountain located at the foot of Philadelphia's City Hall so as to terminate the monumental Benjamin Franklin Parkway that cuts across the city diagonally (pl. b). This is because that site has been the locus of quite a few later VRSB projects as well, for Philadelphia, with both the severity of its Champs-Elysées in the center, and the "messy vitality" of South Street, has always been the natural focus of the Venturis' interest in urban form. Another reason that this early project warrants interest is that it happens to have an ironic parallel to Le Corbusier's career. After the organizers of the Paris Salon d'Automne had invited him to submit an urbanistic project in 1922, they allegedly asked, "Why don't you design

a fountain for us?" Le Corbusier accepted—but not without a symptomatic afterthought: "Very well, I will create a fountain and, behind it, a city for three million inhabitants."[1]

"Urbanism" versus "Urban Design"

The project to which he referred was the *ville contemporaine pour trois millions d'habitants* ("contemporary city for three million inhabitants"), one of modern city planning's archetypes (pl. a). As Corbusier later joked, the fountain was "forgotten." For him, as well as for most other pioneers of modern architecture, "urbanism" meant drawing up a master plan for an urban infrastructure, including everything from the transportation system to details of the architecture. A city was to be conceived just as a large palace complex

a Le Corbusier: *Ville contemporaine pour 3 millions d'habitants* (1922)

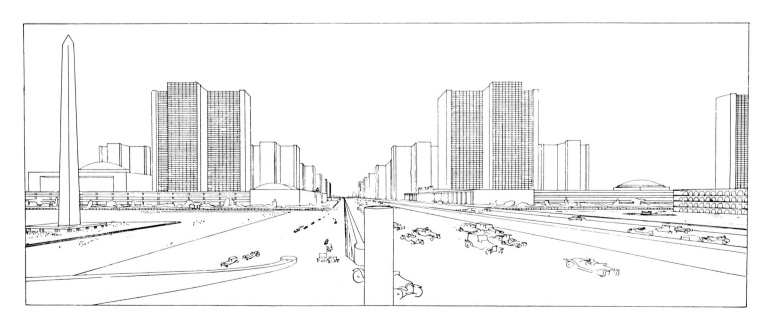

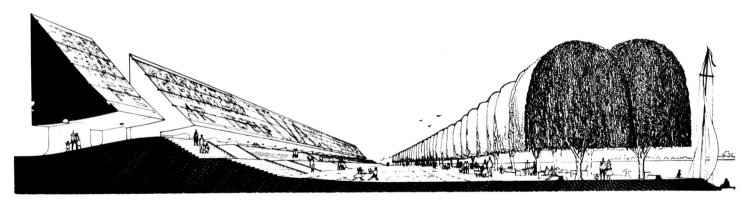

c   Venturi and Rauch (with N. Gionopulos): F. D. R. Memorial Park, Washington, D.C., perspective drawing (competition project, 1960)

would have been in the seventeenth or eighteenth century: as a self-contained entity whose form and organization are rigorously controlled.

It was two or three decades before the urban ideals of Le Corbusier's era were overtaken by reality, especially in America. As a comparison with Stuyvesant Town in Manhattan (1947) or with CO-OP City in Queens (1965–1970) can demonstrate, no project from the heroic period of modern architecture other than the *ville contemporaine* seems to have had such a lasting impact on the imagery of urban renewal in the United States. In cities such as Boston, Chicago, New York, or St. Louis, however, the social benefits of this technocratic model for urban renewal proved dubious in many ways. This was certainly true for residents of neighborhoods that had been "sanitized," leaving them no choice but to flee to other parts of the city threatened by decay. Beginning in the late 1950s and early 1960s, Lewis Mumford, Jane Jacobs, Herbert Gans, and others began to publish their studies on the effects of functionalist dogma on city planning in the United States. Later, after the spectacular debacle of a publically funded modern housing project in St. Louis, Charles Jencks even went so far as to announce "the death of modern architecture."[2]

That the Venturis' career as urban designers and planners should have focused on projects for fountains, squares, and portions of cities—rather than plans for an entire city—is

therefore not without deeper meaning. In fact, the concept of city planning adopted by Venturi and Scott Brown openly challenges the ideals developed with Le Corbusier's help in the 1920s and codified in the Athens Charter drawn up in 1933 by the *Congrès Internationaux d'Architecture Moderne* ("International Congresses for Modern Architecture").[3] Many of Venturi and Rauch's urban design proposals are "monumental" in a classic academic sense. They are public recreational sites to which sculptural and architectural elements lend a ceremonial character. This was as true of the spectacular design for an F.D.R. Memorial on the Potomac River in Washington, D.C. (1960; pl. c) as it was much later for the parks and promenades planned to replace Manhattan's Westside Highway in VRSB's project (1978–1985; not built; see pp. 128–33).

Rome and a Welsh Mining Town

In this firm's work, large urban axes therefore do not represent the backbone of a utopian vision, as they did in Le Corbusier's urban imagery. Rather, they stand for specific localities that have evolved through time and that are in need of architectural and sculptural accentuation. Examples are Franklin Parkway or Broad Street in Philadelphia (see pp. 98f.), Pennsylvania Avenue in Washington, D.C. (see pp. 116–21), and New York's Broadway.

In Europe, city planning had indeed more often been a question of circumscribed correction and enrichment than of all-encompassing "total design." A paradigmatic example

◀

b   Philadelphia: City Hall (below) and Benjamin Franklin Parkway

79

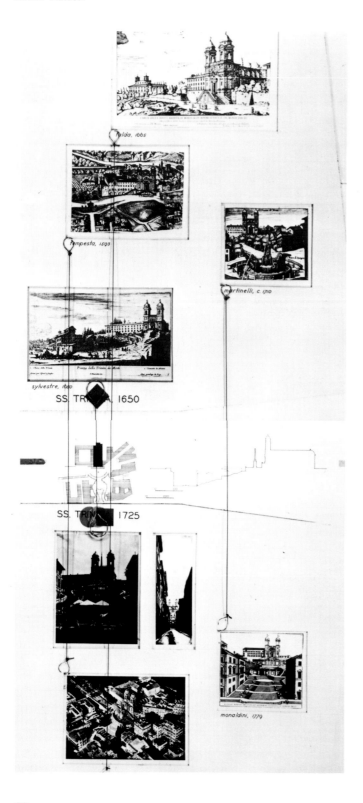

is Michelangelo's modernization of the Roman Palazzo dei Senatori on the Campidoglio in the sixteenth century. The square in front of the palace was transformed into an urban focal point by the addition of one building (the Palazzo dei Conservatori) and an ingeniously patterned pavement in front of it (not executed until the 1930s; see p. 145). Subsequent interventions in Rome may also serve as examples, including the Spanish Steps, which provide both a termination for the Via Condotti and a transition to the piazza in front of Trinità dei Monti, the church at the top of the stairs. In his 1950 Master's thesis for Princeton University, Venturi had analyzed the architectural form of both these urban spaces (pl. d) and other Roman squares.[4]

A few years later (1954) Denise Scott Brown and Brian Smith chose to design a residential neighborhood for a small Welsh mining town as their thesis project at the Architectural Association. In this project the role of New Brutalist "socio-plastics" and a reassessment of CIAM urbanism were both evident. Although the development of a transportation artery was central to the study and although the design had elements of the late Hilberseimer and early megastructure, its housing clusters were resolutely kept close to the ground. Interestingly enough, one part of the residential area was deliberately left undefined (pl. e) so that the town's development would not be preordained by the architects' overall design (see also p. 280).

Pop Art and Social Science

In the early 1950s, Pop Art in England, and subsequently in the United States, had begun to study and assimilate images of everyday commercial culture and to use them for artistic ends (see pp. 52 f.). At the same time in America, John B. Jackson started to substitute the curiosity and the scholarly methods of the cultural historian for the stereotyped professional disinterest, if not disdain, that architects still seemed to cultivate for the "ordinary" commercial environment in general and for "suburbia" in particular. "For it looks," so he argued, "as if suburbs and a suburban way of life would be with us for a long time to come; and if we somehow learned to see them as belated American versions

d Robert Venturi: "Context in Architectural Composition." Trinità dei Monti in Rome before and after the building of the Spanish Steps. Panel accompanying the Master's thesis at Princeton University (1950)

of an ancient and relatively effective worldwide community form instead of as nightmares induced by land speculation, we might adjust to them a little more gracefully and intelligently than we are doing now."[5]

In any case, the era of large-scale master plans based on the modern paradigm of free-standing slabs bathed in sun and air seemed to be over. Under the impact of the civil rights movement and social struggles of the late 1950s and early 1960s, sociologists and social planners decried the urban problems that resulted from a reductionist application of functionalist ideas, problems that led to considerable political unrest. Even architects felt an urgent need to know more about the mechanisms of visual communication, about social behavior, about the articulation of political will, and about status symbolism as they actually operate in cities. The call for alternative, cooperative planning strategies known as "advocacy planning" was only the most radical consequence of the new sociopolitical sensitivity,[6] but it was one with which Denise Scott Brown was closely involved, for the social planning movement in America had its origins at the University of Pennsylvania in the urban planning department while she was a student and faculty member there.

It is from this point that the Venturis started off, convinced that only a readiness to relinquish the position of a moralistic, norm-setting cultural pioneer would make a new and fruitful reading, and ultimately an improvement, of the American landscape possible. Because commissions were long in coming, Venturi and Scott Brown decided to initiate their own studies of the imagery of the American city. In so doing, they slipped, as it were, into the roles of sociologists, anthropologists, cultural geographers of the American environment. Building partly upon the studies of Herbert Gans, Melvin Webber, and others, they documented and analyzed the physical forms and symbols of America's daily environment through a series of case studies undertaken at Yale between 1968 and 1971—studies that focused on two archetypes, Las Vegas and Levittown.[7]

As these studies were initiated, the firm was hired as advocate planners for a low-income Philadelphia community fighting plans for an expressway on South Street (see p. 90). Because the Venturis admired the "messy vitality" of the Las Vegas Strip, community members felt that the firm would

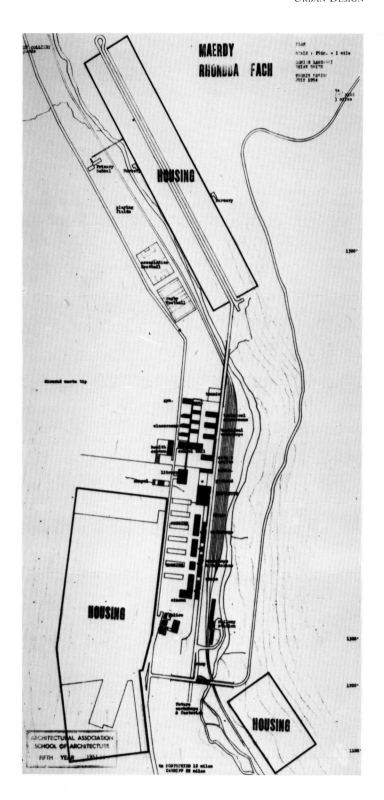

e   Denise Scott Brown and Brian Smith: Planning proposal for a Welsh mining town. Thesis project at the Architectural Association in London (1954)

8218   8220   8222½ 8222   8226   8228   8240   Harper

Marmont   8221   8225   Roxbury

f Edward Ruscha: *Every Building on the Sunset Strip* (1966), detail

accept the reality of community needs and not try to neaten up South Street at the expense of its occupants. Working both as academic researchers and community advocates, the Venturis developed an understanding through which social and economic conditions and the imagination and needs of actors using the environment could be accepted as creative forces. It was this understanding that could simultaneously facilitate the efforts of these architects to orchestrate the public realm with means reminiscent of the forgotten approach that the "City-Beautiful" movement had once taken to architectural form and symbol. As Denise Scott Brown put it: "Urban design must encompass the flower that will bloom tomorrow and an expressway that will last a thousand years."[8] Moreover, "most urban planners today see themselves as strategists, intervening in an ongoing, multivalent, hydra-headed system, working the art of the possible using finely tuned instruments; heading toward an ideal, but shifting vision of the future."[9]

82

8250   8260   8262   8264   8272   8278

8255   8265

1 Le Corbusier, *L'Atelier de la recherche patiente* (Paris: Vincent Fréal, 1960), pp. 62–64; S. von Moos, *Le Corbusier, Elements of a Synthesis* (Cambridge, Mass.: MIT Press, 1979), pp. 187f.

2 J. Jacobs, *The Death and Life of Great American Cities* (London: Jonathan Cape, 1962); L. Mumford, *The Highway and the City* (London: Secker & Warburg, 1964); H. Gans, "The Failure for Urban Renewal," *Commentary*, April 1965, pp. 29–37; C. Jencks, *The Language of Post-Modern Architecture* (London: Academy Editions, 1977).

3 It should be noted, however, that the CIAM had by then considerably modified its earlier positions. See J. L. Sert (ed.), *The Heart of the City* (London: Lund Humphries, 1952). For a detailed discussion of the origins and premises of the firm's ideas on urban design, see DSB, "Between Three Stools" and "A Worm's Eye View of Recent Architectural History," *Arch. Rec.*, February 1984, pp. 69–81. See also below, pp. 145ff.

4 RV, "Context in Architectural Composition," 1950. (Manuscript.) *Idem*, "The Campidoglio: A Case Study," *Arch. Rev.*, May 1953, pp. 333f.; reprinted in *AVC*, pp. 12ff.

5 J. B. Jackson, "The Many Guises of Suburbia," in *Landscapes: Selected Writings*, ed. E. H. Zube (Boston: University of Massachusetts Press, 1970), pp. 113–15.

6 H. Gans, *The Urban Villagers: Group and Class in the Life of Italo-Americans* (New York: The Free Press, 1962); Donald L. Foley, "An Approach to Metropolitan Spatial Structure," in Melvin M. Webber *et al.*, *Explorations into Urban Structure* (Philadelphia: University of Pennsylvania Press, 1964), pp. 21–78; Melvin M. Webber, "The Urban Place and the Nonplace Urban Realm," in Webber, *Explorations into Urban Structure*, pp. 79–153; H. Gans, *The Levittowners* (New York: Pantheon, 1966); R. Goodman, *After the Planners* (New York: Simon and Schuster, 1971).

7 DSB, "On Pop Art, Permissiveness and Planning," *AIP Journal*, May 1969, pp. 184–86; *LLV; LLT*, see here, pp. 17ff.

8 DSB, "The Public Realm in Urban Design," 1985. (Manuscript.)

9 *Ibid.*

ANATOMY OF THE STREET

The traditional urban street, unlike Route 66 and the urban residential street, is laterally enclosed by the facades of buildings that line it.

Walls seen in perspective rather than points seen in perspective, define the geometry of the street; they may be the high cliffs of Wall Street of the continuous brick walls of Beacon Hill, but in each case walls are the major definers of the urban street space. The street differs from the piazza in that street space is directional; it must communicate with people moving in one or two directions. All urban street communication is inflected to this movement, as is communication on the strip. Urban street facades and their signs are therefore designed to be seen obliquely rather than broadside, and they are designed to be seen by pedestrians, transit riders, and slowly moving automobile passengers.

As most American cities have a grid iron plan, city streets are usually straight. The winding Medieval street is visually terminated by buildings on the curve, and frequently a church spire or important building dominates the view. In formal European planning, important buildings terminate vistas and piazzas break the linearity of the street. The facades of buildings may be designed symmetrically to be seen on axis from the street or from a distance across the piazza. Even the urban expressway, in that it curves and winds, affords more vistas than does the urban street. Billboard advertisers use this fact, and some expressway billboards can be seen on axis by automobile users for over half a mile.

g "Signs of Life." Panels from the "City Room" in the 1976 exhibition (see pp. 49, 305)

THE CITY BEAUTIFUL

In Washington, monumental diagonal avenues link important national shrines and governmental buildings. At the turn of the twentieth century the City Beautiful Movement swept America and many other cities got their local Champs Elysees. Perhaps the greatest example was Chicago, where urban improvements were linked with the World's Columbian Exposition of 1893.

The 1909 plan for Chicago by Daniel Burnham employed most of the forms or urban symbolism we have discussed. Grandiose building complexes in the Beaux Arts style were designed to the greater glory of an ever-expanding Chicago. Important civic buildings were tied to a monumental road system that was tied, in turn, to a regional park and parkway system. The plan projected an image of Chicago spreading ever outward fading into the distance. It was a symbolic image of civic boosterism, unlikely ever to be equalled.

THE STREET ON THE STRIP

In Los Angeles people ride to where they want to walk.

Throughout the city and reachable by expressways are enclaves scaled to pedestrian use. Disneyland, the most outstanding, is located in the heart of suburban Los Angeles. Walt Disney claimed that he found "Nowhere to take the kids on a Sunday afternoon," therefore he reproduced a traditional, small-town Main Street in suburbia. Disneyland is a fantasy version of Main Street, whose pastiche buildings and quaint stores are 5/8 normal size. This gives Main Street an intensified "human scale." Disney achieves a more "human" scale (if that is the right word) that Modern architects achieve when they aim for the same quality. The intensified "humanity" may be a sentimental reaction to the freeway outside, but it seems to be appreciated by the public if the public can be said to vote with its feet.

The most pervasive users of the "extra human" environment are suburban shopping malls. Mall stores, like medieval streets, rely on an immediacy of contact between goods and purchasers. Malls provide ornamental plants, ponds, ducks, fountains, quaint signs, banners, boutiques, kiosks, and puppet shows.

The lobbies of some hotels simulate urban piazzas. The common spaces of some suburban townhouse clusters evoke medieval towns or urban piazzas, at 5/8 scale. Many architect-designed piazzas strain to achieve "human scale," yet do not seem to attract human beings.

1   Fairmount Park Fountain Competition

Competition project for a fountain in Philadelphia,
Pennsylvania (1964)
In collaboration with Denise Scott Brown
In charge: Robert Venturi
with Gerod Clark and Frank Kawasaki

This cap-shaped fountain was proposed for a site at one end
of Philadelphia's Champs-Elysées, the Benjamin Franklin
Parkway, an urban arterial that runs to the center of the city.
The project's form and scale has clearly been influenced by
the nature of the site in various ways. As the architects put
it:

> The form is big and bold so that it will read against its
> background of big buildings and amorphous space, and
> also from the relatively long distance up the Parkway. Its
> plastic shape, curving silhouette, and plain surface also

contrast boldly with the intricate rectangular patterns of
the buildings around, although they are analogous to
some of the mansard roof shapes on City Hall. This was
not meant to be an intricate Baroque fountain to be read
only close-up, or from a car stalled in traffic.[1]

At the foot, the fountain is inscribed: "Here Begins
Fairmount Park." From the Franklin Parkway only the words
"Park Here" can be read, information not inappropriate to a
monument built above an underground garage. In this
manner, the project explicitly enhances this urban space, the
essence of which is best perceived from an automobile.

1   *CCA*, pp. 122–23.

Literature
*South Carolina AIA Review of
Architecture*, 1965, pp. 29–31.
Perspecta 11 (New Haven, 1967): 103,
106–7.
New Directions, pp. 51–52.

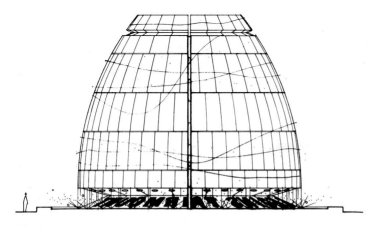

Elevation

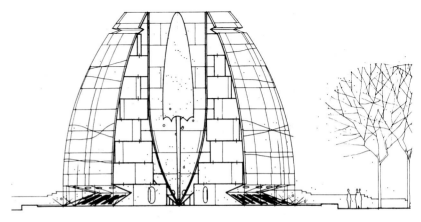

Section

View of the Benjamin
Franklin Parkway, photo-
montage

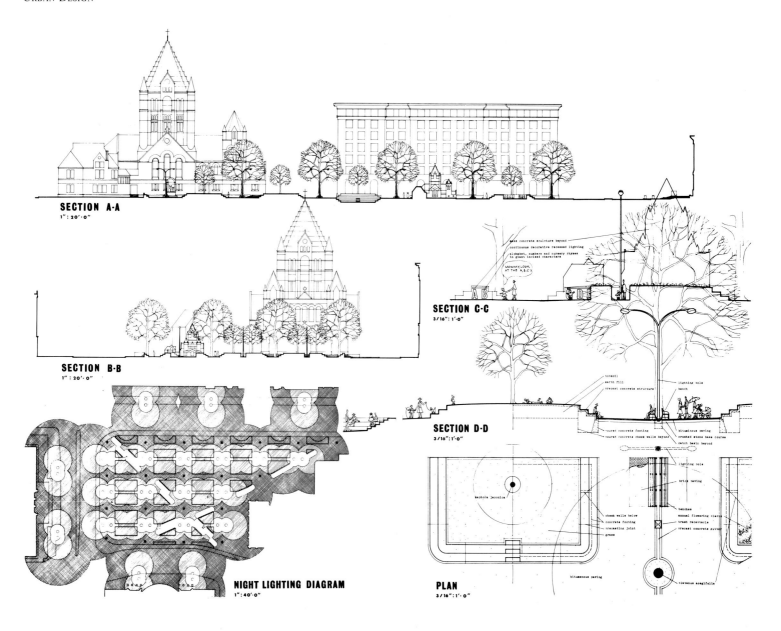

SECTION A-A
1" : 20'-0"

SECTION B-B
1" : 20'-0"

SECTION C-C
3/16" : 1'-0"

SECTION D-D
3/16" : 1'-0"

NIGHT LIGHTING DIAGRAM
1" : 40'-0"

PLAN
3/16" : 1'-0"

2   Copley Square Competition

Project for Boston, Massachusetts (1966)
In charge: Robert Venturi
with Gerod Clark and Arthur Jones

Unlike the project for the fountain in Philadelphia (pp. 86 f.), this one is focused on the pedestrian. At first glance, it is difficult to categorize the concept in terms of most American architectural concerns of the 1960s, for it proposes an alternative to the then current predilection for wide, open plazas.

Venturi considers the "piazza compulsion" another lamentable crutch of modern architecture. Despite an architect's justifiable love for Italian cities, the open piazza "is seldom appropriate for an American city today, except as a convenience… for diagonal shortcuts" from one block to another. "The piazza," according to Venturi,

◀ Plan and sections

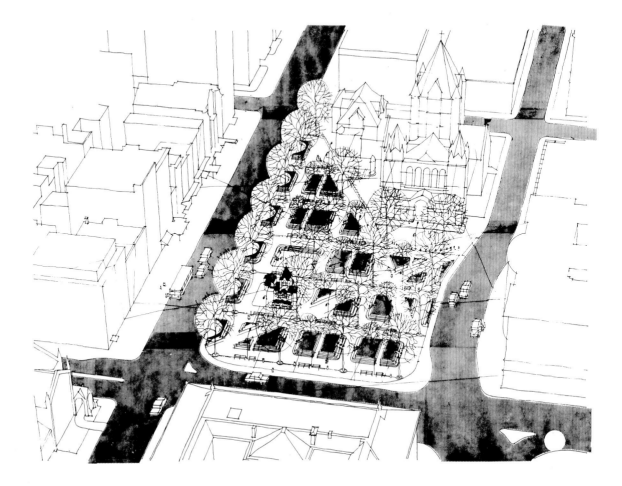

Bird's eye view
(drawing: Gerod Clark
and Arthur Jones)

is in fact un-American, just like the *passegiata*. Americans feel uncomfortable sitting in a square: They should be working at the office or sitting with the family in front of the television. . . . [E]mpty piazzas are intriguing only in early de Chiricos.[1]

The project is an attempt to define public space through a plaid-like articulation of the ground plane. Paths, greenery, visual connections, and furniture are used to this effect, whereas the more typical definers of urban space, the existing, surrounding structures, are deemphasized. For example, the trees on the square were not employed as "sculptural forms sitting *in* a space because that would compete with Trinity Church" (one of H. H. Richardson's major works). Instead, the trees form an evenly distributed, three-dimensional pattern without any particular point of climax. As the architects intimate: "In the context of the 'boring' consistent grid inside the square the chaotic buildings to the north become 'interesting' and vital elements of the composition."[2]

The square also contains a replica of Trinity Church in miniature. "The miniature imitation is a means for explaining to a person the whole which he is in, but cannot see all of."[3]

1 *CCA*, pp. 129–31.
2 *Ibid.*
3 *Ibid.*

Literature

Perspecta 11 (New Haven, 1967): 108–11.

New Directions, pp. 52–53.

Die Revision der Moderne, pp. 331–33.

Moderne und Postmoderne, pp. 179–80.

A. Krieger and L. J. Green, *Past Futures: Two Centuries of Imagining Boston* (Cambridge, Mass.: Harvard University, 1985), pp. 46–53.

The status quo

3   The Philadelphia Crosstown Community

A planning and urban design study for South Street (1968)
In charge: Denise Scott Brown
with Steven Izenour and David Manker

When in the 1950s South Street Philadelphia, famous in the history of jazz, was designated as the last segment of a proposed freeway, it fell progressively into decay but also became the center for important low-income communities in Philadelphia.

Early in 1968, under threat of renewal for the expressway, a neighborhood coalition, the Crosstown Community, requested a planning study by Venturi and Rauch. As one of their consultants put it: "If you can like the Las Vegas Strip, we trust you not to try to neaten up South Street at the expense of its occupants."[1]

The study involved three major steps: a detailed analysis of social, economic, and physical conditions of the community; assistance with instituting a process of democratic participation in planning; and careful design aimed at bringing a high degree of imagination to the most infrangible of urban realities.

1   *LLV*, pp. 126–33.

Literature

M. Osborn, "Saving Picturesque South St.," *Philadelphia Evening Bulletin*, September 1968.

M. Osborn, "The Crosstown and City Planning," *Philadelphia Evening Bulletin*, March 1969.

J. Mathe, "Philadelphia's Mason-Dixon Line," *Distant Drummer*, May 4, 1969, p. 3.

E. L. Meyer, "Residents Envision 'Promenade of Negro Culture' Along South St. If Expressway Fails," *Philadelphia Evening Bulletin*, June 11, 1969.

V. Donohoe, "Advocacy Planners Put Hope in Ghetto," *The Philadelphia Inquirer*, July 6, 1969.

L. Berson, "South Street Insurrection," *Philadelphia Magazine*, September 1969, pp. 87–91.

N. Nelson, "Couple to Unveil Remodeling Plan for South St. Tonight," *Philadelphia Daily News*, January 12, 1970.

L. Berson, "Dreams for a New South Street are Spun at Theater Meetings," *Center City Philadelphia*, February 1970.

American Heritage, August 1970, p. 119.

DSB, "An Alternate Proposal that Builds on the Character of South Street," *Arch. Forum*, October 1971, pp. 42–44.

M. Osborn, "The Crosstown is Dead. Long Live the Crosstown," *Arch. Forum*, October 1971, pp. 38–42.

AA 159 (January 1972): 94–97.

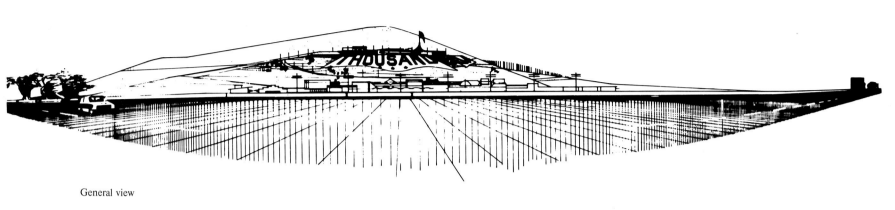

General view

4 Thousand Oaks Civic Center

Competition project for Thousand Oaks, California (1969)
In charge: Robert Venturi
with John Anderson, Denise Scott Brown, W.G. Clark, James Greifendorf, Steven Izenour, Anthony Pett

Thousand Oaks was a rapidly growing suburb. For its Civic Center, the architects "tried to make civic architecture out of low, modest buildings, parking lots, symbols people like and can understand, and the signing systems they know from driving the freeway."[1]

For City Hall, a simple steel frame structure was chosen for maximum flexibility. At the entrance to the council chamber this structure evolved into a ceremonial tower, whose construction suggested a live oak, which, in turn, became a flagpole at the top. Along the length of the building, signs in Roman lettering signal the location of city departments to people arriving by car in the parking lot.

The architects call the design "camp Mies." They point to the experimental character of their project:

> Our design has learned from and comments upon Las Vegas and the A&P parking lot, more specifically than we would want or expect in the developed project, because a building should be more than the embodiment of a theory.... Perhaps a better point of departure and at least as rich a source for inspiration and comment would have been suburban housing, rather than the suburban strip.[2]

1 *LLV*, pp. 142–43.
2 *Ibid.*

Literature

S. Izenour, "Civic Center Competition for Thousand Oaks, California ...," *AD* (February 1971): 113–14.

werk-archithese 7–8 (1977): 35–36.

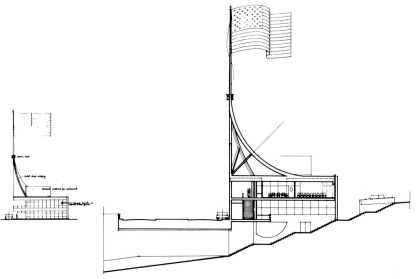

City Hall, section and elevation

Bird's eye view

Arts Center, plan and elevation

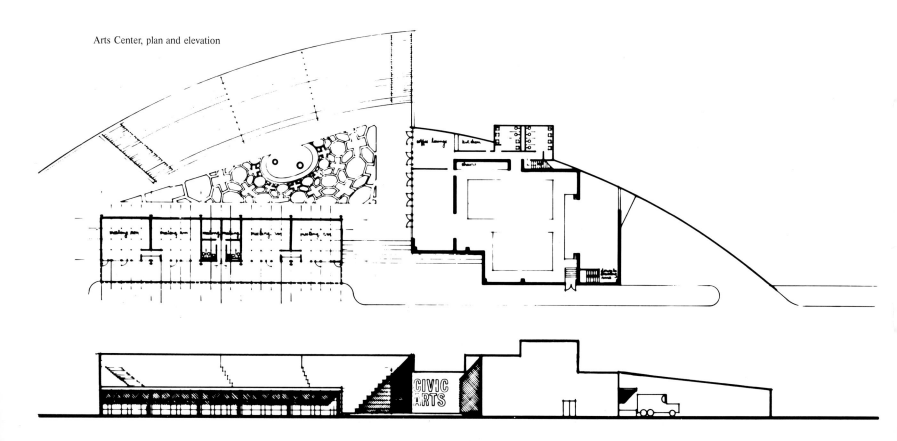

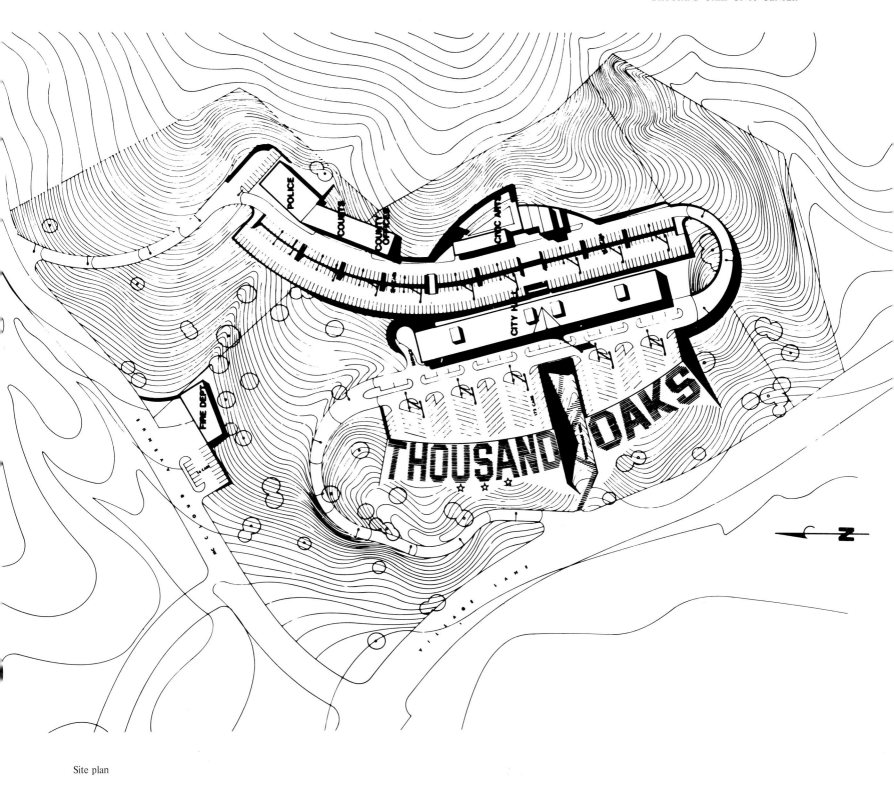

Site plan

5 California City Planning and Urban Design Study

General plan and design proposal for California City, California (1970)
In charge: Denise Scott Brown
with W.G. Clark, Giovanni Cosco, James Greifendorf, Paul Hirshorn, Steven Izenour, Robert Venturi

California City is located approximately 100 miles north and east of Los Angeles in the Mojave Desert. When the planning of the city was commissioned in 1970, many of its 2,000 inhabitants were living in mobile-home parks. Given its location and context, the planning study paid particular attention to questions of ecology and to the need to provide a well-developed public infrastructure and adequate recreational and leisure facilities. One of their planning tasks was to design a set of signs to be placed along Twenty Mule Team Parkway, the main road to an outlying residential area. They also submitted designs for various office buildings, a supermarket, a city hall, and a cemetery.

Large signs recalling the Las Vegas strip were employed to call the attention of prospective investors and residents to the attractions and advantages of the new city. In the words of the architects:

> We knew too that to hold people's attention these signs must look "beautiful" and therefore must not resemble billboards since people do not find billboards beautiful.... We chose desert flowers as our theme, partly because flowers are regarded as beautiful (they are also uncontroversial), partly to reinforce our own aim to push desert gardening to save the ecology.[1]

The architectural expression chosen for the sales office of the Great Western United Corporation (see p. 38) was made to conform to the conventions of civic buildings. The City Hall stands as a reflecting glass cube in the middle of the desert landscape like a modern variation on the archetypal pyramid in an empty desert.

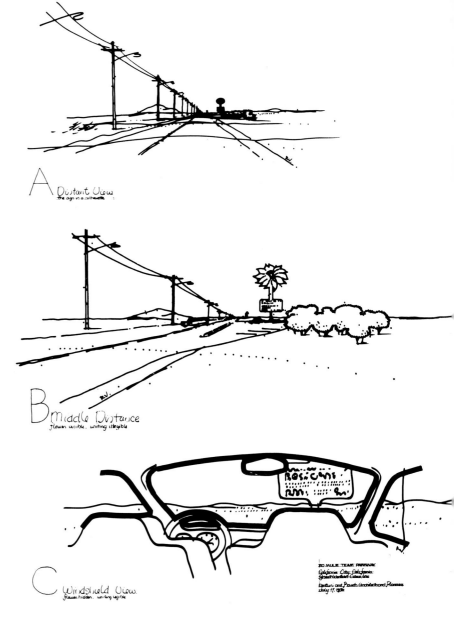

Signs along the Twenty Mule Team Parkway: distant view (top), middle distance view (center), and windshield view (bottom) (drawing: RV)

1 *LLV*, pp. 176–87.

Literature
Arch. Rec., June 6, 1971, pp. 117–20.

AA 159 (January 1972): 98–104.

A. Sky and M. Stone, *Unbuilt America* (New York: McGraw Hill, 1976), p. 275.

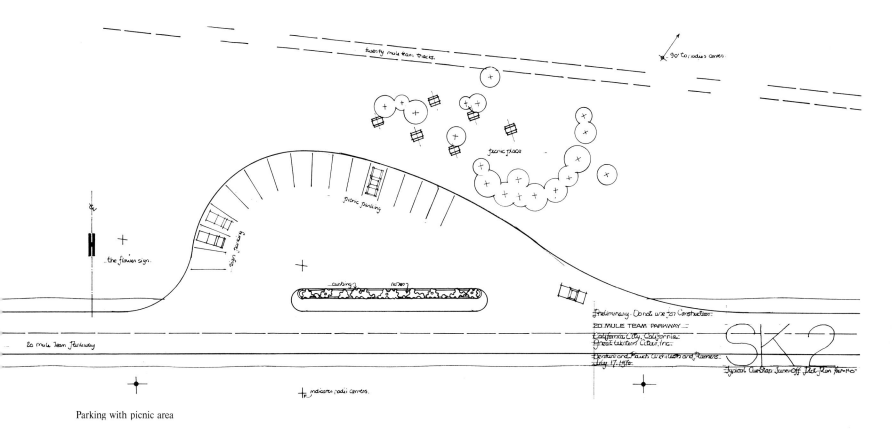

Parking with picnic area

Twenty Mule Team Parkway

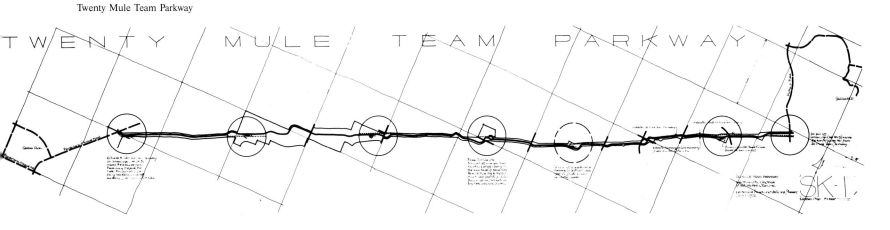

MOJAVE ASTER
Machaeranthera Tortifolia
Habitat : S. California, Arizona, Utah

California City
HOLIDAY INN
By The Lake

Approaching Galileo Hill

Approaching the First Community

SOUTHEAST ELEVATION

City Hall, elevation

◄ Signs of "Mojave Aster" and "Holiday Inn" (drawing: Paul Hirshorn)

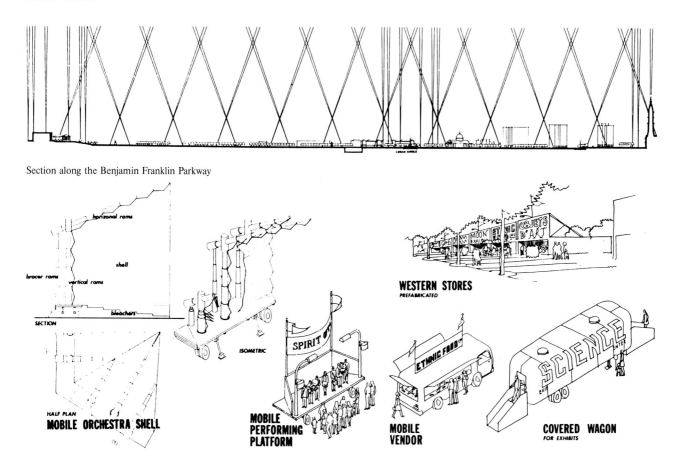

Section along the Benjamin Franklin Parkway

Movable kiosks

6   Benjamin Franklin Parkway Celebration for 1976

Project for celebration and exhibition architecture for the American Bicentennial, Philadelphia (1972)
In charge: Robert Venturi
Project Manager: Steven Izenour
with W. G. Clark

The Benjamin Franklin Parkway, Philadelphia's monumental axis, is a major work of the "City-Beautiful" movement (see also p. 78). The project called for keeping this "Champs-Elysée" intact and for organizing a number of activities to enhance its vitality and glamour. The architects concluded that the Parkway's ceremonial character could hardly be improved upon by day. By night, however, moving lights, not available when the street was designed, could be used to dramatize this setting.

The architects also proposed that movable kiosks, booths, a system of signs, stages for improvized concerts, and other features be erected along both sides of the monumental boulevard.

Literature

RV and DSB, "Bicentenaire de l'indépendence américaine," *AA*, November 1973, pp. 63–69.

a+u 11 (1974): 62–67.

A. Sky and M. Stone, *Unbuilt America* (New York: McGraw Hill, 1976), p. 261.

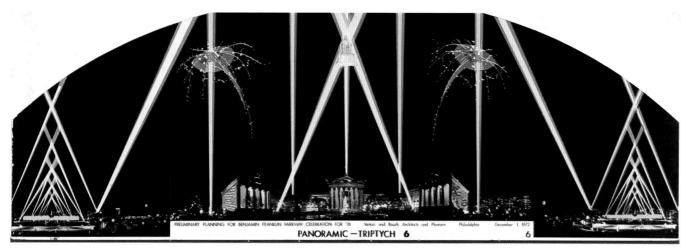

Panoramic triptychon (color collage by Steven Izenour)

Site plan

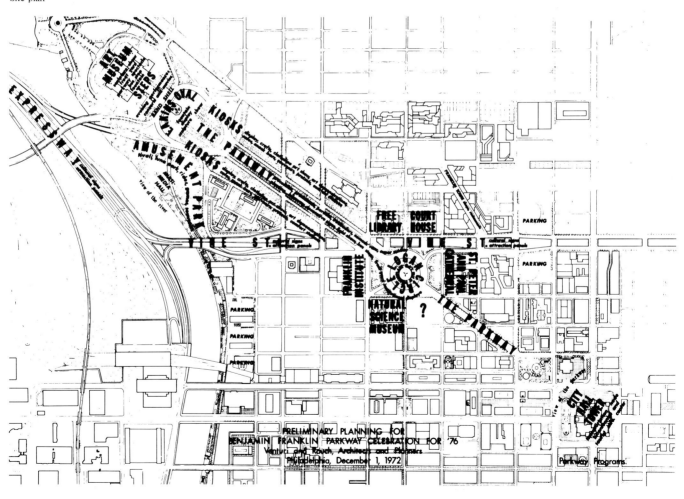

7 City Edges Planning Study

Planning study for Philadelphia, Pennsylvania (1975)
In collaboration with Murphy, Levy, Wurman, Architects
In charge: Denise Scott Brown
Project Manager: Mary Yee
with Paul Hirshorn, Steven Izenour, Missy Maxwell

This planning study analyzes possible visual improvements along major traffic arteries that follow the Schuykill River and skirt the center of Philadelphia. In a detailed report the architects began by inquiring into existing "conditions" along the river and traffic arteries. They compiled an inventory of the city's appearance as seen from an automobile. Statues and memorials along river banks, dating from the years 1875–1970, were as much a part of this picture as the nineteenth- and twentieth-century bridges. The list also included industrial buildings, oil tanks, autobody graveyards, and, finally, billboards.

The main aim was to describe the character of different reaches of the river corridor and to suggest improvements in line with each. Maintenance and renewal of the existing fabric of this corridor was seen as requiring creative attention more than new design. Several practical ideas were suggested for improving the directional signs along the two traffic arteries—not least in the interest of traffic safety. New signs were created both to promote the Bicentennial and to advertise Philadelphia's cultural sites.

Literature

DSB, "City Edges Planning Study," 1973. (Unpublished manuscript.)

a+u 11 (1974): 87–92.

T. Hine, "Pretzel-Land Welcomes the World," *The Philadelphia Inquirer, Today Magazine*, April 13, 1975, pp. 35–42.

AA, June 1978, pp. 83–85.

Moderne und Postmoderne, pp. 168–69.

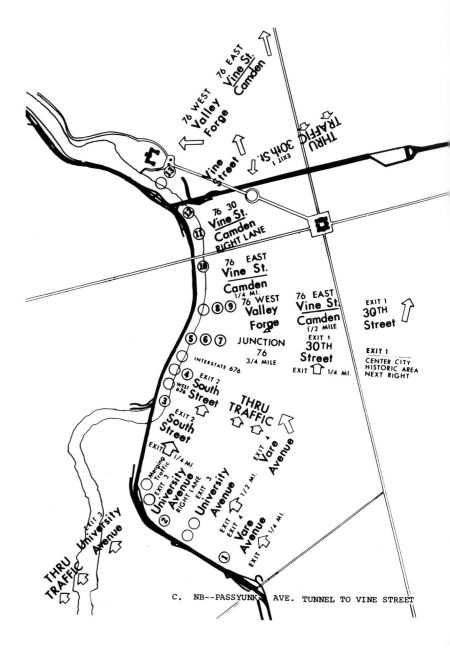

Philadelphia: the two main access highways (with exits)

Proposed signs for the Schuykill River Parkway: William Penn

Proposed signs for the Schuykill River
Parkway: Skyline, Pretzels, Independence
Hall, and a painting from the Philadelphia
Museum of Art

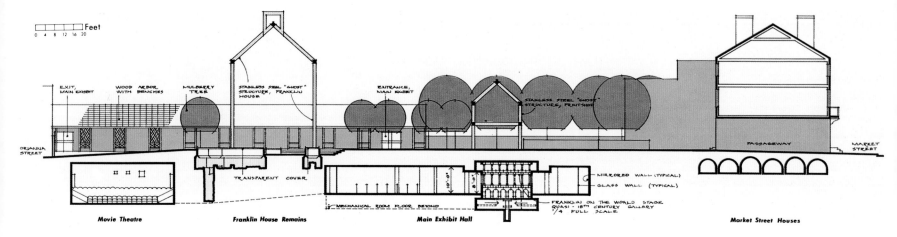

EXIT, MAIN EXHIBIT   WOOD ARBOR WITH BENCHES   MULBERRY TREE   STAINLESS STEEL "GHOST" STRUCTURE, FRANKLIN HOUSE   ENTRANCE, MAIN EXHIBIT   STAINLESS STEEL "GHOST" STRUCTURE, PRINTSHOP

ORIANNA STREET   PASSAGEWAY   MARKET STREET

TRANSPARENT COVER   MECHANICAL ROOM FLOOR BEYOND   MIRRORED WALL (TYPICAL)   GLASS WALL (TYPICAL)   FRANKLIN ON THE WORLD STAGE QUASI - 18TH CENTURY GALLERY 3/4 FULL SCALE

Movie Theatre   Franklin House Remains   Main Exhibit Hall   Market Street Houses

Section

8   Franklin Court

Benjamin Franklin Memorial in Philadelphia (1972)
In collaboration with George Patton Associates, Landscape Architects; National Heritage Corporation, Restoration Architects; deMartin-Marona and Associates, Exhibit Designers
In charge: Robert Venturi; John Rauch
Project Manager: David Vaughan
with Denise Scott Brown, Stanford Hughes, Missy Maxwell, Robert Renfro, Dick Rice, Terry Vaughan

Franklin Court is located on Market Street in Philadelphia, on the site once owned by Benjamin Franklin (1706–1790). The National Park Service commissioned Venturi and Rauch to restore Franklin's house as a museum and national landmark for the Bicentennial in 1976.

The row of brick houses on Market Street, which had been rented out by Franklin, was entirely reconstructed and has since been used for exhibitions. Today, one of the houses contains an operating post office in the style of the 1700s.

A carriageway leads from Market Street into the garden, in the middle of which once stood the three-story mansion that Franklin had built for himself. Because the house has long since been destroyed and because the original plans have not survived, an exact reconstruction was not even considered. In place of the Park Service's suggested museum building the architects recommended an under-

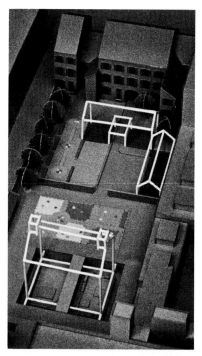

Model view

ground museum with a small, urban park placed above it. In the park, they installed an open steel frame, at the site of the house, depicting its original contours. Thus the architects created a "ghost" house and an extra city park (with an implicit tribute to Giacometti).

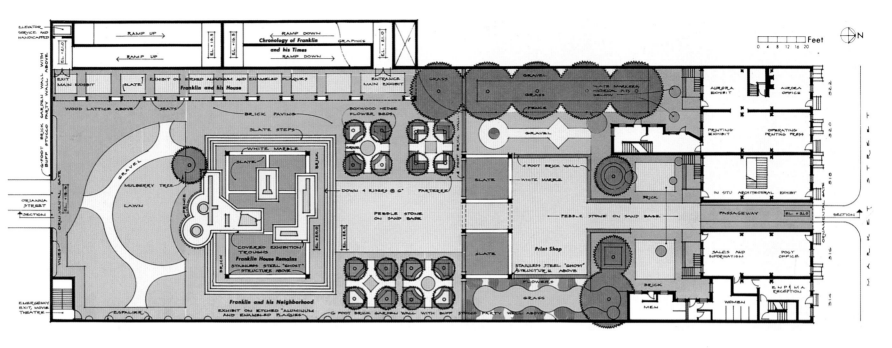

First floor plan

Underground level plan with exhibition

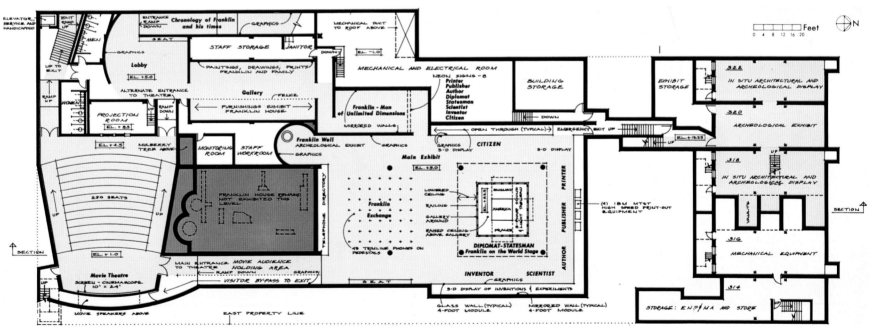

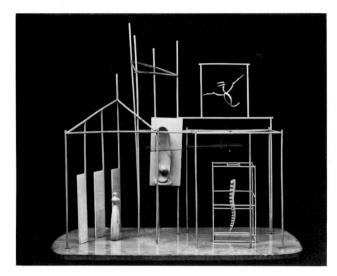

The furnishings in the park (pergolas, poles, fences, and benches) were intended to evoke the atmosphere of an eighteenth-century garden while avoiding the effect of purely historical replicas. An extensive exhibition on the life, work, and times of Benjamin Franklin is housed in the basement of Franklin Court.

Alberto Giacometti: *Palace at 4 o'clock in the Morning* (1932). The Museum of Modern Art, New York

Facades on Market Street ▼   General view ▶

View towards houses on Market Street

Literature

T. Hine, "Franklin Shrine to Center on Abstract 'Ghost' House," *The Philadelphia Inquirer*, July 19, 1974, pp. 1-D, 3-D.

Exponent, National Park Service Quarterly, October 1974, Vol. 1, no. 1, p. 2.

T. Hine, "Shrine for Now, A Park Forever," *Philadelphia Inquirer*, April 18, 1976, pp. 1, 8 b.

S. Stephens, "Franklin Court," *PA*, April 1976, pp. 69-70.

E. K. Carpenter, "Salute to the National Park Service—Exhibits at Franklin Court," *Design and Environment*, Fall 1976, pp. 32-33.

J. Vrchota, "Preservation," *Design and Environment*, Fall 1976, pp. 30-31.

C. Knight III, "Park Service Opens Franklin Court," *Preservation News*, August 1976, pp. 1, 6.

"Non la ricostruzione ma l'idea," *Domus*, March 1977, p. 53.

M. Fox and E. K. Carpenter, *Print Casebooks 2, Second Annual Edition: The Best in Exhibition Design* (Washington, D. C.: R. C. Publications, 1977), pp. 5, 6, 28-30, 56-59, 76-79.

"Franklin's House" above remains of foundations

"Venturi and Rauch: pour Franklin Court un acte poétique," *Architecture Intérieure*, December 1977–January 1978, pp. 72-73.

a+u 1 (1978): 53-62.

B. Zevi, *Cronache di architettura*, 21 (1978): 29-31.

T. Hine, "A Yearning for the Old Ways Finds Expression in New Ruins," *The Philadelphia Inquirer*, March 16, 1980, p. L1.

Y. Futagawa (ed.), *GA Document Special Issue 1970-1980*, 1/1980, pp. 220-21.

J. Sidener, "Franklin Would Appreciate Franklin Court," *The Philadelphia Inquirer*, September 20, 1981.

a+u 12 (1981): 82-86.

D. Graham, "Not Post-Modernism: History as Against Historicism, European Archetypal Vernacular in Relation to American Commercial Vernacular, and the City as Opposed to the Individual Building," *Artforum*, December 1981, pp. 50-58.

P. Goulet, "La Troisième Génération," *AA* (1984): 2-9.

View of the Strand

9 Galveston Development Project

Revitalization plan for "The Strand" in Galveston, Texas (1974)
In charge: Denise Scott Brown
Project Manager: Stanley Taraila
with Stanford Hughes, Steven Izenour, Robert Venturi

For years Galveston's wharf street, "The Strand," once a lively business area, had been decaying. Fortunately, however, a great number of attractive warehouse buildings from the Victorian era, and some original Art Déco buildings were well preserved.

When, in the early 1970s, a portion of Galveston's downtown district was redeveloped, The Strand regained attention. A local historical foundation commissioned Venturi and Rauch to study the area to see whether new uses in keeping with the existing social structure and buildings could be found.

This project resulted from detailed analyses, made in collaboration with area residents and merchants, of Galveston's projected economic development, accessibility, and need for parking space.

New stores, housing, and cultural services were envisioned for The Strand—a mixture of activities that would enliven the street, day and night. A small square was designed, combined with a children's playground adorned by a miniature replica of a historical Galveston street front.

Literature

A. Holmes, "The Pop Artist Who Isn't Kidding Plans to Give Vitality to the Strand," *Houston Chronicle*, November 24, 1974, Part A, Section 4.

M. Blatt, "Historical Foundation Picks Strand Planners," *The Galveston Daily News*, November 24, 1974, p. 1.

P. Papademetriou, "News Report: Report from Galveston," *PA*, December 1976, pp. 26–27.

A. L. Huxtable, "The Fall and Rise of Main Street," *NYT Magazine*, May 30, 1976, pp. 12–14.

AA 197 (June 1978): 80–82.

PA, November 1978, pp. 72–77.

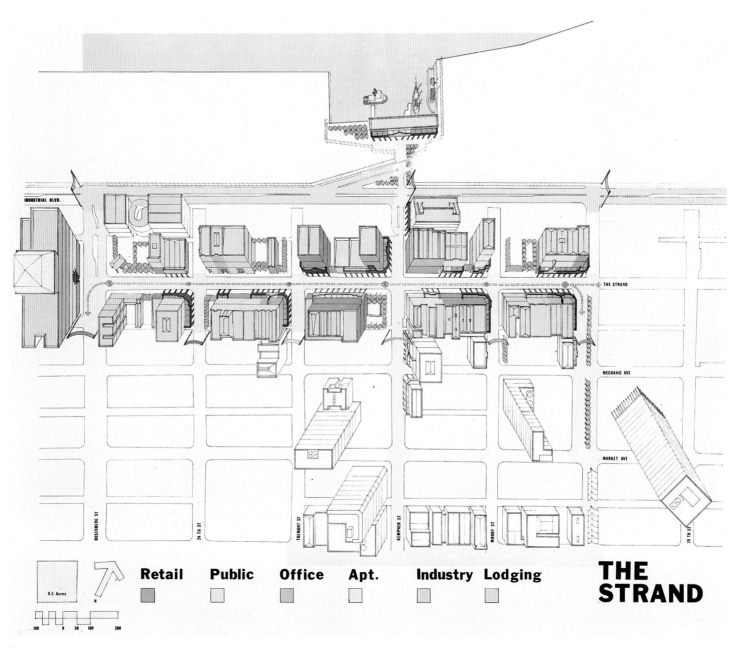

Retail Public Office Apt. Industry Lodging

0.5 Acres

N

100 0 50 100 200

INDUSTRIAL BLVD.

ROSENBERG ST

24 TH ST

TREMONT ST

KEMPNER ST

MOODY ST

19 TH ST

THE STRAND

MECHANIC AVE

MARKET AVE

THE STRAND

Site plan

View from the Strand towards the harbor (drawing: Stanford Hughes)

The Strand

Downtown Galveston: today

10 Scranton Murals

Project for a mural in Scranton, Pennsylvania (1976)
In charge: Robert Venturi
with Stanford Hughes, Steven Izenour

"This outdoor mural is our suggestion for a small town in Pennsylvania where they wanted to enliven the side of a narrow street. It consists of porcelain-enamel panels with very bright colors set out from the wall and well lighted at night."[1]

1 RV, "Learning the Right Lessons from the Beaux-Arts," *AVC*, pp. 70–95; 88 f.

FAMOUS ARCHITECTURE IN THE WORLD
ELEVATION
WEST WALL OF MILLER BUILDING
NOTE: INTERRUPTIONS IN FRIEZE PANELS WILL ACCOMMODATE EXIT DOORS THERE.

SCALE 3/16" = 1'-0"

DOWNTOWN
SCRANTON
MURAL-PROJECT
Venturi and Rauch, Architects + Planners
September 23, 1976
2

Mural project with motifs from the history of architecture (drawing: Steven Izenour and RV)

11   Jim Thorpe
Mauch Chunk Historic District Study

Planning study for the preservation and restoration of a
mining town
Pennsylvania (1977)
In charge: Denise Scott Brown
Project Manager: David Marohn
with Frances Hundt, James H. Timberlake, Mary Yee

The subject of this study is the preservation of a small town
tucked between mountains in upstate Pennsylvania. Built
from 1860 to 1900 around a now abandoned coal mine, the
town is today a historical site popular with visitors for its
picturesque location and its Victorian architecture. The

challenge to the architects was to find ways to preserve the
historic town and increase its economic viability without
pricing out local residents and merchants.

The plan recommends the careful conversion of
nineteenth-century buildings to new commercial and
cultural uses. The aim is not to "restore" the industrial
architecture to its original state, but to preserve its character
as a relic of the past while making it accessible to the public.

Literature

J. Quinn, "Jim Thorpe Is Alive and Well
and Blooming in Pennsylvania," *PM*,
November 1979, pp. 178–83, 282–88,
290.

DSB and F. Hundt, "Erhaltung histori-
scher Bauten und wirtschaftliche Neu-

belebung," *archithese*, March 1980,
pp. 20–24.

PA, January 1981, p. 98.

DSB, assisted by F. Hundt and D.
Marohn, "Historic Jim Thorpe,"
Solutions, Fall 1981, pp. 31–32.

a+u 12 (1981): 87.

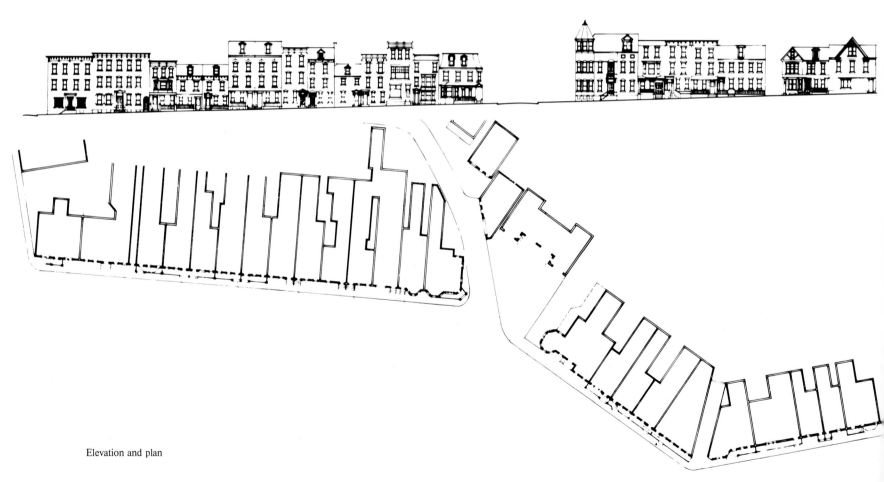

Elevation and plan

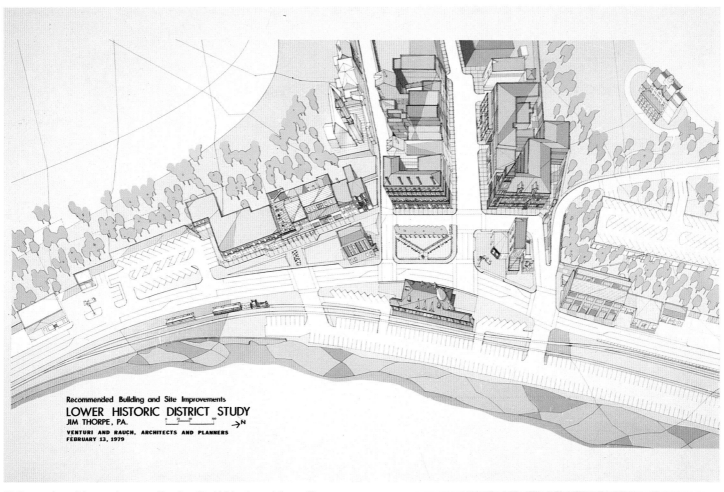

Recommended Building and Site Improvements
LOWER HISTORIC DISTRICT STUDY
JIM THORPE, PA.
VENTURI AND RAUCH, ARCHITECTS AND PLANNERS
FEBRUARY 13, 1979

Bird's eye view of the town's center (drawing: David Marohn and James H. Timberlake)

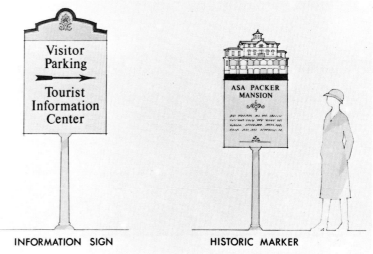

Proposed publicity signs (drawing: James H. Timberlake)

115

12   Pennsylvania Avenue Project

Project for the redesign of Western Plaza
in Washington, D.C. (1977)
In collaboration with George Patton Associates, Landscape Architects
In charge: Robert Venturi; John Rauch
Project Managers: Jeffrey Ryan, Stephen Kieran, Ronald McCoy
with Denise Scott Brown, Janet Colesberry, Steven Izenour, David Marohn, Missy Maxwell, Frederic Schwartz, James H. Timberlake

Pierre Charles L'Enfant's original plan for Washington, D.C. (1791) provided a direct visual link between the Capitol building and the White House. These structures were meant to terminate opposite ends of the monumental axis of Pennsylvania Avenue. During the nineteenth century, however, the construction of the new Treasury Building, which flanks the White House, obstructed this visual link.

View with proposed pylons (drawing: James H. Timberlake)

Venturi and Rauch's project attempts to restore something of L'Enfant's plan. The project was commissioned by the Pennsylvania Avenue Development Corporation (PADC) and focused on the redesign of Western Plaza. According to the initial proposals, the plaza was to become a lowered pedestrian square, boasting small cafés and other facilities to create interest and activity for passersby—for instance during their lunch break. The sunken plaza surface was to be iced over for skating in winter. In reality, however, an alternative to this plan was executed in which the plaza was raised a few steps above street level and L'Enfant's plan was depicted in its paving. Small models of Washington's principal buildings—the Capitol and the White House—were to be placed at their corresponding sites on the paving for the pleasure of visitors, young and old. Actually the tourists liked the provisional wooden models (pl. p. 119) better than the commissioners did; the stone models are yet to be made.

In addition to the square's furnishings, the intimate scale of which recalls the 1966 project for Copley Square in Boston (see pp. 88 f.), the architects also designed elements that would relate to the monumental scale inherent in L'Enfant's original plan for the city as a whole. There are, in particular, two slablike pylons, which do not serve as a

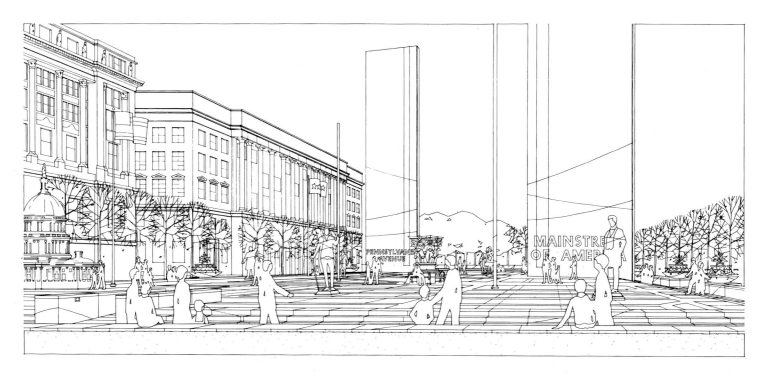

colossal termination of the main axis, but rather as an effective frame for the view towards the Treasury Building. Upon closer inspection, the visitor realizes that both pylons are placed asymmetrically so as to direct the viewer's eyes to the large park at the foot of the White House as well. Thus the plaza was meant to become a kind of hinge connecting the city's two major geometrical orders: the diagonal axes of the avenues and the rectangular grid pattern of the street blocks.

The architects explain:

> But our framed image doesn't make a bad picture—and it is picturesque in several ways. It is an asymmetrical composition, a Romantic scene of a Classical portico in a rural landscape whose prettiness Mills in mid-century would have appreciated. It is reminiscent too of the oblique view of the portico of San Giorgio across the lagoon framed by the two columns on the Piazzetta of San Marco. And it is a symbol of American pragmatism, perhaps—framed in a Baroque plan and developed not with the authority of a prince but through the vagaries of checks and balances.[1]

Paradoxically, the project's systematic character has turned out to be the reason for its fragmentary execution so far. Not only the architectural replicas mentioned above (see pl. p. 119) are still absent, but so too are the pylons designed to give the plaza its monumental identity.

1   VRSB project description.
(Unpublished.)

The Capitol and the city's three main axes, Pennsylvania Avenue to the right

Pennsylvania Avenue with proposed pylons (photomontages)

Proposed pylons

Western Plaza with wooden mock-up of miniature replica of the Capitol building

Literature

B. Forgey, "The Continuing Battles of Pennsylvania Avenue: An Artist, Wounded, Withdraws," *The Washington Star*, April 11, 1978, p. D 2.

P. Richard, "New Design for A National Square," *WP*, May 24, 1978, p. C 13.

W. von Eckardt, "Focus for the Avenue," *WP*, May 27, 1978, pp. B 1, B 6.

"Monumental Main Street," *PA*, May 1979, pp. 110–13.

The Federal City in Transition (Washington, D. C.: The Barbara Fiedler Gallery, exhibition catalogue), 1979.

AA, February 1980, pp. 17–20.

R. Goldberger, "Western Plaza in Washington Gets a Somewhat Flat Reception," *NYT*, December 18, 1980.

W. von Eckardt, "Bare & Square," *WP*, December 20, 1980, pp. D1, D5.

B. Forgey, "The Plaza that Might Have Been," *The Washington Star*, December 28, 1980, pp. D 11–13.

"A Grander Vista for Inauguration Crowds," *U.S. News & World Report*, January 19, 1981, pp. 48–49.

B. Forgey, "Magnets for People: Planning the Parks Along Pennsylvania Avenue," *WP*, December 19, 1981.

a+u 12 (1981): 76–81.

Engineering News Record, June 24, 1982, pp. 24–25, 28.

B. Forgey, "Tarnished Brilliance. Western Plaza: No Wonder It's 'Not Quite Right'," *WP*, June 18, 1983, pp. C 1, C 4.

RV, "Learning the Right Lessons from the Beaux-Arts," *AVC*, pp. 70–95, especially pp. 92 ff.

Washington, D.C.: plan of 1762, detail

Western Plaza, general view towards the White House

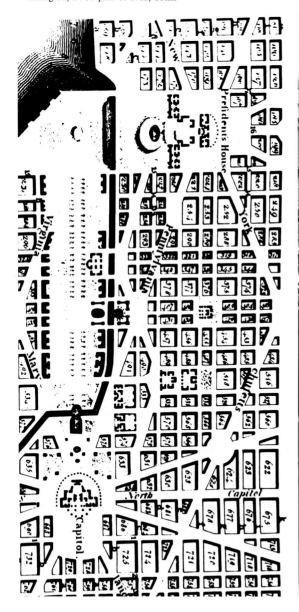

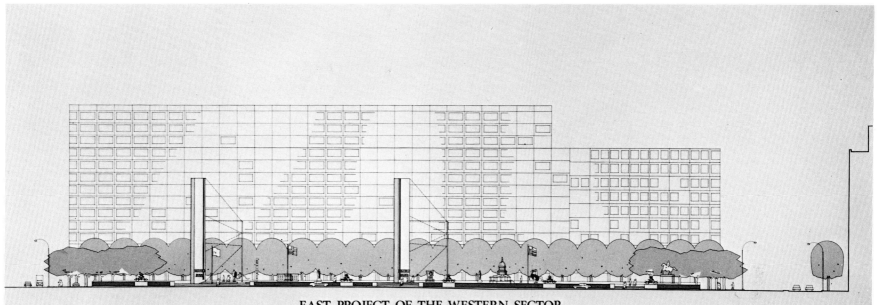

EAST PROJECT OF THE WESTERN SECTOR

PENNSYLVANIA AVENUE DEVELOPMENT CORPORATION
425 13TH STREET, N.W. WASHINGTON, DC 20004

SCHEMATIC DESIGN / SOUTH ELEVATION

GEORGE E. PATTON, INC. / VENTURI AND RAUCH · SEPTEMBER 8, 1978

South elevation
Section

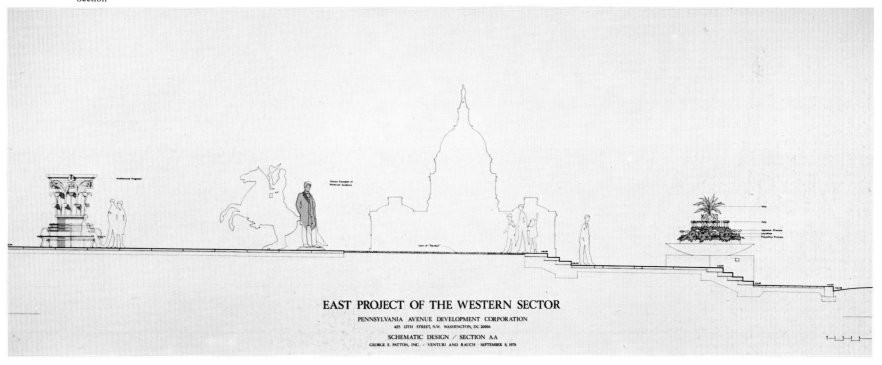

EAST PROJECT OF THE WESTERN SECTOR

PENNSYLVANIA AVENUE DEVELOPMENT CORPORATION
425 13TH STREET, N.W. WASHINGTON, DC 20004

SCHEMATIC DESIGN / SECTION AA

GEORGE E. PATTON, INC. / VENTURI AND RAUCH · SEPTEMBER 8, 1978

13 Washington Avenue Revitalization Plan

Planning study for the preservation and redecoration of a shopping street in Miami Beach, Florida (1978)
In charge: Denise Scott Brown
In collaboration with David Jay Feinberg and Richard Rose, Architects
Project Manager: Mary Yee
with David Brisbin, Frances Hundt, Steven Izenour, James Allen Schmidt, Frederic Schwartz, James H. Timberlake

The subject of this planning study is a commercial spine running through Miami Beach's "Art Déco District" which serves as its main street. The study involved an analysis of the street's diverse economic, social, and transportation functions and a description of possible improvements in the architecture and landscaping. The neighborhood's main features had to be considered: the demographic mix of its inhabitants—mainly senior citizens and an ethnic population—the Art Déco architecture, and the tropical landscape, which together create the symbol of "Miami Beach," as depicted in Hollywood in the 1930s and 1940s.

The architects recommended only small-scale improvements after recognizing the existing street's positive aspects (its human scale, its interesting variety of stores) as well as its problems (the economically marginal character of many stores, and the dearth of amenities for pedestrians). For the public sector, designs were made for new paving, street furniture, and planting that would bolster the tropical-Déco image of Miami Beach. For the private sector, design guidelines were suggested for painting and renovation that would retain the Art Déco character but not put too much stress on the finances of small merchants.

A drastic bulldozing and recreation are not necessary to make Washington Avenue a pleasant place to shop or stroll, a street that business people and neighborhood residents can be proud to be associated with.[1]

1 VRSB, project description.

Literature

E. Edwards, "Architects Arrive to Tackle Washington Avenue Project," *The Miami Herald*, August 11, 1978, p. 4D.

DSB, "Rivitalizing Miami," *Urban Design International*, January–February 1980, pp. 20-25.

D. Morton, "Miami Beach," *PA*, August 1980, pp. 64–65.

a+u 3 (1931): 139-45.

AIA Journal, June 1981, pp. 18–20.

a+u 12 (1981): 39.

DSB, "Zeichnen für den Deco-Distrikt," *archithese* 2/1982, pp. 17–21.

PA 1 (1983): 122-23.

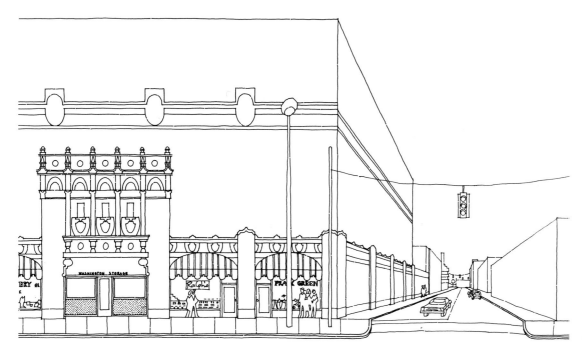

Store front (drawing: Steven Izenour and Steven Kieran)

Proposed signs for entrance in the "Art Déco District"

Existing shop fronts (drawing: Steven Izenour and Janet Colesbury)

123

Existing buildings in the "Art Déco District"

Proposed pedestrian area (drawing: James H. Timberlake)

"Rambla," the proposed pedestrian street (drawing: Miles Ritter)

14   Republic Square District Master Plan

Renewal plan for a downtown district in Austin, Texas (1983)
In collaboration with Halcyon, Ltd., Economists
In charge: Denise Scott Brown
Project Manager: Vincent Hauser
with Gabrielle London, Miles Ritter, David Schaaf, Robert Venturi

The subject of the master plan developed for the Watson-Casey Companies is a district located in the southwest quadrant of Austin's business center. The twenty-five or so blocks contain warehouses for the most part. The area's projected uses range from creating space for private offices and public administration to providing recreational services. The task was to plan for future community, cultural, and commercial facilities and to point out ways to establish appropriate economic, visual, and transportation connections between elements of the district.

As part of their study, the architects recommended planting a tree-lined avenue beside West Third Street to serve as the main axis of the new business district. They suggested naming the street "The Rambla," alluding to Barcelona's famous avenue "Las Ramblas." This planning study paralleled the design study for the Laguna Gloria Art Museum (see pp. 212–14), to be built within the district.

Literature

VRSB, "A Plan for the Republic Square District, Austin, Texas," 1984. (Unpublished.)

DSB, "Visions of the Future Based on Lessons from the Past," *Center*, vol. 1, 1985, pp. 44–63; also published in *The Land, The City, and The Human Spirit*, Larry Fuller, ed. (University of Texas: LBJ Library, 1985), pp. 108–14 and panel discussion, pp. 128–36.

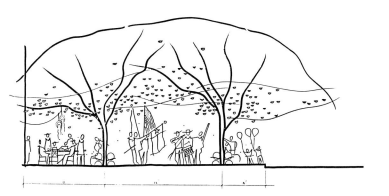

Detail studies (drawing: David Schaaf)

Site plan

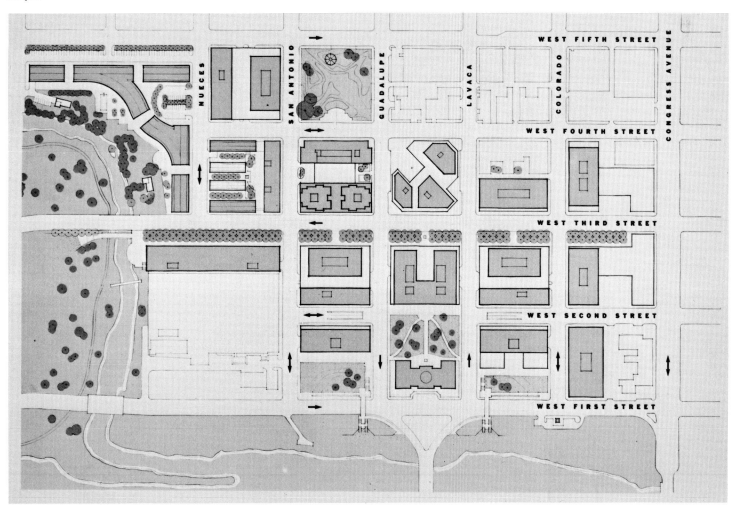

15   Westway Urban Design Project

Masterplan for the West Side Highway and renewal of the Hudson River waterfront in Manhattan, New York City (1978–1985)
In collaboration with Clark and Rapuano, Landscape Architects; Salmon Associates, Engineers; Craig Whitaker, System Design Concepts, Inc.
In charge: Robert Venturi; John Rauch
Project Manager: Frederic Schwartz
with Denise Scott Brown, Eric Fiss, Perry Kulper, Ronald McCoy

Built between 1934 and 1937 and connecting downtown New York City with the Westchester Park System and the city's northwestern environs, the West Side Highway has been the major traffic artery of Manhattan's West Side for decades. In the early 1970s parts of the elevated expressway in Lower Manhattan were found to be in serious disrepair. When sections of the highway eventually collapsed, the entire southern arm had to be closed to traffic. Since then, this part of the Westside has survived as a gigantic ruin.

For years it had been debated whether the expressway ought to be rebuilt in its old form, torn down entirely, or replaced by an underground highway. In the late 1970s, while the discussion was still in progress, the New York State Department of Transportation began planning a subsurface, six-lane, interstate highway intended to replace the four-mile section of the old elevated expressway. At the same time, VRSB and the landscape architects Clark and Rapuano were asked to prepare a proposal for the vast riverfront area that would be freed once the old highway was demolished. The idea was to develop the ninety-seven acre landfill as a continuous riverfront park and to link it to the residential and downtown districts beyond. The programing and design of the park, the development of a new street system, and the designs for ventilation building, tunnel portals, signs, lighting, and finishes were the most salient features of the project. Traditional park and public design in New York City and, in particular, the design of Central Park, were the context for the design of Westway.

In the summer of 1985, the Governor of New York State decided to stop the plans, which by then were in an advanced stage, and to omit the construction of the subsurface Westside Highway from the list of transportation projects.

Westside Highway with existing docks

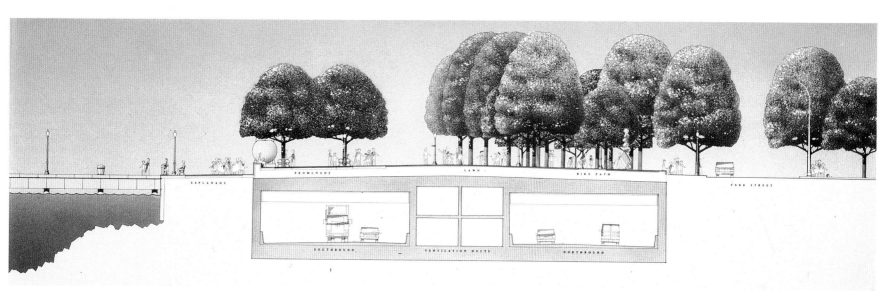

Proposed park above highway tunnel (drawing: James Kolker, Perry Kulper, Frederic Schwartz, and James H. Timberlake)

Literature

P. Goldberger, "Westway Architect Selected by State," *NYT*, February 24, 1978, p. 16.

"The New Westway Math," *NYT*, March 4, 1978, p. 20.

R. Johnson, "Top Pop Thinker on Westway," *New York Post*, July 20, 1978.

F. Werner, "8 Einsichten an 16 Beispielen," *Bauwelt*, January 8, 1982, pp. 22–35.

Arch. Rec., February 1984, p. 51.

P. Goldberger, "Three Design Plans Being Considered for Proposed Park over the Westway," *NYT*, March 28, 1984, B 1/B 4, pp. 131, 134.

D. Carmody, "Westway Park Design Goes Public," *NYT*, June 21, 1984, B 1, p. 131.

G. Anderson, "Big Park for the Big Apple," *Arch. Rec.*, January 1985, pp. 124–31.

A. Lubasch, "U. S. Appeals Court Upholds Decision to Halt Westway," *N Y T*, September 12, 1985, pp. A1/B4.

M. Oreskes, "House Votes by Big Margin to Bar Funds," *NYT*, September 12, 1985, p. B8.

M. Oreskes, "New York Leaders Give Up Westway and Seek Trade-In," *NYT*, September 20, 1985, pp. A1/B2.

Site plan with proposed park (in green)

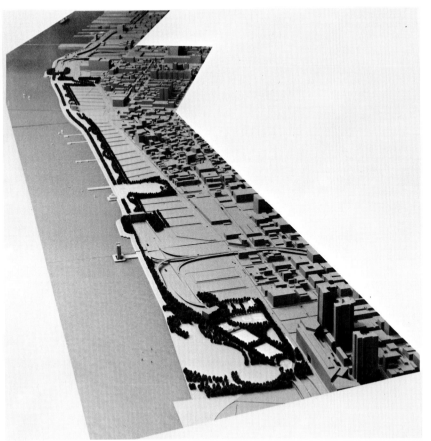

Model view

Proposed park at the height of 42nd Street, photomontage

Embankment, detail (drawing: James H. Timberlake)

Quay with miniature "big Apples" (drawing: Miles Ritter and Simon Tickell)

Esplanade (drawing: James Kolker, Perry Kulper, Robert Marker, David McCoubrey, Richard Mohler, Miles Ritter, and Ivan Saleff) ▶

Exhibition of the project in New York City, 1984

Detail of park (drawing: Timur Galen and Miles Ritter)

132

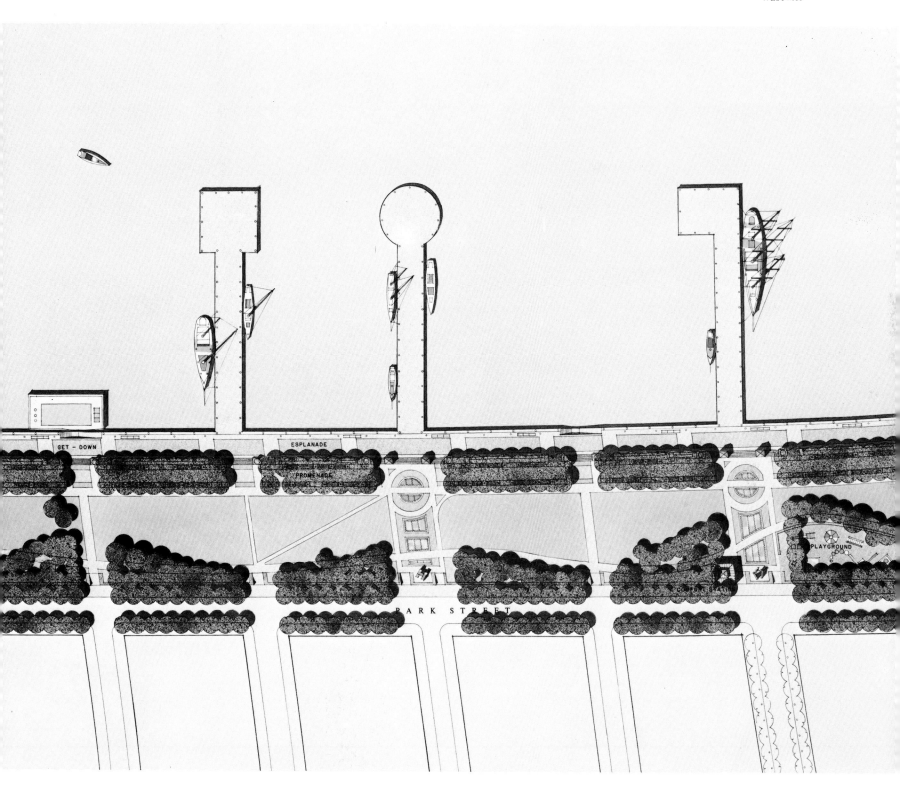

GET - DOWN

ESPLANADE

PROMENADE

PARK STREET

PLAYGROUND

16   Times Square Plaza Design

Proposal to redesign Times Square in New York City (1984)
In charge: Robert Venturi; John Rauch
Project Manager: Frederic Schwartz
with Denise Scott Brown, Eric Fiss, Steven Izenour, John Rauch, Miles Ritter

For several years the future of New York's Times Square has been under discussion. When the Park Tower Realty Corporation commissioned the architect Philip Johnson to conceive a master plan for the square, Johnson proposed a design consisting of four office buildings of varying heights. Opinion on this project was divided. In particular, it was felt that the fairlike atmosphere characteristic of Times Square was about to be sacrificed. At this point, VRSB was asked to create a design for an element at the center of the square that would be in keeping with the square's traditionally popular, glittering, commercial-sign architecture but that would also contain qualities consistent with the scale of the proposed highrise buildings. The architects write:

> This design proposes a Big Apple for Times Square: a piece of representational sculpture which is bold in form yet rich in symbolism,... [a] realism with a diversity of associations. It is popular *and* esoteric—a Big Apple symbolizing New York City and a surrealistic object evoking René Magritte or a Pop-art monument in the manner of Claes Oldenburg....
> Contrasts and ambiguities in scale along with unusual juxtapositions are traditional means of creating surprise, tension and richness in urban architecture. Some New

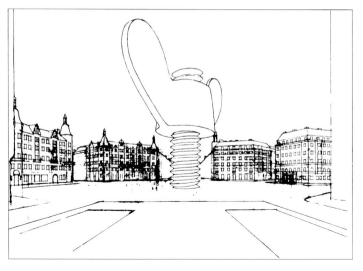

Claes Oldenburg: project for a monument in Karlaplan, Stockholm (1966)

York examples are the Statue of Liberty, the Little Church around the Corner and Trinity Church on Wall Street....
This 90 ft.-plus diameter apple is the modern equivalent of the Baroque obelisk that identifies the center of a plaza.[1]

1   VRSB, project description. (Unpublished.)

Literature

Quaderns, July–September 1984, pp. 126–27.

P. Goldberger, "Design for Times Square: Problems Remain," *NYT*, July 5, 1984, pp. B1/B5.

P. Goldberger, "Picking a Centerpiece for a New Times Square," *NYT*, September 17, 1984, pp. B1/B5.

"The Big Apple" in gold, model view

"The Big Apple," night- and daytime view, and an earlier version of the project with globe and light shaft (drawing: Perry Kulper, Miles Ritter [top right], Eric Fiss, Perry Kulper, and Miles Ritter [below])

"The Big Apple," model view

137

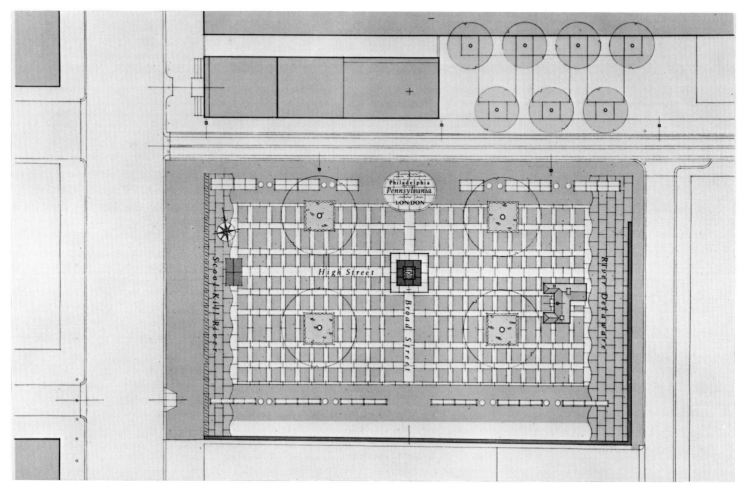

Site plan

17   Welcome Park

William Penn Memorial, Philadelphia (1982)
In charge: Robert Venturi; John Rauch
Project Managers: Ronald McCoy, Frances Hundt

Welcome Park (named after the *The Welcome*, the ship that brought William Penn to Philadelphia in 1682) is located on the site of the Slate Roof House in the heart of Philadelphia. This house—a miniature bronze replica of which is mounted on a pedestal—served as Penn's residence and Pennsylvania's seat of government in 1700–1701.

The square's paving depicts the original plan of Philadelphia, drawn up by Penn's surveyor, Francis Holmes. One of the walls surrounding the park carries a mural with a seventeenth-century view of the Delaware River from this spot. The adjacent wall contains historical quotations and pictures. Benches and greenery make the square a popular site on the "doorstep" of historic Philadelphia.

Literature

C. Romano, "Finally, a Memorial to Penn," *The Philadelphia Inquirer*, October 29, 1982, p. 1C.

T. Hine, "Welcome Park's Exposed Look Overshadows its Tribute to Penn," *Philadelphia Inquirer*, January 14, 1983, pp. 1D, 8D.

General view towards Society Hill

Welcome Park: view towards
Society Hill Towers

Welcome Park: mural with
Delaware river and miniature
replica of Slate Roof House

18   Ponte dell' Accademia

Competition project for renovating the Ponte dell' Accademia in Venice (1985)
In charge: Robert Venturi
with Timur Galen, Steven Izenour, Robert Marker, Miles Ritter

The architects write:

> The competition brief for the Ponte dell' Accademia of 1843 stated that the designers be limited to "reputable engineers." The subsequent checkered history of over a hundred years of proposals and alterations illustrates that engineers, reputable or not, were not immune from the conflicts and contradictions of structural efficiency, cost, style and public taste. The problem, then, as we see it, is a remedial one—to give the architects who were "relegated only to the design of the ornamentation" an opportunity to do just that....
>
> ... We recommend stabilizing and legitimizing the "temporary" wood and steel structure with the addition of a "permanent" layer of monumental decorative civic symbolism. Our proposed decorative additions recall the tradition of Cosmati ornamentation and that of Venetian marble facades like those of S. Maria dei Miracoli and the diminutive Palazzo Dario on the Grand Canal.[1]

For materials, the architects proposed prefabricated molded fiber-glass panels affixed to the existing structure with steel angles.

Literature
"Venturi, Rauch, Scott Brown," *Terza Mostra internazionale di architettura III* (exhibition catalogue) (Milan: Electa, 1985).

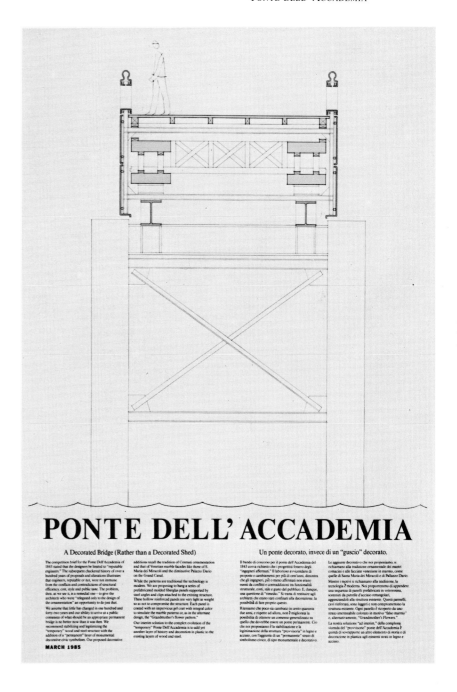

Section

Pages 142–43: competition project

19   Marconi Plaza Monument

Proposal for a monument honoring the Italian-American community or the 500th anniversary of Christopher Columbus's discovery of the New World (1492)
Philadelphia (1985)
In charge: Robert Venturi
with David Fox, Steven Izenour

The site of the proposed monument is Marconi Plaza, a public park in South Philadelphia, a part of the city inhabited by many Americans of Italian descent. Given the fact that the existing plaza straddles Broad Street (with the city hall as the vanishing point), it is not possible to transform it into a "piazza" in the classical Italian sense of the word. The architects propose the erection of two large stone and marble pylons that both frame the axis and the view toward the city center and subdivide the present space to give it a dimension that would make it useful for public functions. Seen from the outside, that is, by the visitor approaching the city, the pylons appear as two-dimensional, representational abstractions of two classic pieces of Italian architecture from the time of Christopher Columbus. The inside surfaces of the pylons are adorned with inscriptions.

View along Broad Street

2 Public Buildings

Buildings used by the public can be subdivided into those that serve shared but essentially private needs (department stores, for example) and those that have an explicitly political function because they serve people in their capacity as "citizens." The Greek temple, the cathedral, and the medieval town hall are historical archetypes of "public" architecture. Church, school, museum, bank, and office building are their modern, democratic counterparts. Viewed "from the Campidoglio,"[1] they are the types of building that inevitably attract the attention of architects concerned with the contemporary city.

"New Monumentality" and Communal Palaces

The search for forms of a "New Monumentality" for public buildings became almost an obsession in the 1950s and 1960s, especially in the United States.[2] During that period American variations on the Piazza del Campidoglio in Rome (pl. a) and medieval communal palaces "with glandular problems" were built[3]: the Lincoln Center for the Performing Arts in New York (1957–1966) and City Hall in Boston (Competition 1953; see p. 54) come to mind. It is symptomatic that Venturi avoided any direct allusion to Rome or Siena in his own project for the Town Hall in North Canton, Ohio (1965). Perhaps this was precisely *because* he had been familiar with the Italian architects of the

a Rome: Piazza del Campidoglio (18th-century engraving)

145

Renaissance and the Baroque since his years as a student at Princeton (see p. 80) and as a fellow at the American Academy in Rome (1952–1953). Instead, Venturi drew on one of modern architecture's American pioneers, Louis Sullivan, and on his Midwestern bank buildings—so modest in scale yet heroic in posture (b).

Robert Venturi's Master's Project

Nor does Venturi's Master's project (1950) reveal anything of his preoccupation at that time with the Roman Baroque (see pp. 22f.). Rather, the project seems to combine memories of Mies van der Rohe's country house project of 1924 with the shed roof of Albert Kahn's Chrysler Plant in Detroit. It seemed to strive for restraint in a manner that recalls designs by Eero Saarinen (with whom Venturi later worked). Commenting later on his Master's project, Venturi said: "I am rather proud that an early design of mine contained a thing within a thing representing an aesthetic of enclosure and redundancy that was unusual in an era of flowing space and simplicity…"[4]

The subject of the project was a church to be built on the grounds of a Protestant high school in Pennsylvania. Venturi made no attempt to impose the new structure on the existing complex of formally disparate Victorian school buildings; rather, the form and position of the church was meant to unify the existing buildings and thus enhance their presence (pl. c). In this light, the church at first appears to be little more than a backdrop, a large garden wall. Venturi writes: "I think I felt my building should not be just a simplistic proof of a theory on the outside, and so behind the parapeted wall appear hints of complexities of scale and form within."[5]

b Columbus, Wisconsin: Farmers' and Merchants' Union Bank (architect: Louis Sullivan, 1919)

Interior and Exterior

In later projects, the dialectic between interior and exterior was more often realized in reverse: Large facades or decoratively highlighted elements of a facade belied the ordinary, sometimes very modest office buildings or garages that lay behind them (see pp. 39ff.). In the firm's more recent designs, however—particularly for the museum in Austin, Texas (see p. 45)—the images of the Roman Baroque, so long restrained, finally find expression.

VRSB's contribution to the genre of "public buildings" has thus far been limited essentially to those sandboxes of modern American architects—the campuses of a few universities.[6] Except for very early projects in Bridgetown, New Jersey, or Columbus, Indiana (see pp. 152f., 158f.), VRSB have thus far had few opportunities to make an impact on America outside the restricted university world. It seems, however, as though the museum projects that the firm is planning are about to change this situation.

146

1   Not by coincidence, the Venturis have published a recent anthology of articles under the rather exacting title of *A View from the Campidoglio* (New York: Harper & Row, 1984).

2   For a critical evaluation of this phenomenon, see S. Giedion. *Space, Time, and Architecture* (Cambridge, Mass.: Harvard University Press, 1941; 5th ed., Cambridge Mass.: Harvard University Press, 1965), pp. xxxii–xxxiii; and—referring to the "New Monumentality" and its theory—*Architecture, You and Me* (London and New York: Oxford University Press, 1957).

3   DSB, "A Worm's-Eye View...," p. 71, where Scott Brown attributes glandular problems to "some White architecture."

4   RV, 1979. Unpublished project description.

5   *Ibid.*

6   See in this context P. V. Turner, *Campus: An American Planning Tradition* (Cambridge, Mass.: MIT Press, 1984).

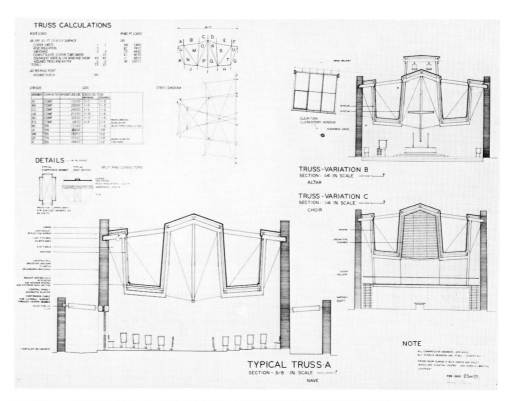

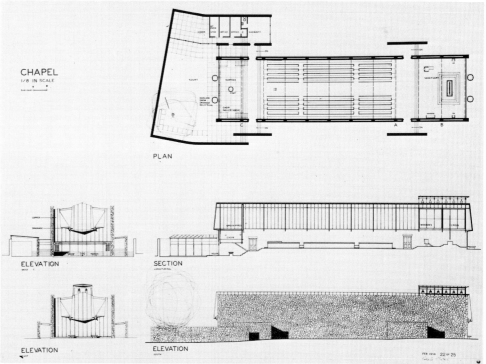

c   Robert Venturi: Chapel for a high school in Pennsylvania (thesis project, 1950)

General view

20 North Penn Visiting Nurses' Association Headquarters

Nurses' Offices in Ambler, Pennsylvania (1961)
Architects: Venturi and Short
In charge: Robert Venturi
Project Manager: John Rauch

The program for these nurses' offices dictated a number of reception and living rooms as well as storage space. The parking lot for five cars, bounded by a retaining wall, cuts into the terrain. The wall's curvilinear form, with its foot leading the way towards the entrance, contrasts with the angular building and creates a duality.

The public character of the relatively small building is reflected by the "portal," by the large upper-story windows, and, at the street level, by doubled window frames, an extremely unusual feature in the architectural language of that time (see p. 41). Playing on Frank Lloyd Wright's words, Venturi states that he has "destroyed the box, not through spatial continuities, but by circumstantial distortions."[1]

1 *CCA*, (1977 ed.): 109–10.

Literature
"Pennsylvania Clinic," *Arch. Forum*, October 1963, p. 17.
Perspecta 9–10 (1965): 34–37.
Moderne und Postmoderne, pp. 148–50.

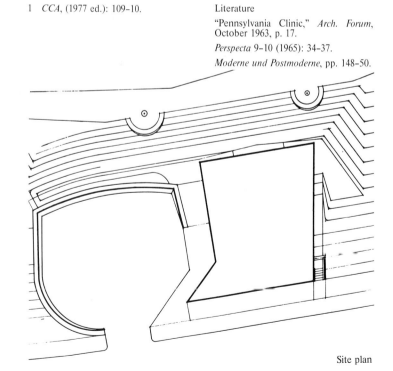

Site plan

148

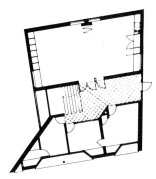

Second floor plan

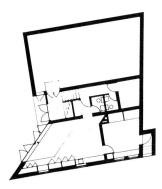

First floor plan

View along street

Entrance

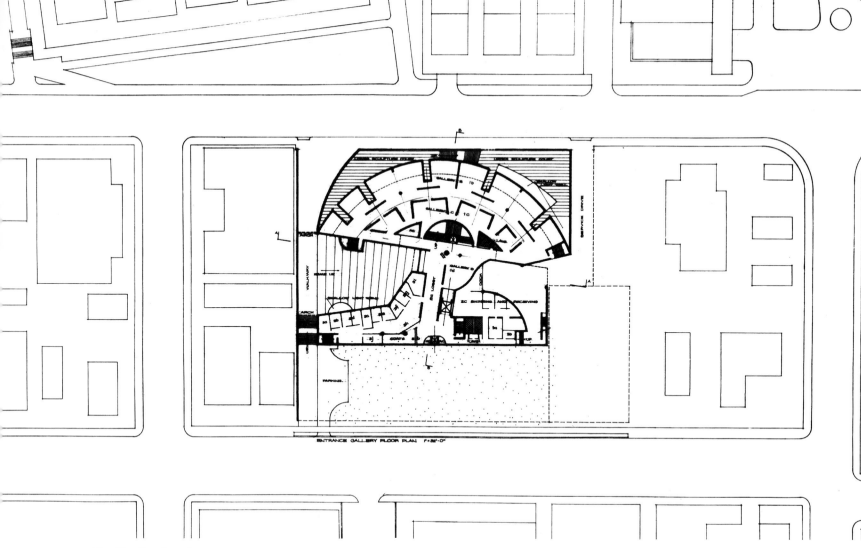

Site with gallery floor plan

21 Berkeley Museum and Art Gallery Competition

Competition for an art museum in Berkeley, California (1964)
In charge: Robert Venturi
with Gerod Clark

The building's external form is derived essentially from the organizational diagram proposed for the museum. The exhibition hall, which is linked to an arc of offices facing north at the back of the building, is "modern" in its openness and flexibility. Additional exhibition space is provided by a traditional "enfilade" gallery, which has, in itself, a definitive architectural character.

Entry foyer, seminar rooms, and lecture room are situated in an extended wing facing south. Should the building need to be expanded later, an additional exhibition wing could be comfortably accommodated.

Literature
werk-archithese 7–8 (1977): 20–21.

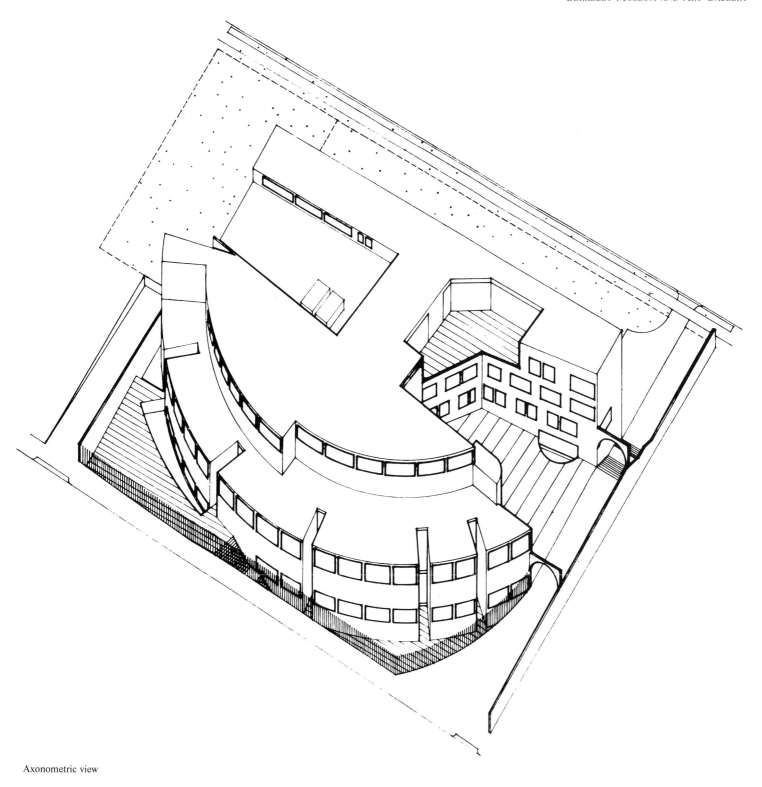

Axonometric view

22 Varga-Brigio Medical Office Building

Doctors' offices in Bridgeton, New Jersey (1966)
In charge: Robert Venturi; John Rauch
Project Manager: Gerod Clark

A doctors' office in a small town: a "decorated shed," suitable for its corner site and expandable. In the words of the architects:

This little shed's big, conventional elements and decorated entrance were an attempt at monumentality....

The building as a whole is carefully ordinary; the one arty amenity is applied to the entrance. It has been likened to a little factory that has rented space to a Chinese restaurant.[1]

1 *LLV*, p. 113.

Literature
PA, November 1968, pp. 124–25.
werk-archithese 7–8 (1977): 29.

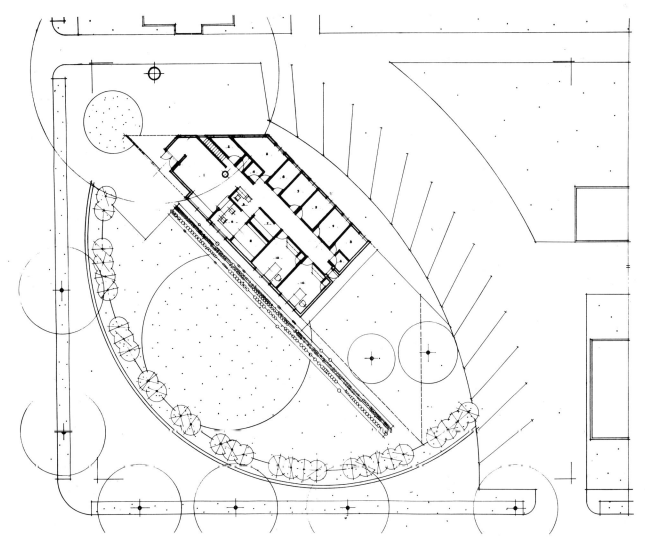

Site with first floor plan

Entrance facade

Plan and facades studies (drawing: RV)

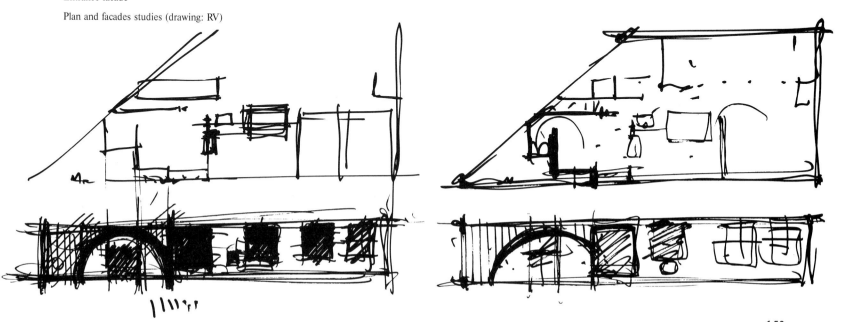

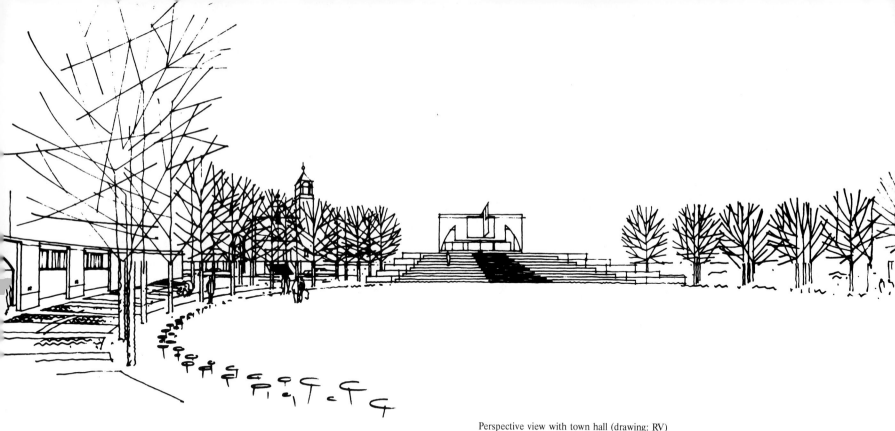

Perspective view with town hall (drawing: RV)

23   North Canton Town Center

Three public buildings for North Canton, Ohio (1965)
In collaboration with Clark and Rapuano, Landscape
Architects
In charge: Robert Venturi; John Rauch
with Gerod Clark, Arthur Jones, John Thrower

This project was part of a master plan for New Canton, a
small town in the mid-Western United States. It involved
plans for a town hall, a YMCA, and the expansion of an
existing library. The enlargement of a shopping center was
also proposed, although it was first introduced in a later
phase of the project.

The first proposal (see pl. above) placed the town hall next
to the church in a dominant position terminating the axis of
a large plaza in the center of town.

> ... the town hall is like a Roman temple in its general
> proportions, and also because it is free-standing, but—in
> contrast with a Greek temple—a directional building
> whose front is more important than its back....
>
> I like Louis Sullivan's use of the giant arch to give
> image, unity, and monumental scale to some of his late

banks which are important but small buildings on the
main streets of mid-Western towns.[1]

The design for the YMCA adheres strictly to the established guidelines for a youth center of this size. Its appearance was determined by its position on the "piazza" across
from an old factory:

> This building had to be big in scale to complement and
> not to be overpowered by the factory opposite....
>
> And it is appropriately secondary to the small city hall
> on the other side of the plaza.[2]

In its spatial configuration the town center recalls the "group
form" of an archaic Greek temenos, enlivened by clashes of
small and big scales in the facades that help to differentiate
the three buildings and lend them identity. The masonry
screen wrapped around the existing library building and
leading along the YMCA's main facade serves to add civic
scale.

1 *CCA*, pp. 124–28.
2 *Ibid.*

Literature
Zodiac 17 (1967): 138–51.

New Directions, pp. 56–59.

D. Dunster, "Drei Bauten für eine Stadt
in Ohio," *werk-archithese* 7–8 (1977):
25–28.

Model view

Town Hall, facades

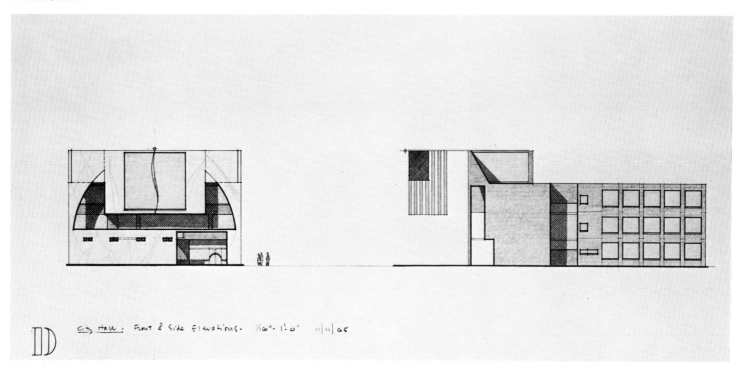

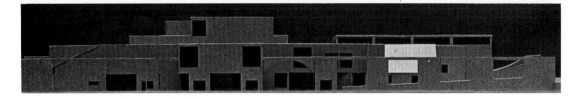

YMCA, model view

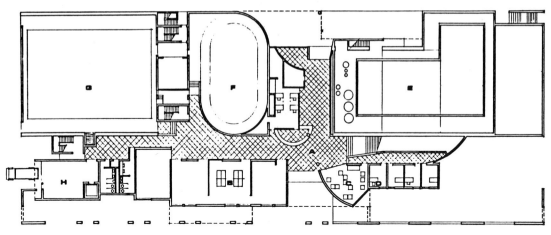

YMCA, plan

Library, model view

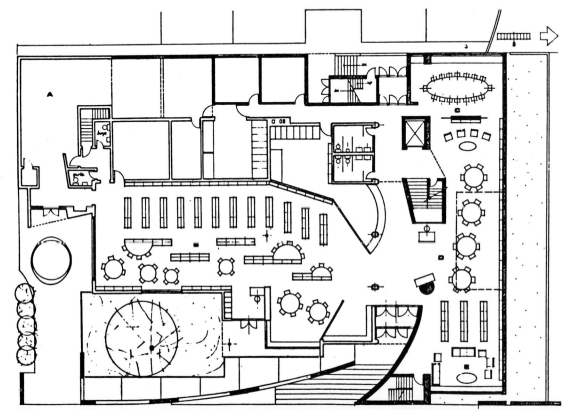

Library, plan

YMCA (left) with view towards church and town hall (drawing: RV)

24 Fire Station No. 4

Fire station in Columbus, Indiana (1966)
In charge: Robert Venturi; John Rauch
Project Manager: Gerod Clark

The plan is simple: duality between the apparatus room on the right, and the storage and living quarters on the left. In the center of the building is a hose-drying tower.

> Because the dormitory is lower than the apparatus room, we applied a parapet to the facade on its side in order to simplify the front and enhance the scale.[1]

The architects applied a second "graphic" facade of white-glazed brick to screen the building's squat, supermarketlike proportions and signify the station's importance as a public building.

1 *LLV*, p. 112.

Literature

M. Wellemeyer, "An Inspired Renaissance in Indiana," *Life*, November 17, 1967, pp. 74–84.

R. Zurier, *The American Firehouse: An Architectural and Social History* (New York: Abbeville Press, 1982), pp. 222, 224, 237.

werk-archithese 7–8 (1977): 22–23.

H. Takase, "Columbus, Indiana: Museum of Modern American Architecture," *Space Design*, June 1984, pp. 27–41, especially p. 38.

PA, November 1968, pp. 118–23.

Cathedral, Crema   Views ▶

Plan

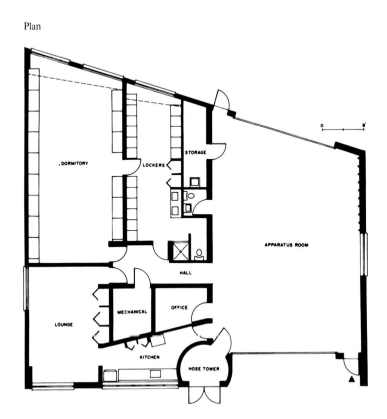

159

Model view

25 National Football Hall of Fame Competition

Competition for a Football Hall of Fame, Rutgers University, New Brunswick, New Jersey (1967)
In charge: Robert Venturi
with Gerod Clark and Frank Kawasaki

The President of the National Football Foundation has described the Hall of Fame as:

> an Ideological Center, serving our social and educational structure and our competitive economy.[1]

The foundation is convinced that:

> at a time of the long hair, beard, [and] beatnik revolt on the campus... the disciplines of football make it the biggest and best classroom in the nation for teaching leadership.[2]

The heroes of American football were therefore to be beatified and canonized in a subtle hierarchy within this sanctuary of mass sport. The architects proposed a "Bill-Ding-Board" (see also pp. 67 f.) comprised of an ominously oversized billboard connected to an exhibition—or, rather, cult-worship room:

> The constant vaulted space of the gallery is like the gallery space in Tintoretto's *Finding of the Body of St. Mark*, where the quality of light is all that varies along the exaggerated length. (R. V.)[2]

In this gallery, slide shows and films about football history were to be shown.

1 *LLV*, p. 116.
2 *Ibid.*

Literature

RV, "A Bill-Ding Board Involving Movies, Relics and Space," *Arch.*

Forum, April 1968, pp. 74–76. (Reprinted in *AVC*, pp. 14–17.)

C. Jencks, "Points of View," *AD*, December 1969, p. 644.

A. Sky and M. Stone, *Unbuilt America* (New York: McGraw Hill, 1976), p. 275.

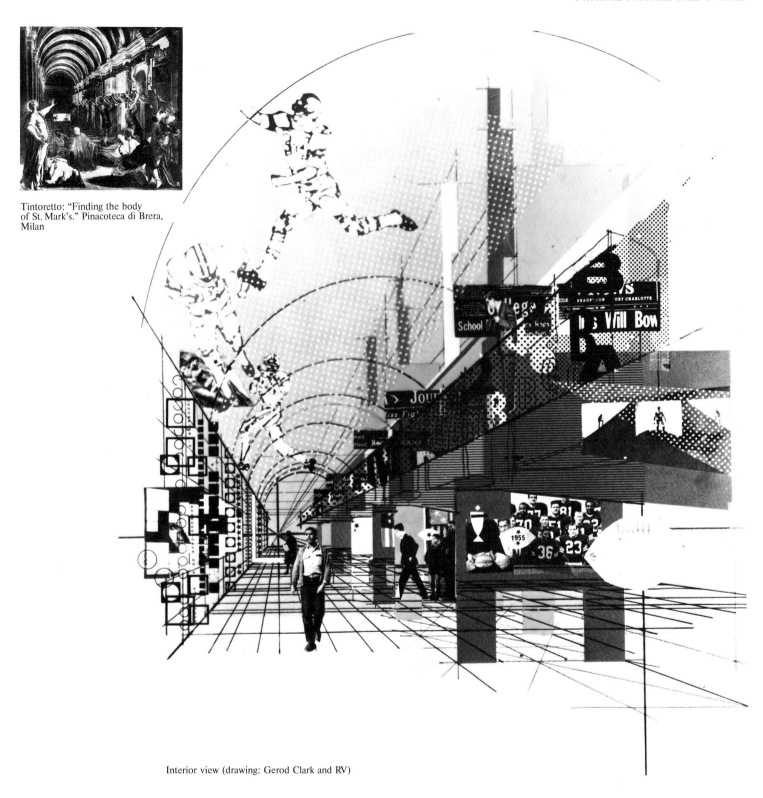

Tintoretto: "Finding the body
of St. Mark's." Pinacoteca di Brera,
Milan

Interior view (drawing: Gerod Clark and RV)

161

National Football Hall of Fame, model view

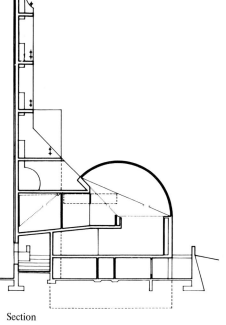

Site plan

Section

Turku, concert platform (architect: Alvar Aalto, 1929)

162

26   Humanities Building

Department of Humanities, State University of New York in Purchase, New York (1968)
In charge: Robert Venturi; John Rauch
Project Manager: Arthur Jones

West facade

with John Anderson, Denise Scott Brown, Gerod Clark, W.G. Clark, James Greifendorf, Steven Izenour, Anthony Pett, David Vaughan

As is the case with many American universities built or enlarged during the construction boom of the 1960s, the S.U.N.Y. campus at Purchase is something of an architec-

tural museum. In addition to Venturi and Rauch's work, that of the Architects' Collaborative, Edward L. Barnes, Gunnar Birkerts, Charles Gwathmey, Philip Johnson, and Paul Rudolph is represented by various buildings.

Edward L. Barnes's master plan attempts nonetheless to subordinate individual buildings to an overall concept based on Thomas Jefferson's University of Virginia (see pl. p. 64). An arcade, similar to that in Charlotteville, Virginia, circumscribes the campus's large, open, central place and links the individual buildings to one another.

The master plan also dictates the use of a specific dark brick for all the buildings. Where the buildings are tangent to

Munkkiniemi near Helsinki: studio building for own architectural office (architect: Alvar Aalto, 1955)

Open-air arena facing north . . .

. . . and facing east

Lobby ▶

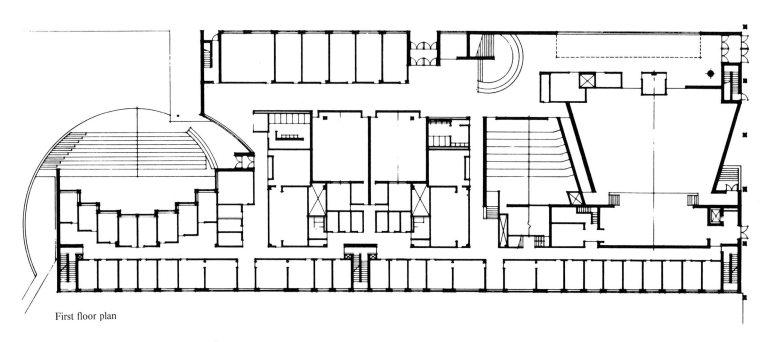

First floor plan

the arcade, permitting one to inspect the architecture at close range, Venturi and Rauch have used glazed brick to accentuate the facades decoratively.

The Humanities Building is a big box from which pieces have been removed—in particular to form an open-air arena at the building's south end. It is no coincidence that this solution is reminiscent of Alvar Aalto's own studio in Munkkiniemi, Finland (see p. 164).

Seminar rooms, offices, and lecture halls, all of which need daylight, are placed along the outer walls. Auditoriums and rooms that need acoustic insulation rather than windows are in the building's core.

This building was the first in a series of campus buildings; its plan is a prototype of the series. In it, an internal "street" links the heavily used lecture spaces to the entrance and proceeds through the building to the arena behind. Along the street are sitting places, telephones, notice boards, and coffee machines. It provides extra common-room space and is planned to allow for informal meeting and talking.

The architects were not entirely pleased with the execution of the building, yet their prognosis was completely correct:

> We think this ordinary building, in the context of all the extraordinary buildings, will look extraordinary.[1]

1   *LLV*, pp. 146-49.

Literature

Arch. Forum, November 1970, pp. 38–39.

Architecture for the Arts: The State University of New York College of Purchase (New York: Museum of Modern Art, 1971).

G. Allen, "Venturi and Rauch's Humanities Building for the Purchase Campus of the State University of New York," *Arch. Record*, October 1974, pp. 119–24.

DSB, E. Izenour and S. Izenour, "A Post-Construction Evaluation," *Arch. Record*, October 1974, pp. 122–24.

East elevation ▼

Entrance section, detail

Seminar room ▶

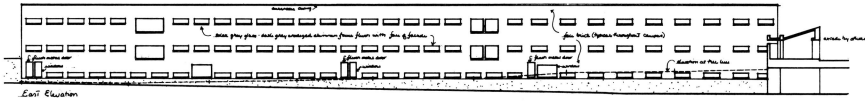

East Elevation

27   Social Sciences Building

Department of Sociology, State University of New York in Purchase, New York (1970)
In charge: Robert Venturi; John Rauch
Project Manager: David Vaughan
with Gerod Clark, W.G. Clark, Arthur Jones

This building's basic form is, like that of the Humanities Building (see pp. 163–67), a simple box. Small, regularly placed windows in the continuous plane of the building's eastern flank emphasize the wall's size. The treatment of the west elevation is different. It brings out the intricate arrangement of seminar rooms and laboratories. Its scale suits its function as an entrance and as a backdrop for the outdoor seating area.

Literature
LLV, pp. 146–49.
a+u 12 (1981): 136–40.

Site plan of University campus: 1. Humanities Building, 2. Social Sciences Building

Floor plans

168

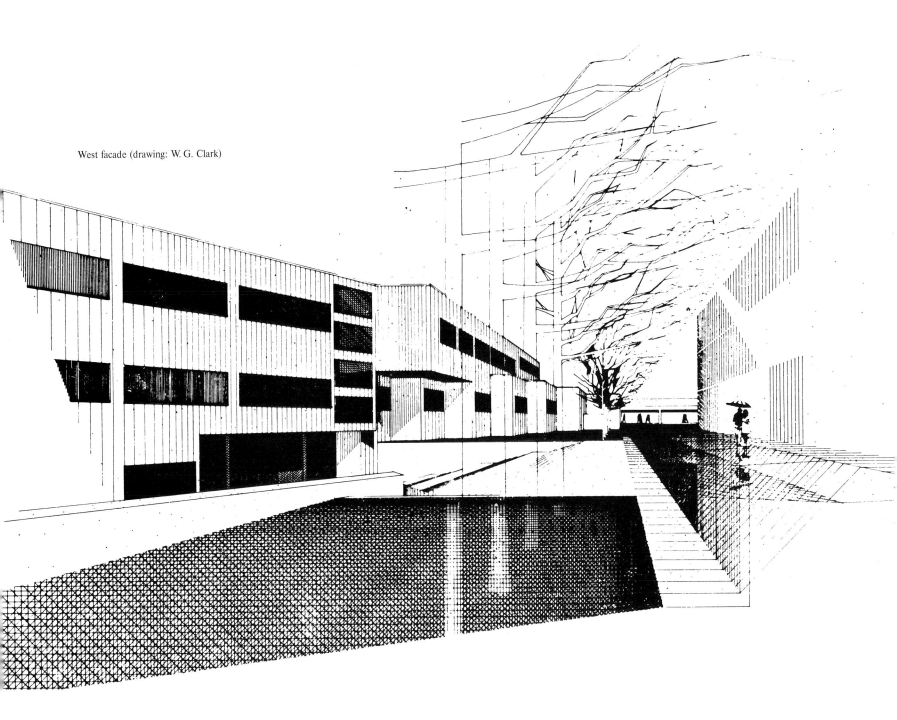

West facade (drawing: W. G. Clark)

West facade

North facade, detail

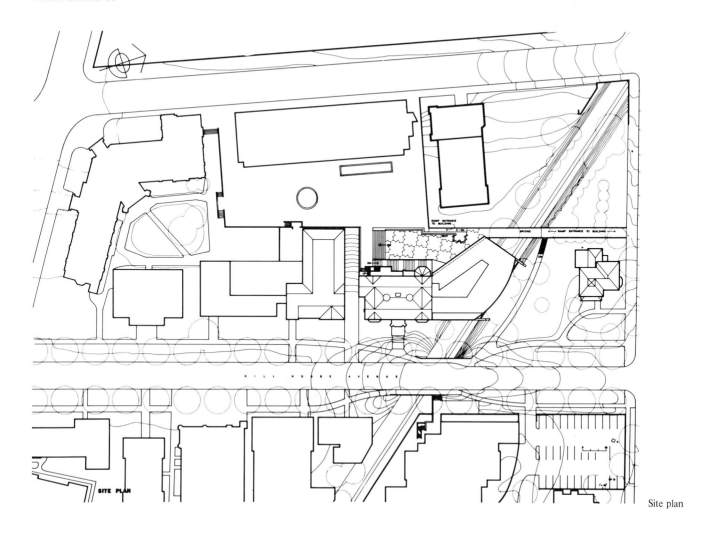

Site plan

28   Yale Mathematics Building Competition

Competition for a new building for the Department of Mathematics at Yale University, New Haven, Connecticut (1969)
In charge: Robert Venturi
with Denise Scott Brown, W.G. Clark, Steven Izenour

The architects' task was complicated by the difficult urban situation. Here, too, they attempted to define an architecture that could exist within the cultural and ideological context of the 1960s: unheroic, skeptical about the relevance of the "monumental" within contemporary culture, and both curious and respectful in its approach to history and to the social and cultural aspects of scholarship.

Unlike the various Modern "masterpieces" on the Yale campus (including work by Paul Rudolph, Philip Johnson, Marcel Breuer, and Gordon Bunshaft), this building tries to look and be ordinary. In the opinion of the architects, this quality of "ordinariness" is also inherent in the campus's Neo-Gothic buildings. They stress that "architecture for a time of questioning cannot be monumental. It cannot be a barracks either. But it must be more than a loft."[1]

In spite of the extremely extensive program, they attempted to give the building a size and scale compatible with that of Hill House Avenue. Such decorative elements as the quatrefoil paving in the rear courtyard and the Neo-Gothic tracery at the rear entry relate directly to the

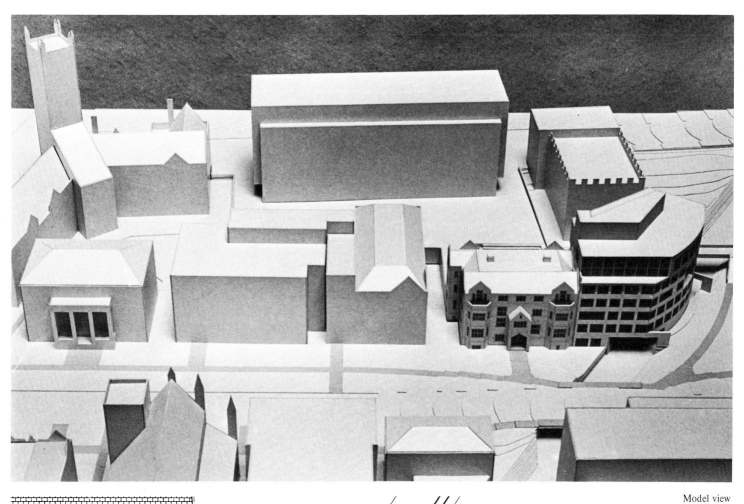

Model view

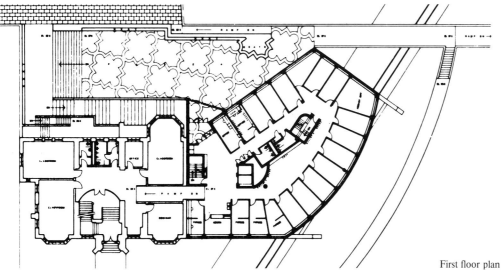

First floor plan

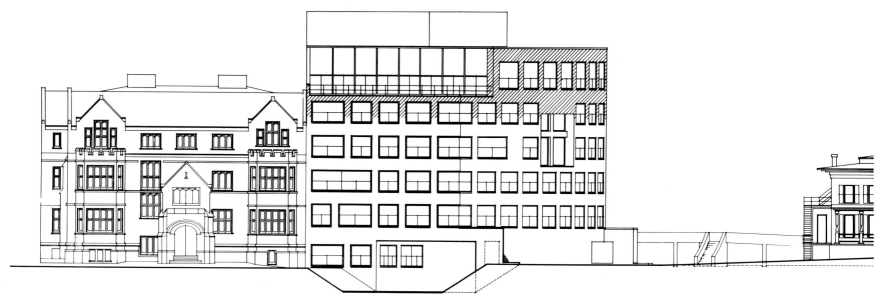

East facade

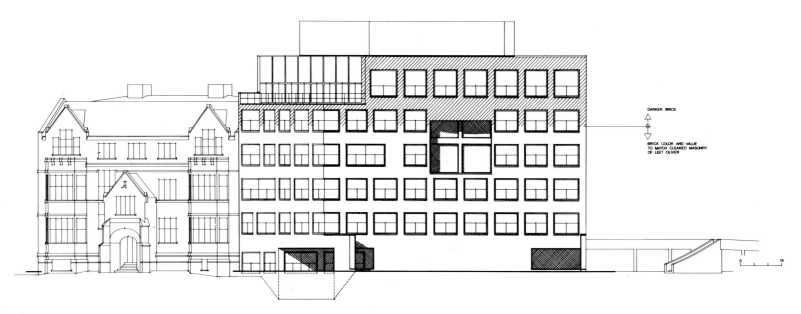

Northeast facade

DARKER BRICK

BRICK COLOR AND VALUE
TO MATCH CLEANED MASONRY
OF LEET OLIVER

174

Northwest facade

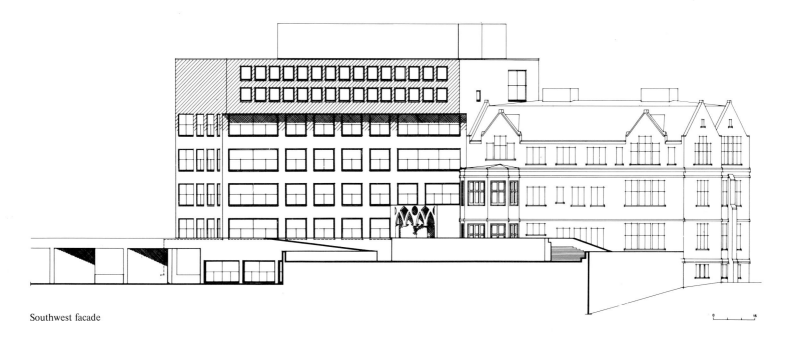

Southwest facade

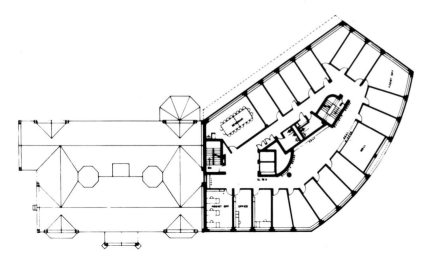

Fourth floor plan

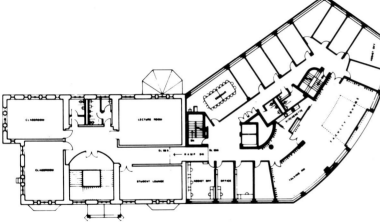

Third floor plan

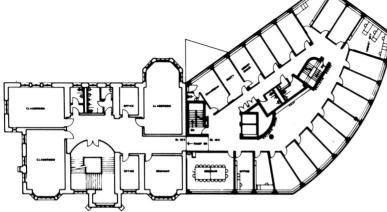

Mezzanine floor plan

surrounding campus buildings. This was an early, perhaps the first, "postmodern" use of historic elements as collage for purposes of allusion.

The architects clarify their approach further:

> Exaggerated urbanism attached to a small building in the manner of Le Corbusier's Carpenter Center or Mill-owner's House, involving near-vehicular scale for mass circulation of pedestrians, is magnificent for the heroic fifties but out of order for the ordinary seventies.[2]

1 *LLV*, pp. 150–55.
2 *Ibid.*

Literature

"Choosing A Non-Monument," *Arch. Forum*, June 1970, p. 22.

AIA-Journal, July 1970, p. 8.

E. P. Berkeley, "Mathematics At Yale," *Arch. Forum*, July–August 1970, pp. 62–67.

Arch. Forum, October 1970, pp. 64–66. (Readers' Response.)

RV and DSB, "Yale Mathematics Building," 1971, (Unpublished manuscript.)

AA 159 (1972): 86–91.

C. W. Moore and N. Pyle, *The Yale Mathematics Building Competition* (New Haven–London: Yale University Press, 1974), pp. 68–85.

C. Rowe, "Robert Venturi and the Yale Mathematics Building," *Oppositions* 6 (1976): 11–19; C. W. Moore, "Conclusion," *ibid.*, pp. 20 f.; V. Scully, "The Yale Mathematics Building: Some Remarks on Siting," *ibid.*, pp. 22 ff.

Fifth floor plan (library)

West facade

29 Dixwell Fire Station

Fire Station in New Haven, Connecticut (1967)
In charge: Robert Venturi; John Rauch
Project Manager: Robert Renfro
with Leslie Delong, Steven Izenour, Arthur Jones

The Dixwell Fire Station is situated diagonally on the site to give the fire trucks efficient access to and egress from the building. The curved facade, with lettering that identifies the building as a fire station, is given a base, shaft, and cornice by changes in color and in surface treatment. Part of the facade appears to peal away from the building, suggesting a traffic sign or a billboard. Unofficially, Venturi likes to compare this building to a Palladian *barchessa* (part of an industrial building on the grounds of a villa).

Literature

LLV, p. 144.

R. L. Miller, "New Haven's Dixwell Fire Station by Venturi and Rauch," *Arch. Rec.*, July 1976, pp. 111–16.

M. Queen and P. Tucker, "Dixwell Fire Station," *Drawings for Modern Public Architecture in New Haven.* (exhibition catalogue) (New Haven, 1976), pp. 19–24.

"La Caserma dei Pompieri," *Interni*, April 1981, pp. 44, 45.

R. Zurier, *The American Firehouse: An Architectural and Social History* (New York: Abbeville Press, 1982), pp. 242–47, 255.

Interior view

Recreation room

Site plan

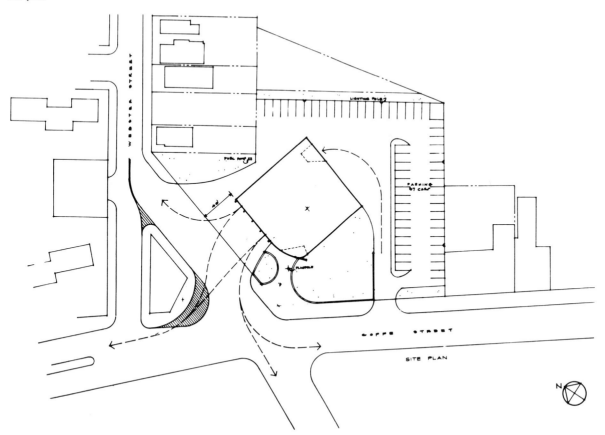

Entrance

30 Allen Art Museum, Oberlin College

Expansion of the Allen Art Museum, Oberlin College, Ohio (1973)
In charge: Robert Venturi; John Rauch
Project Manager: Jeffrey Ryan
with Tony Atkin, Denise Scott Brown, Janet Colesberry, Stanford Hughes, Richard Rice

The Allen Memorial Art Museum is a solid Neo-Renaissance building designed by Cass Gilbert and built in 1917. In 1937 a wing for seminars and studios was added. The extension by Venturi and Rauch included new facilities for the library, the restoration laboratory, a sculpture studio, a large exhibition hall, offices, and a climate-controlled storage room.

The formal challenge inherent in the project was to achieve an appropriate balance between the new and the existing buildings. Venturi and Rauch did not propose a "reinterpretation" of historical forms, much less an exact reconstruction of historical styles. For them, it was a question of expressing the dialectic between the old and the new buildings within a complex and contradictory whole. In this sense, their solution recalls Gunnar Asplund's addition to the Göteborg City Hall (1937). The new gallery wing was set back from the existing museum, however.

Pink granite and red sandstone cladding were used to create a decorative facade that plays composite elements against the whole in a reinterpretation of the main building's character. Venturi says: "we tried to harmonize with his masterpiece in ways not too obvious."[1]

The long "International Style" strip windows of the school and workshop wing make for an uninteresting facade, as the architects themselves acknowledge, since it was intended to simulate loft buildings that house studios for artists and to please the occupants by not infringing on their creativity by an excess of architectural zeal.

1 RV, project description.

Addition to the Göteborg Town Hall (architect: Gunnar Asplund, 1937)

Detail of the museum wing by Cass Gilbert, with gallery addition (right)

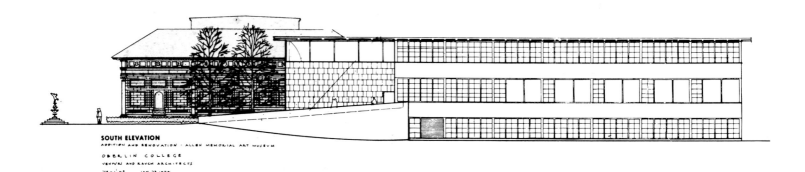

SOUTH ELEVATION
ADDITION AND RENOVATION · ALLEN MEMORIAL ART MUSEUM
OBERLIN COLLEGE
VENTURI AND RAUCH ARCHITECTS
⅛" = 1'-0"   JAN 28 1974

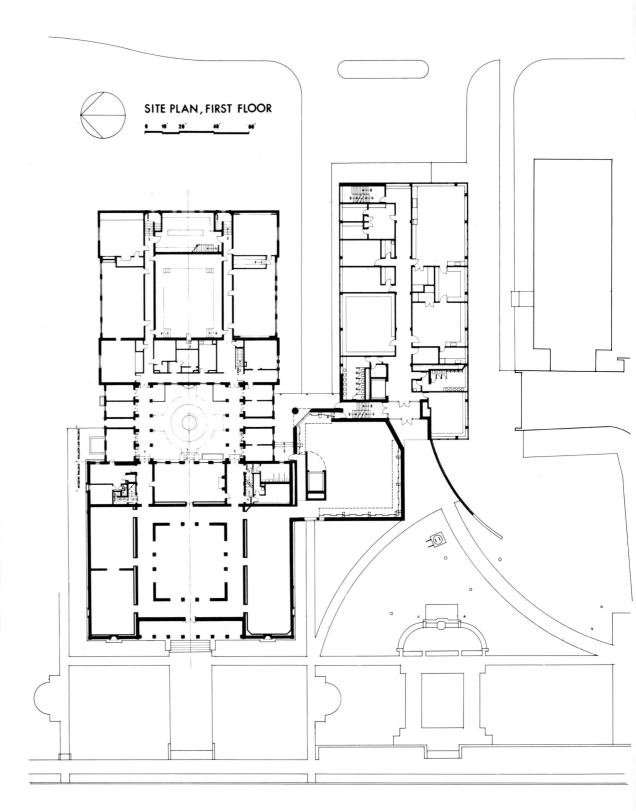

SITE PLAN, FIRST FLOOR

Entrance

First floor plan

Gallery wing

Literature

"Allen Art Building New Wing Dedication," *Oberlin Alumni Magazine*, March–April 1974, pp. 9–14.

RV, "Plain and Fancy Architecture by Cass Gilbert at Oberlin," *Apollo*, February 1976, pp. 6–9; *Allen Memorial Art Museum Bulletin*, 2 (1976–77): 83–104.

"First Photos of Allen Art Buildings's New Addition," *Oberlin Alumni Magazine*, September–October 1976, pp. 13–15.

H. Gallagher, "Allen Museum Completes Expansion," *Tempo*, January 7, 1977, pp. 1, 3.

H. Cullinan, "Allen Museum's Wing Adds Dimensions in Modern Dress," *Cleveland Plain Dealer*, January 9, 1977, section 5, p. 20.

A. Ruckman, "Big Donors a Museum Make," *Oberlin News Tribune*, January 13, 1977, pp. 1, 6f.

A. L. Huxtable, "The Venturi 'Anti-Style' of Architecture," *NYT*, January 30, 1977, pp. 27, 36 D.

J. Wood, "Art Museum at Oberlin Shocks the Eye, Wins the Heart," *The Cleveland Plain Dealer*, February 13, 1977, pp. 1, 4.

"Allen Art Building New Wing Dedication," *Oberlin Alumni Magazine*, March–April 1977, pp. 9–14.

T. Hine, "It's Not Easy to Put Modern Addition on Traditional Building," *Philadelphia Inquirer*, April 10, 1977, p. 13 G.

S. Cohen, "A Summing Up," *PA*, October 10, 1977, pp. 50–54.

D. Gebhard and D. Nevins, *200 Years of American Architectural Drawing* (New York: Architectural League and American Federation of Arts, 1977), pp. 292–93.

"Our Museum," *Oberlin News-Tribune*, January 5, 1978, p. 4.

a+u 1(1978): 63–76.

Bauen & Wohnen, July–August 1978, pp. 289–91.

RV, "Une Galerie d'art à Oberlin, Ohio," *werk-archithese*, January–February 1979, pp. 31–32, 96.

F. Schulze, "Plain and Fancy out on the Prairie," *ARTnews*, April 1979, pp. 42–45.

F. Schulze, "On Campus Architecture," *Portfolio*, August–September 1979, pp. 34–39.

C. van Bruggen, C. Oldenburg, R. H. Fuchs, *Claes Oldenburg: Large-Scale Projects, 1977–1980* (New York: Rizzoli, 1980), pp. 38–43.

"Forum Discussion," *The Harvard Architecture Review*, vol. 1, Fall 1980, pp. 228–39.

A. Colquhoun, "Sign and Substance: Reflections on Complexity, Las Vegas and Oberlin," *Oppositions* 14 (Fall 1978): 26–37; *Essays in Architectural Criticism: Modern Architecture and Historical Change* (Cambridge, MA, 1981), pp. 139–51.

a+u 12 (1981): pp. 22–29.

B. Zevi, *Cronache di architettura*, vol. 24, 1981, p. 17, chapter 1332.

Entrance to library and workshop wing

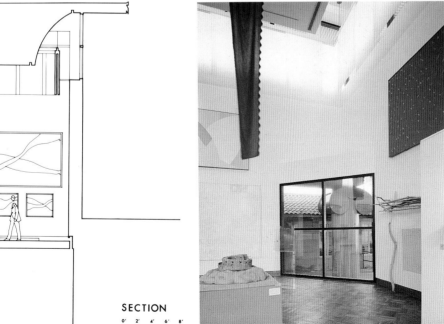

SECTION

0' 2' 4' 6' 8'

Gallery wing, section of exterior wall with fenestration

Gallery with view towards "symbolic column"

Gallery, interior view

31 Penn State Faculty Club

Faculty clubhouse, Pennsylvania State University,
University Park, Pennsylvania (1974)
In charge: Robert Venturi; John Rauch
Project Manager: Robert Renfro
with Denise Scott Brown, Janet Colesberry, Missy Maxwell,
Richard Rice

In this project the architects draw on the archetype of the
stately, shingled nineteenth-century manor (see p. 240 f.).

The program included dining facilities for approximately
100 people, a kitchen, bar, and lounges. The location of the
building was largely determined by the university, and a
particularly important point was to preserve as many of the
trees on the site as possible.

The well-planned and contrasting relationship between
the various elements helps to lend the clubhouse the air of a
stately building rather than that of a commercial eatery. The
form of the long dining hall derives from the banqueting
halls of medieval English colleges, while that of the large
lunette opening that dominates the room recalls the Gothic
clerestories of English refectories (see also pp. 311–13).

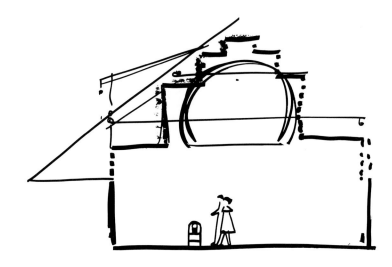

Section (drawing: RV)

Literature
a+u 11 (1974): 103.

a+u 1 (78): 37–46.

M. Filler, "Seeing the Forest for the
Trees," *PA,* 10, October 1977, pp. 56–59;
reactions: *PA*, 12, December 1977, p. 8.

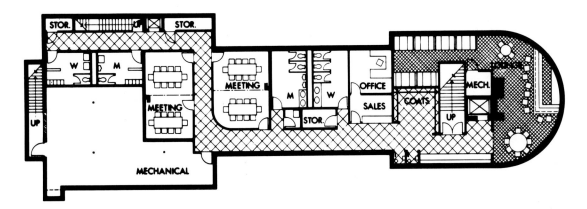

Basement plan

Dining hall, interior view

First floor plan

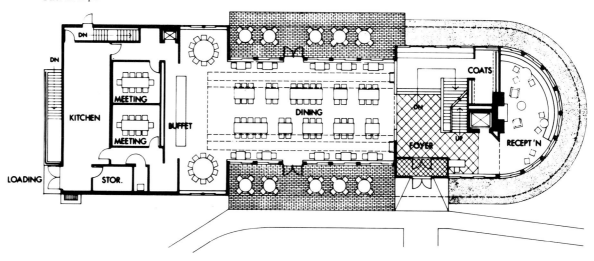

Exterior view

Sitting room on the upper floor

First floor reception room

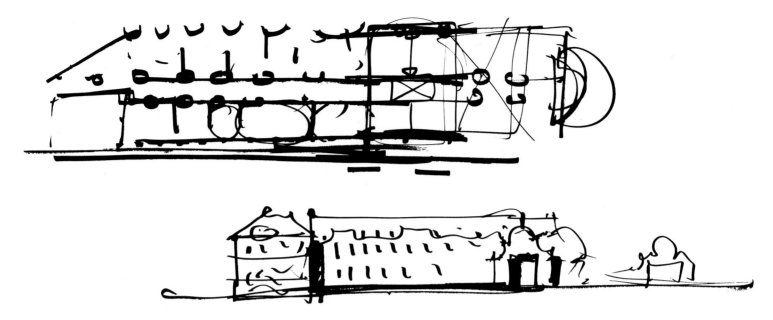

Facade studies (drawing: RV)

32   Museum of Arts and Crafts

Competition entry for the new section of the Frankfurt Museum of Arts and Crafts (Museum für Kunsthandwerk) (1979)
In charge: Robert Venturi
Project Manager: David Vaughan
with James Bradberry, Denise Scott Brown, Lee Rayburn, Frederic Schwartz, James H. Timberlake

It was specified in the competition that the new Arts and Crafts Museum be connected to the Villa Metzler (built shortly after 1800) and that the splendid trees of the park on the Schaumainkai were to be preserved. The project proposed placing the museum building to bar off the river-front, thus creating an unbroken street facade similar to that on the opposite quay. This strategy made it possible to preserve the park as it was while integrating it into the museum grounds as "an intimate garden, away from the busy street along the river."[1]

With its series of relatively closed, linear galleries, the interior organization resembles that of a traditional museum. Special care was given to the design of the entrance and foyer, which incorporate individual architectural references and decorative elements suggestive of the type of objects on exhibit.

Despite what they described as "the high artistic and intellectual standards of its references to historical as well as to contemporary architecture,"[2] the jury found "its subtle dialectic not easily understood."

Apparently easier to understand, Richard Meier's unambiguous "idealistic" design was built instead (see pp. 68 f.).

1   VRSB, project description.
2   F. Werner; see Literature.

Literature

F. Werner, "Der Wettbewerb für das Museum für Kunsthandwerk in Frankfurt am Main," *Jahrbuch für Architektur* (Brunswick-Wiesbaden: Vieweg, 1980), pp. 22–52.

Museum für Kunsthandwerk. Architektenwettbewerb für den Erweiterungsbau (Frankfurt am Main: n.d.), pp. 17 ff.

a+u 12 (1981): 66–69.

Baumeister, August 1980, pp. 766–75.

DSB, "Competition Feature: Venturi, Rauch and Scott Brown," *AD*, December 1981, pp. 124–29.

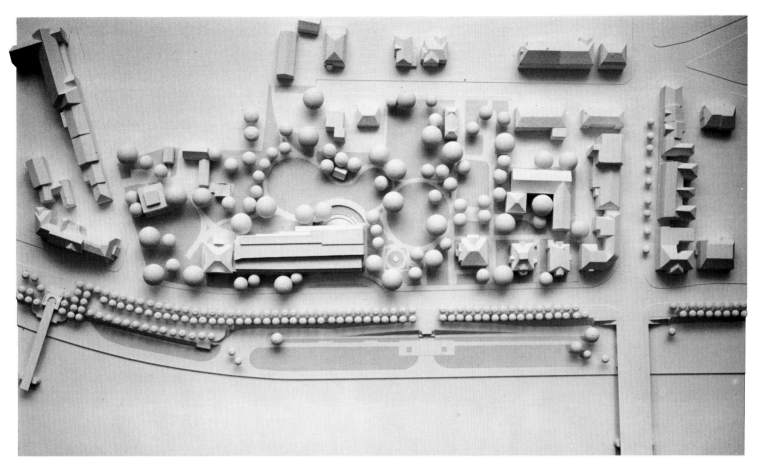

Model view

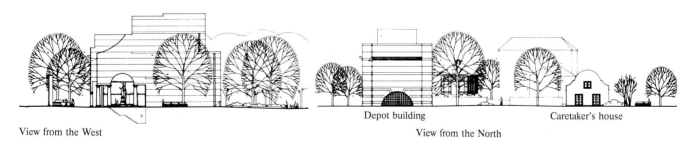

View from the West   Depot building   Caretaker's house

View from the North

Elevations

191

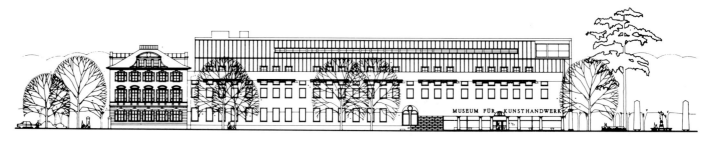

View from the North

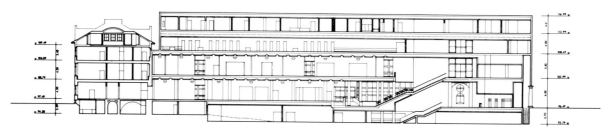

Section A-A

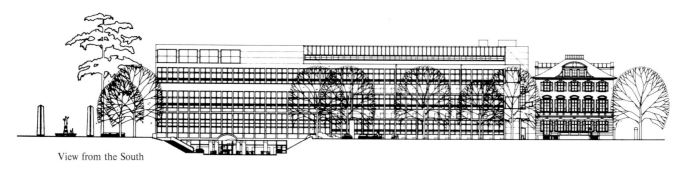

View from the South

Elevations and section

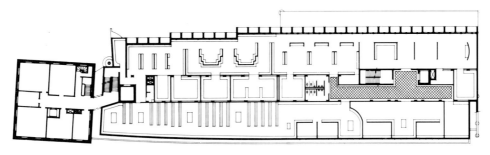

Second floor

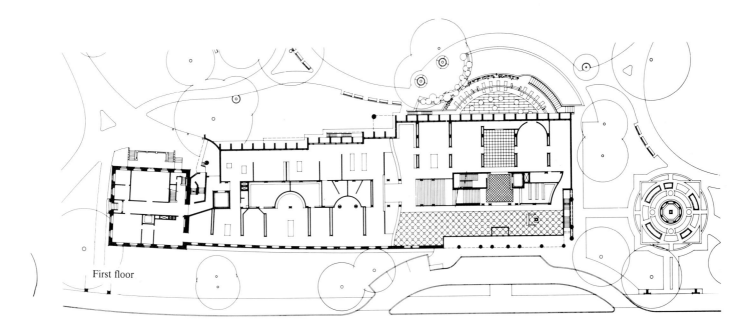

First floor

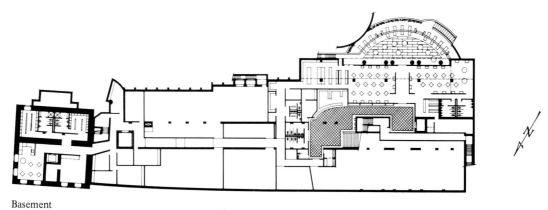

Basement

MASSTAB 1:200

Plans

193

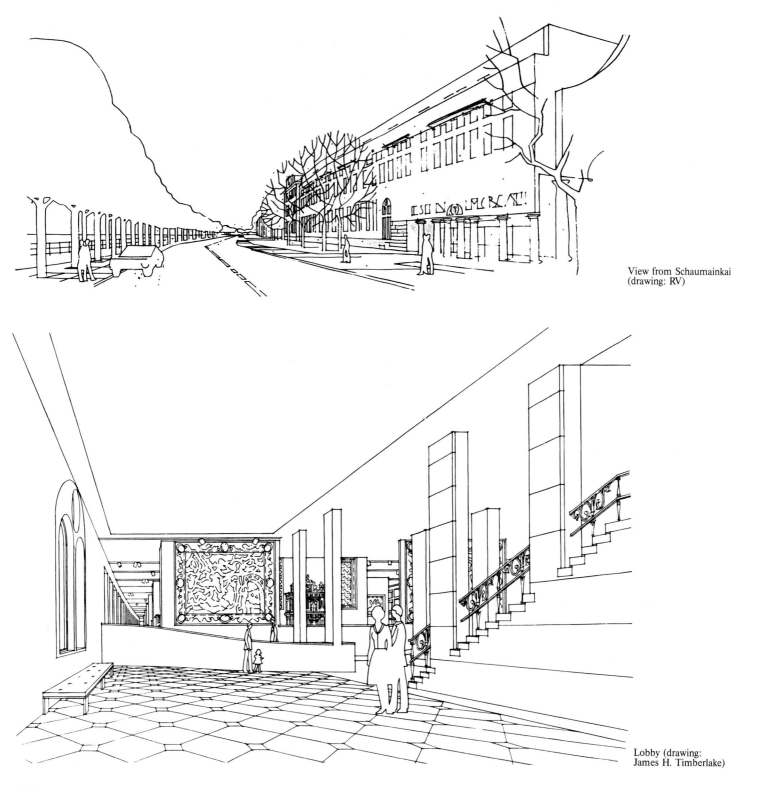

View from Schaumainkai
(drawing: RV)

Lobby (drawing:
James H. Timberlake)

194

33 Canberra Parliament House Competition

Competition entry for the government center of Canberra, Australia (1979)
In charge: Steven Izenour
with James Bradberry, Christine Matheu, Paul Muller, Frederic Schwartz, James H. Timberlake, Robert Venturi, Noriyinki Yasuyama

Like a Baroque facade, Walter Burly Griffin's plan for Canberra (1911) combines two orders: the "giant" order of the great diagonal avenues and the auditorium of mountains that terminates them, and the "minor" order or the grid of local streets. The interplay of these two scales has been the key idea in the design for Parliament House, too. As the architects put it: "We have taken his selective and discreet use of a Baroque tradition as a sound basis for dealing with a complex building and difficult site."[1]

The longitudinal axis is marked by a barrel vault that spans the public areas of the building. The main body of the building forms a cross axis to the vault and is massed on either side of it asymmetrically, owing to the disproportionate size of the House and Senate. The northeast facade along the cross axis is slightly curved to guarantee maximum illumination even in winter, to afford as many offices as

Model views and photomontages

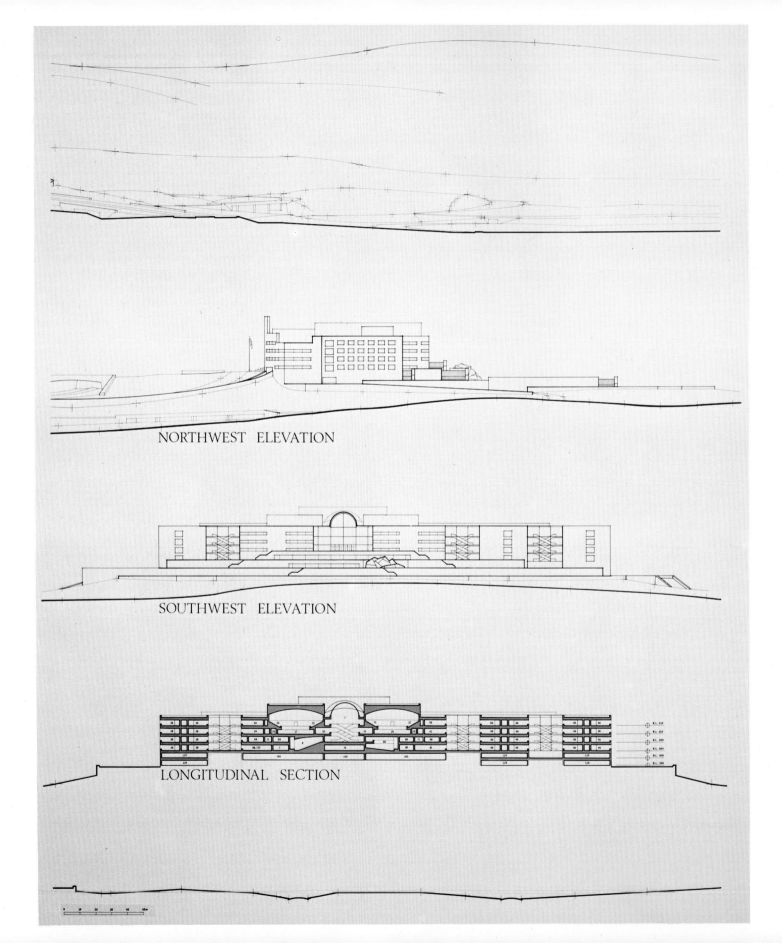

NORTHWEST ELEVATION

SOUTHWEST ELEVATION

LONGITUDINAL SECTION

◀ Sections and elevations

Bird's eye view (drawing: James H. Timberlake)

possible a panorama of the auditorium, and to emphasize the grand scale of the "giant" order in the most monumental facade of Parliament House. "From a distance, that facade should appear like a cliff at the top of a hill: of great presence but of indeterminable size. From close up, it should seem a little smaller than you expected, and friendly and urbane."[2]

1 RV, project description, 1979. (Unpublished manuscript.)
2 *Ibid.*

Literature
a+u 12 (1981): 130-32.

34 State Mosque of Iraq Competition

Competition entry for a national mosque in Baghdad (1982)
In charge: Robert Venturi; Steven Izenour
Project Manager: David Marohn
with James Bradberry, Denise Scott Brown, Rick Buckley, Erica Gees, John Hayes, David Hinson, Reyhan Larimer, Tim Lisle, Robert Marker, Christine Matheu, John Rauch, Fran Read, Miles Ritter, Louis Rodolico, Simon Tickell, Maurice Weintraub

In late 1982 Iraq's Ministry for Cultural and Religious Affairs, in cooperation with the city of Baghdad, invited seven architects to submit proposals for a national mosque. The building was to accommodate a congregation of 30,000 worshippers, If built, the structure would be the largest Moslem shrine in the world. The results of the competition were never made public and, in the light of the political situation, it is more than uncertain that any of the projects will be built.

The project under discussion is inspired by precedents in Islamic monumental art. It evokes images of the mosques in Isfahan, Samarkand, Córdoba, and Samarra. Venturi himself carefully studied the Ibn Tulun Mosque in Cairo; the great mosque of Kairouan, especially its interior space; and the dome of Imam Dur in Samarra.

The architects did not derive their design from any one of these precedents, or any single period or style. They were concerned with using historical associations to lend meaning to a building constructed with modern industrial techniques. The goal was to build a mosque that would be "at once profound, to speak to future ages, and popular, to be loved by the people of Iraq today."[1]

The primary feature of the ground plan is a hypostyle, created by rows of closely spaced columns. This repetitive and nonhierarchical order permits each worshipper to relate to the interior space without being overwhelmed by its monumentality.

The dome, the faceting of which is a variation on the stalagtite form of Islamic domes, rises above the interior courtyard or "sahn," which is surrounded on three sides by the shrine's hypostyle.

1 VRSB, project description

Literature

RV, "Proposal for the Iraq State Mosque, Baghdad," *AA*, September 1983, pp. 28–35; XLV.

"Regenerative Approaches to Mosque-Design: Competition for Stage-Mosque, Baghdad," *Mimar* 11 (January–March 1984): 44–63.

M. Schmertz, "Design Competition Entry for the State Mosque by Venturi, Rauch and Scott Brown," *Arch. Rec.* June 1984, pp. 142–49.

O. Grabar, "From the Past into the Future: On Two Designs for State Mosques," *Arch. Rec.*, June 1984, pp. 150–51.

A. de Bonis, "Under Two Cultures," *Eupalino*, Fall 1984, pp. 6–13.

Quaderns 162 (1984): 128–29.

Art and Design, February 1985, pp. 34–35.

"State Mosque of Iraq, Invited International Design Competition," *a+u* (August 1985): 12–15.

Historic models and patterned ornaments

Main facade with dome, detail (drawing: Richard Buckley, Michael Levin, and Miles Ritter)

Model view

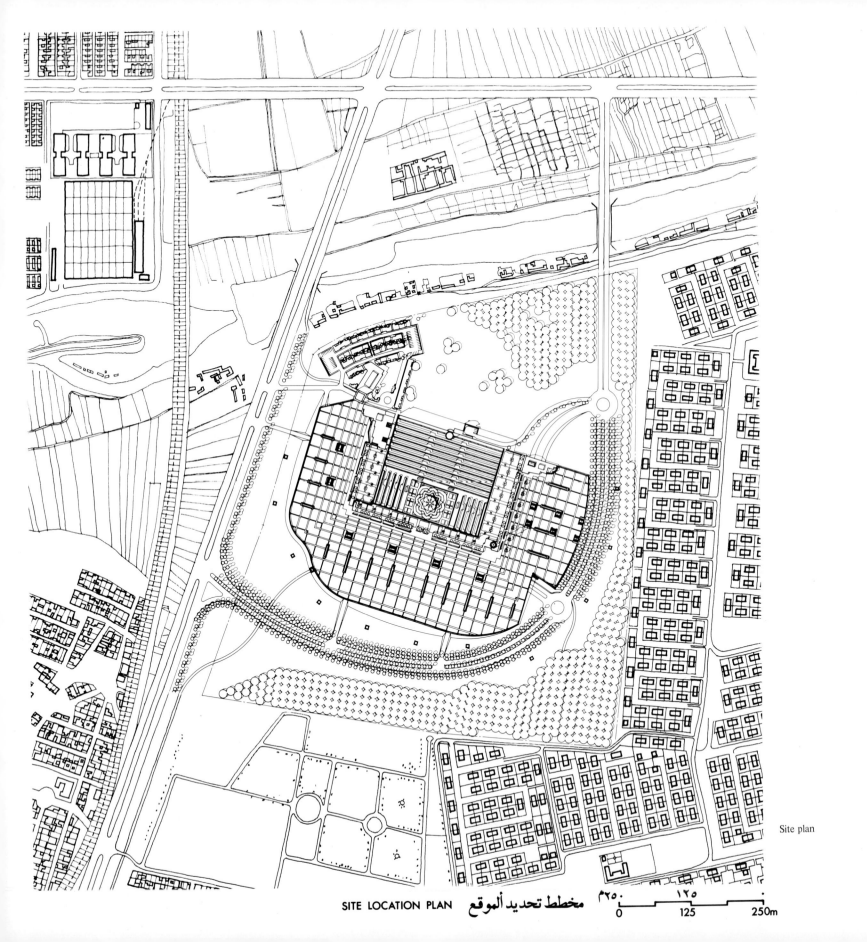

Site plan

SITE LOCATION PLAN مخطط تحديد الموقع

٢٥٠   ١٢٥

0   125   250m

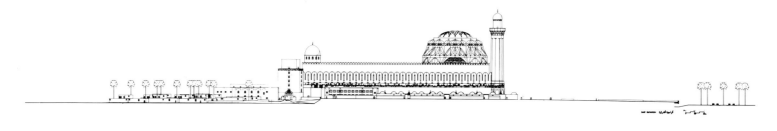

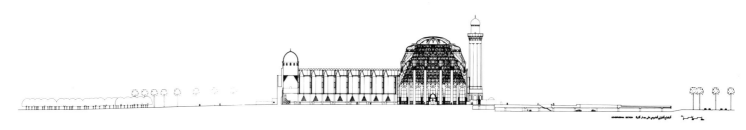

Elevation and section

PERSPECTIVE FROM SAHN لمنظور من أصحن

Interior perspective view of hypostyle (drawing: David Hinson)

35 Gordon Wu Hall

New dormitory for Butler College, Princeton University,
Princeton, New Jersey (1980)
In charge: Robert Venturi; John Rauch
Project Managers: Arthur Jones, Missy Maxwell
with Sam Harris, Christopher Smith

In recent years, VRSB have received commissions for a
variety of large-scale planning projects, two new buildings,
and the renovation of several undergraduate colleges at
Princeton University (see pp. 311–13). Gordon Wu Hall was
perhaps the most difficult of these projects.

The problem lay in creating a new center for Butler
College. The architects write:

> The building's design takes important cues from what is
> around it, but it promotes also an identity of its own. Its
> long shape and central position make it a visual hyphen
> that connects the dormitories and unites them. The brick,
> limestone trim, and strip windows adhere to the
> traditional gothic architecture of Princeton. The main
> entrance, set off-center and broadside in the building, is
> marked by a bold marble and gray granite panel recalling
> early Renaissance ornament and symbolizing the entrance
> to the College as a whole as well as to the building itself.[1]

Sixteenth-century chimneypieces, English variations on the
Bolognese architect and painter Serlio, and the gabled
doorways of Elizabethan country houses served as inspi-
ration.

> Inside, the long dining hall recalls those English Gothic
> halls traditional at Princeton. Bay windows two stories
> high at each end of the building create some spaciousness
> and scale typical of historical prototypes....[2]

The building was intended to provide opportunities for

Wooton Lodge: Entrance with decor
ated portal (ca. 1600)

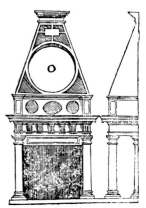

Chimneypiece from Serlio's
VIIth book

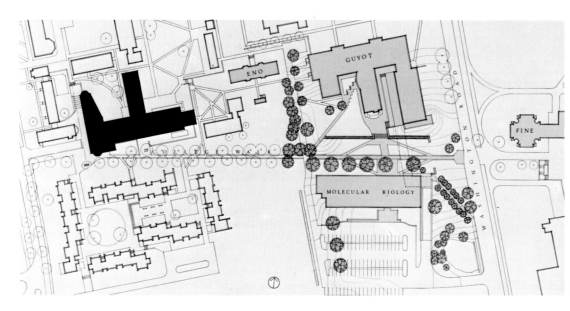

Site plan with Gordon Wu Hall (left) and
Microbiology Building (right)

Entrance with "sign" made
of marble and gray granite

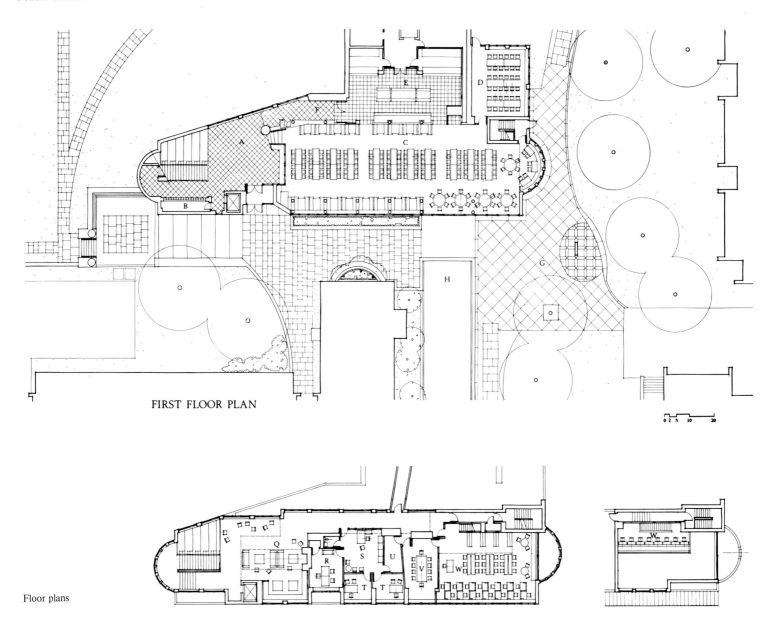

FIRST FLOOR PLAN

Floor plans

casual contact among students. This purpose is certainly served by the staircase to the left of the entrance:

The stairway itself serves several purposes. As the first flight leads to a landing and the foot of the bay window, the stairs extend to one side becoming larger, higher steps suitable for sitting.[3]

This space functions as a grand staircase, as an informal waiting and gathering place, and as an indoor amphitheater.

View from the East

1 VRSB, project description. On sixteenth-century English architecture, which influenced the forms, see M. Girouard, *Robert Smythson and the Elizabethan Country House* (New Haven and London: Yale University Press, 1983). On the Campus of Princeton University: P. V. Turner, *Campus: An American Planning Tradition* (New Haven and London: MIT Press, Cambridge, Mass., 1984), pp. 227–33.
2 *Ibid.*
3 *Ibid.*

Literature

P. Goldberger, "Small Building, Big Gestures," *NYT*, June 19, 1984, pp. 35–36.

A. Chimacoff and A. Plattus, "Learning from Venturi," *Arch. Rec.*, September 1983, pp. 86–97.

R. Gutman, "Venturi's Masterclass," *The Architects' Journal*, September 7, 1983, pp. 36–39.

T. Hine, "New Princeton Building Links Past to Future," *The Philadelphia Inquirer*, October 30, 1983, p. 20.

S. Stephens, "Gordon Wu Hall, Butler College, Princeton University, Princeton, New Jersey," *Vanity Fair*, October 1983, pp. 135–36.

D. Boles, "What Does Wu Mean?" *PA*, October 1983, p. 38.

M. L. Scalvini, "Learning from Princeton," *Domus*, December 1983, pp. 18–23.

M. Swenarton, "Venturi in Princeton," *Building Design*, December 2, 1983, pp. 14–16.

M. M. Keenan, "An Architect's Tour of Wu Hall," *Princeton Alumni Weekly*, January 25, 1984, pp. 11–15.

G. Macrae-Gibson, "The Ironies of the Difficult Whole: Venturi, Rauch and Scott Brown's Gordon Wu Hall", *a+u* 1 (1984): 85–86.

R. Janjigian, "Contextual Credit," *Interiors*, January 1984, pp. 146–47.

AA, February 1984, pp. 92–94.

AD 3-4 (March–April 1984): 56–59.

GA Document 10 (May 1984): 76–81.

G. Nannerini, "Gordon Wu Hall for Butler, Princeton University, New Jersey," *L'Industria delle costruzioni*, May 1984, pp. 40–45.

A. O. Dean, "Cerebral Campus Center that Abounds in Contradictions," *Architecture*, May 1984, pp. 200–3.

Quaderns 162 (1984): 107–11.

A. F. Alba, "In the Beginning Was the Word," *Quaderns*, 162 (1984): pp. 112–14.

T. Hine, "Laurels for Phila. Architects," *The Philadelphia Inquirer*, June 22, 1984, p. 1C.

"The Ironies of the Difficult Whole," in G. Macrae-Gibson, *The Secret Life of Buildings. An American Mythology for Modern Architecture* (Cambridge, Mass.: MIT Press, 1985), pp. 142–69.

Dining Hall

Second floor sitting room

Second floor library with *finestra termale*

View from the West

36 Lewis Thomas Laboratory for Molecular Biology

Laboratory for the Institute of Molecular Biology, Princeton, New Jersey (1983)
In collaboration with Payette Associates, Architects; George Patton Associates, Landscape Architects
In charge: Robert Venturi; John Rauch
Project Managers: Ronald McCoy, David Schaaf

In this project, VRSB were only responsible for the facade and for the design of the building's immediate context. The facade's scale, rhythm, and proportions were predetermined by the complex technical requirements of the laboratory.

Design ideas were thus expressed primarily in the building's alternating bands of patterned brick facing and cast-stone-framed strip windows. A massive rectangularly patterned cladding wraps the high attic story, which houses the mechanical plant. The windows in the northern facing facade are flush with the wall. Those facing south are recessed in order to prevent direct sunlight from entering the building, a design that has given the facade a sculptural effect.

The architects emphasize:

The variety and texture of the surfaces create several orders of scale, lending interest to the extremely long facade and complementing the traditional collegiate Gothic architecture of Guyot Hall Complex, the existing Geology and Biology Departments.[1]

At the ends, bay windows serve as seminar lounges separated from the lab span: these windows recall the bays of Wu Hall, a short distance along College Walk to the west.

1 VRSB, project description.

Literature
GA Document 1 (1981): 82–83.
PA 10 (1984): p. 93.
Quaderns 162 (1984): 115–17.
V. Gregotti, "A proposito di decorazione," *Panorama*, August 17, 1896, p. 19.

North facade

North entrance

South view

First floor plan

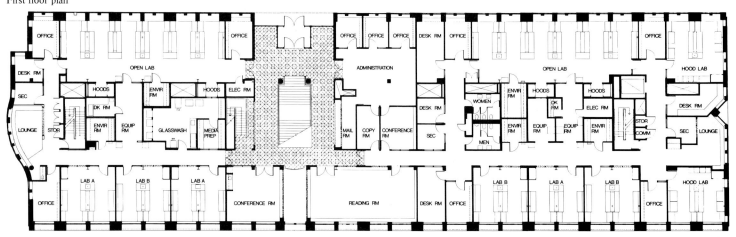

South entrance

37 Laguna Gloria Art Museum

Project for a museum in Austin, Texas (1983)
In charge: Robert Venturi
Urban design: Denise Scott Brown
Project Managers: David Vaughan, Ann Trowbridge

This museum is part of a comprehensive urban planning proposal (see pp. 126f.). It is to be built in the center of Austin, facing Republic Park. These circumstances help to clarify the treatment of the facade, which is both impressive at a distance and rich in details perceptible only from a closer vantage point. A variety of historical precedents is also evoked, such as the facade of the Aqua Paola on the Gianicolo in Rome, and Schinkel's Altes Museum in Berlin (see p. 44), Le Corbusier's Villa Schwob, and Aalto's Enso Gutzeit Building in Helsinki (pl. above, right).
Concerning the project, Venturi writes:

The flaglike panel is creased and curved back at its ends to create a small entrance courtyard on the east and a corresponding courtyard at the western end for a dining patio for the museum restaurant. These big elements, grand in scale to reflect the importance of the building and

Helsinki: Enso Gutzeit Headquarters (architect: Alvar Aalto, 1959)

to be seen from across the park, are juxtaposed with small-scale architectural and graphic elements and decorative patterns to be seen close-up and to make the building appear attractive and inviting to individuals— especially, we hope, to children.[1]

The entry foyer and a sculpture gallery are planned for the ground floor.

On the second floor are two parallel series of art galleries in the long configurations traditional to art galleries, fortuitously dictated here by the elongated shape of the site....

Perspective view
(drawing: David Mohler)

The front galleries are designed to receive natural northern light indirectly from high windows which create ambient light for these spaces; occasional small windows at eye level invite you to look out intermittently on the beautiful park and skyline beyond.[2]

1 RV, project description.
2 *Ibid.*

Literature

Texas Architect, July–August 1983, pp. 23, 25.

J. Hutchinson, "Venturi, Brown Building on Ideas," *Austin-American*

Statesman, December 16, 1984, pp. E1, E18.

A. Holmes, "New Austin Museum Shown as Work in Progress," *Houston Chronicle*, April 20, 1985, section 4, p. 1.

D. Turner, "Austin's New Laguna Gloria Museum," *Site*, Summer 1985, p.5.

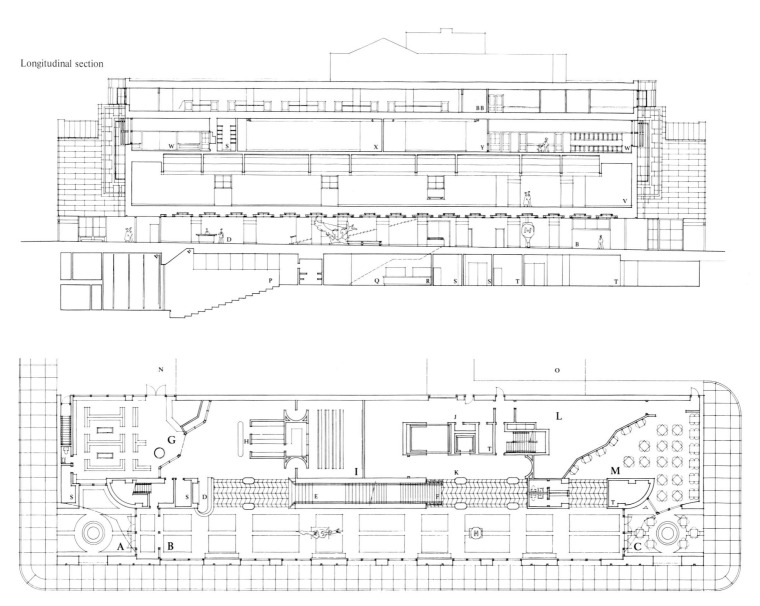

Longitudinal section

First floor plan

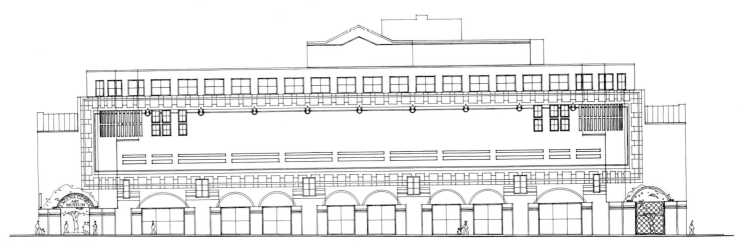

Fourth Street elevation

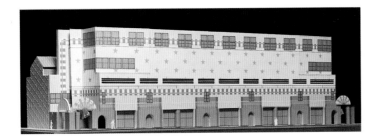
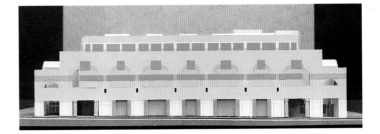

Facade studies (models)

3   Commercial and Office Buildings

If you want to meet the man in the street, go to the market-place. In America, this might well mean going to the supermarket on the "strip." To study the strip itself, go to Las Vegas, where the aesthetic rules for an architecture of commerce and entertainment can be analyzed in their extreme—stretched taut between the necessity of cost-effective, air-conditioned interior environments and conspicuous or spectacular exteriors.[1]

Whether one regards the architecture of Las Vegas and its neon signs as an authentic form of folk art or, as Tomàs Maldonado warns, as "the pseudo-communicative culmination of more than half a century of masked manipulatory violence"[2] is not at issue here. Turning one's back, as most architects ritually do, on the crass symbolism of commercial life would mean retreating from reality. In America the urge to sell goods and services to the motorized consumer by employing every possible strategy to create catchy visual effects and promises of "fun" is older

than modern architecture—and will probably outlast it—quite apart from the fact that modern architecture itself has not entirely abstained from merging its imagery with the commercial glamour of the mechanized metropolis, as shown by work of Eric Mendelsohn and by Oscar Nitzchke's project for a "Palais de la Publicité" in Paris (1934), among others.

"Ducks" and "Decorated Sheds"

What makes the strip's "naive" form of architectural communication interesting to the historian and to the architect with a historical bent is the often hilarious way in which it preserves fossilized forms of expressing function through decoration and symbolism. The McDonald's drive-in, with its bold combination of arch and Hamburger

a   Fast-Food Iconography: the "Diner" (left) and McDonald's Drive-In (right)

215

b   The "duck" as an architectural paradigm

stand, is a classical example.[3] On the other hand, concepts developed by the Venturis and Steven Izenour in their analysis of the typologies of fast-food stands and gas stations can easily be applied to the high art of modern architecture, albeit with a wink:

> A "Duck" is a duck; it can also be a hot dog, a milk bottle, an elephant.... In other words, a "Duck" is a building whose function, structure and material are secondary to its representational quality or sculptural form.[4] (pl. b)

Seen in this way, a large part of modern architecture, especially after 1960, is actually composed of "ducks":

> "Ducks" are sculptural and three-dimensional—the building is the sign. "Decorated Sheds," on the other hand, are

a two-dimensional approximation of a "Duck." The "Decorated Shed" exaggerates or distorts one element, usually the front facade, while the rest of the building remains conventional in appearance.[5]

Not only would the Golden Nugget Casino in Las Vegas be a "decorated shed," but so would the Cathedral of Cremona or the Palazzo Strozzi in Florence. VRSB's projects for shopping centers and office buildings demonstrate what kind of lessons lie concealed in the forgotten atavisms of commercial architecture. The projects also show that these inspirations can dovetail with traditional ideas from the International Style—or from Alvar Aalto's work.

1   See here, of course, R. Venturi, D. Scott Brown, and S. Izenour, *Learning from Las Vegas* (Cambridge, Mass.: MIT Press, 1972).

2   Tomàs Maldonado, *La Speranza progettuale*, Turin, 1970, quoted from K. Frampton, *Modern Architecture: A Critical History* (London and New York: Thames and Hudson, 1980), p. 290.

3   See M. Treib, "Eye-Konism (pt. II): Signs as Buildings as Signs," *Print*, May 1973, and Alan Hess, "The Origins of McDonald's Golden Arches," *Journal of the Society of Architectural Historians*, March 1986, pp. 60–67.

4   SI, "The 'Duck' and the 'Decorated Shed,'" in *Built in the USA: American Building from Airports to Zoos*, ed. D. Maddex (Washington, D.C.: Preservation Press, 1985), pp. 64–67; see *LLV*, pp. 90–91.

5   *Ibid.*

38 Transportation Square Office Building

Competition for an office building in Washington, D.C. (1967)
In collaboration with Caudill Rowlett Scott, Architects
In charge: Robert Venturi; John Rauch
Urban design: Denise Scott Brown
with Gerod Clark, James Greifendorf

Should the "quality" of commercial and office buildings be defined primarily in terms of structural and spatial consistency and abstract form demonstrated with such perfection by Mies van der Rohe and his school? Or would it be appropriate to develop architectural languages that can relate to the historical characteristics of the given site and its specific purpose?

The architects are partial to the latter view. With this project for Washington, D.C., they demonstrated as early as 1967 how they believed a complex of commercial buildings should be integrated into an existing urban setting. The trapezoidal site, a residual space in L'Enfant's rigorous urban plan, is reiterated in the form of the buildings themselves: the slablike office tower follows the rectangular grid of the street axes, whereas the building's lower section nestles against Maryland Avenue, which cuts through the block diagonally.

The slab structure itself, in the manner of the *ville radieuse*, also relates to the urban renewal context of the neighborhood. On the other hand, the building's lower sections extend, in the manner of Baron Haussmann, along the street axis to create a *rue corridor*. The highrise bank building at 20 State Street in Boston (architect: Edward L. Barnes) served as a model for the facade. In the end,

Model view of entrance

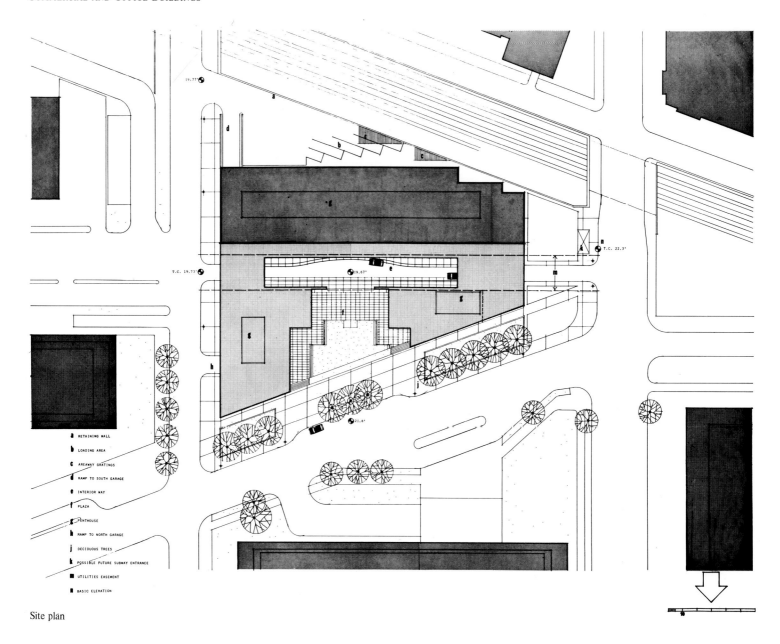

a RETAINING WALL
b LOADING AREA
c AREAWAY GRATINGS
d RAMP TO SOUTH GARAGE
e INTERIOR WAY
f PLAZA
g PENTHOUSE
h RAMP TO NORTH GARAGE
j DECIDUOUS TREES
k POSSIBLE FUTURE SUBWAY ENTRANCE
l UTILITIES EASEMENT
m BASIC ELEVATION

Site plan

however, the urban setting and the way in which the project responds to it reminds one of Alvar Aalto's Pension Building in Helsinki (1952–1956; see p. 34).

Although the project won the redevelopment competition, it was not executed. Even a revised version could not overcome the resistance of the Washington Fine Arts Commission under the architectural leadership of Gordon Bunshaft. What was finally mandated by the Commission could not be built. The dispute over this project has been documented by the architects as an exemplary case study.[1]

1 *LLV*, pp. 138–41.

Literature
New Directions, pp. 54–56.

218

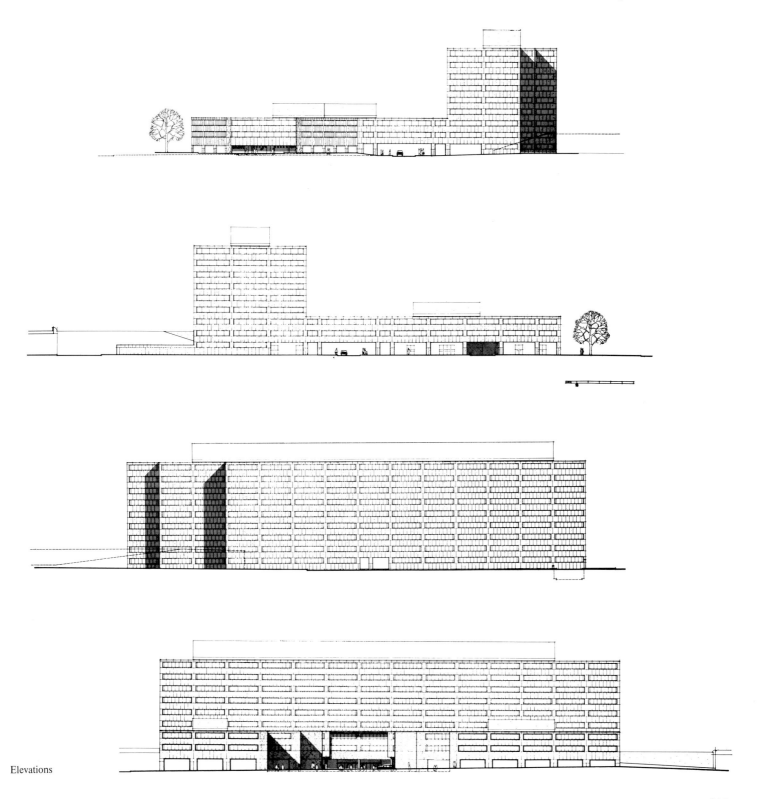

Elevations

39 California City Sales Office

Project for the sales office of the Great Western United
Corporation in California City (1970; not executed)
In charge: Robert Venturi
with W.G. Clark

This building was designed to serve the Great Western
United Corporation as an office from which to promote and
sell real estate in California City, a community on the edge
of the Mojave Desert for which the firm was then
developing a planning study (see pp. 94–97). The architects
state:

> We designed a box with a single window on each main
> facade, recessed and partly covered with lattice for shade
> from the desert sun. The big central windows, which are
> not an entrance, give symmetry and symbolic dignity and
> increase the scale of the relatively small building seen
> from the parking lot and from across the lake.[1]

The architectural *parti* include a lake in front of the building,
an axial plan and elevation, and a low arched opening in the
middle of the main facade. These design elements recall the
formal schemes of the Beaux-Arts Tradition that was still
commonplace in American schools of architecture in the
1930s.

1 *LLV*, p. 183.

Literature

AA (December 1971–January 1972):
84–104.

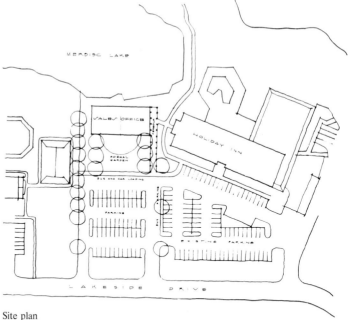

Site plan

Plan

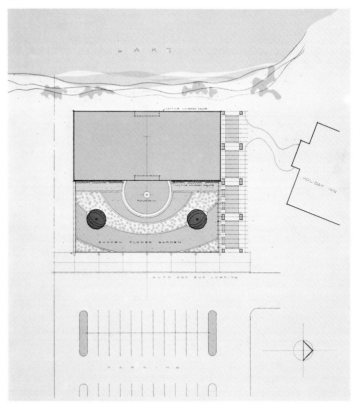

Elevation
(drawing: W. G. Clark)

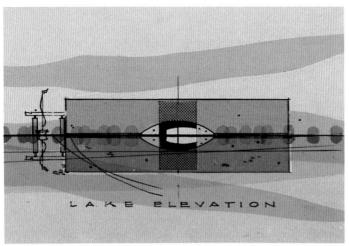

40 MERBISC Mart

Project for a Shopping Mall along the Landsburg-Mojave Road in California City (1970; not executed)
In charge: Robert Venturi
with Denise Scott Brown, W. G. Clark, Paul Hirshorn, Steven Izenour
MERBISC is an acronym for "Most Extraordinary Recreation Bargain In Southern California."

This project was conceived as a row of shops that could later be expanded into a veritable shopping center. In front of the shops is a loggia for shade. Surmounting the loggia is a high lattice backing to support the store signs.

The opening in the middle of the row frames a view towards two buttes in an attempt to relate the architecture to the landscape, as the Greeks seem to have done with their archaic sanctuaries.[1]

This opening is crowned by a large reproduction of a nineteenth-century landscape painting, *New England Summer*. "We hope," the architects emphasize, "that an appreciation of this picture of an Eastern landscape will replace the inclination of citizens to reproduce it in their yards."[2]

1 V. Scully, *The Earth, the Temple and the Gods: Greek Sacred Architecture.* (New York: Frederick A. Praeger, 1962).
2 *LLV*, p. 184.

"Horns" on the horizon of the plain of Thorikos with sanctuary of Demeter and Kore. From Vincent J. Scully, *The Earth, the Temple and the Gods* (1962)

Facade towards parking lot (drawing: Steven Izenour)

41   Jazz Club, Houston

Project for a Dancing and Jazz Club in Houston, Texas (1978)
In charge: Robert Venturi
with Steven Izenour, Missy Maxwell

The specifications for this approximately 2,700 square foot night club call for a bar with boxes as well as a music and dance hall. The interior spaces are inserted into the boxlike shape of the building but maintain their spatial independence. In this way they recall both Aalto's library buildings and the Casino architecture of Las Vegas or Atlantic City. On the outside of the first project the imagery develops the "marine" theme. The facade of the second version relates jazz to the classical archetype of a museum. This was one of the firm's first explicit uses of classical imagery. By means of

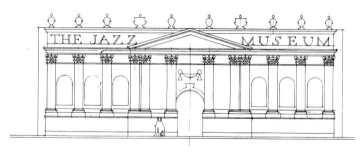

Second project elevation in the form of a "museum" (drawing: Steven Izenour)

slide projections, the inside is meant to evoke the atmosphere of a "museum in which you can relax."

Literature
AA, June 1978, pp. 24-26.
AVC, pp. 82-85.

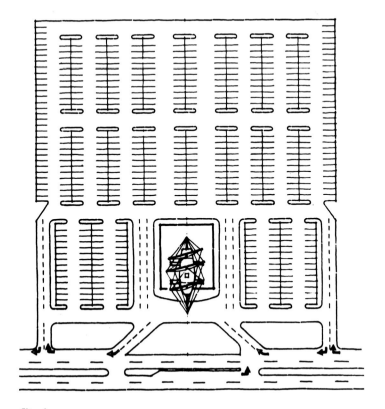

Site plan

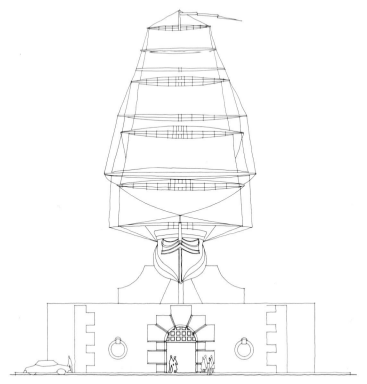

First project elevation with giant ship model (drawing: Steven Izenour)

Model view of main facade with dome of the old Blenheim Hotel

42 Hotel and Casino in Atlantic City

Project to restore and enlarge a hotel in Atlantic City, New Jersey (1977)
In charge: Robert Venturi; John Rauch
Project Manager: Steven Izenour
with John Chase, Janet Colesberry, Stanford Hughes, Virginia Jacobs, Don Jones, Benjamin Kracauer, David Marohn, Amy Weinstein

This project was part of a planning study on strategies for the architectural and economic rehabilitation of Atlantic City, once an elegant beach resort on the East coast of the United States. The site covers the present locations of the hotels

Marlborough, Blenheim, and Dennis. The proposal includes a casino as well as a hotel with 1,500 rooms in the shape of a concave highrise slab.

The project—of which various revised versions exist—proposes to retain the ornamental, domed front section of the Blenheim Hotel (architect: William Price, Philadelphia, 1906). An entrance hall, conference rooms, shops, the casino itself, and a parking garage are on the lower floors. On the "deck" of this flat section and at the foot of the huge hotel slab are terraced gardens, swimming pools, cafés, and recreation areas, all facing the ocean. The old Blenheim Hotel contains suites and conference rooms.

Ornamentation plays a vital role in the architecture of this project. The jewellike fragment of the original building stands in the center, impressively set off by the "hanging gardens" at its foot and the curved wall of the slab behind. The slab itself is decorated with blue tiles of varying hues.

Unfortunately, the project was never executed, and when Atlantic City underwent a boom as the "Las Vegas of the East Coast" in the late 1970s, the old Blenheim Hotel was forced to give way to new development.

Literature

J. Kron, "Hello Atlantic City," *NYT*, April 14, 1977, section 3, p. 3.

S. Stephens, "Casino qua non," *PA*, 10 (October 1977): 67-69.

A. L. Huxtable, "Architectural Drawings as Art Gallery Art," *NYT*, October 23, 1977.

P. Goldberger, "Architectural Drawings Raised to an Art," *NYT*, December 12, 1977.

P. Apraxine, *Architecture I*, 1977. (Exhibition catalogue.)

V. Donohoe, "Saving Marlborough Blenheim, A Chance to Blend Old and New," *The Philadelphia Inquirer*, February 5, 1978, p. 16 K.

R. F. Snow, "The Marlborough Blenheim: A Last Look?" *Americana*, March–April 1978, p. 70.

G. F. Thomas, "Architectural Preservation", *Arts Exchange*, March–April 1978, pp. 6-7.

werk-archithese, May 1978, pp. 53–54.

J. Quinn, "Architecture: Does Everything Have to Go?," *PM*, June 1978, pp. 107–110, 112, 114–15.

AA 197 (June 1978): 32–37.

A. L. Huxtable, "Atlantic City–Analyzing an Urban Phenomenon," *NYT*, September 21, 1980, p. D 29.

a+u 12 (1981): 133–35.

B. Zevi, *Cronache di architettura*, vol. 24, 1981, pp. 14, 17, chapter 1332.

T. Hine, "Learning From Atlantic City," *AIA-Journal*, November 1982, pp. 44–47. (Interview with Robert Venturi and Steven Izenour.)

T. Hine, "Today's Atlantic City, where character is as much at stake as cash," *Philadelphia Inquirer*, 1982, pp. 1D, 4D.

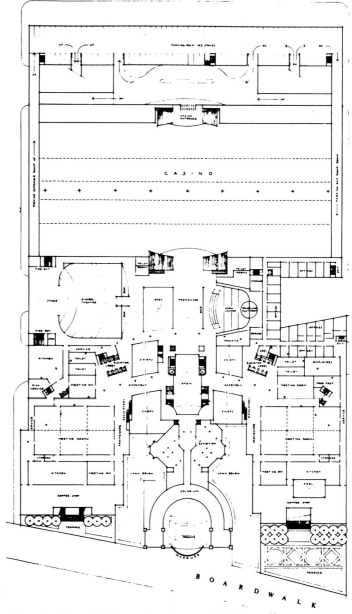

Lower level plan with lobby, casino and congress facilities

▶

Model views of rear side with garage at casino entrance

Facade studies

Lower level plan

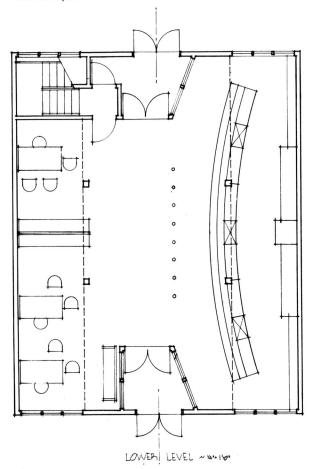

LOWER LEVEL ~ 1/8" = 1'0"

43 County Federal Savings and Loan Association

Transformation of a small workshop house into a bank branch in Westport, Connecticut (1977; not executed)
In charge: Robert Venturi; John Rauch
with Stanford Hughes, Frederic Schwartz

This project involved turning an old mechanics workshop into the branch of a bank. The existing building stands at the fork of two suburban streets lined by numerous commercial buildings, some quite dilapidated. Only the interior of the attractive brick building was to be redone to suit its new function; the exterior was to be cleaned and accentuated by a monumental rooftop in the American colonial style. This rooftop is deliberately "too big" in relation to the house below in order for the logo to be easily legible from a passing car.

Unfortunately, the chairman of the local Fine Arts Commission thought the dome "vulgar," so it was not hard to block the project.

Literature
a+u 1 (1978): 77.
AA (June 1978): 75.
Revision der Moderne, pp. 342–43.

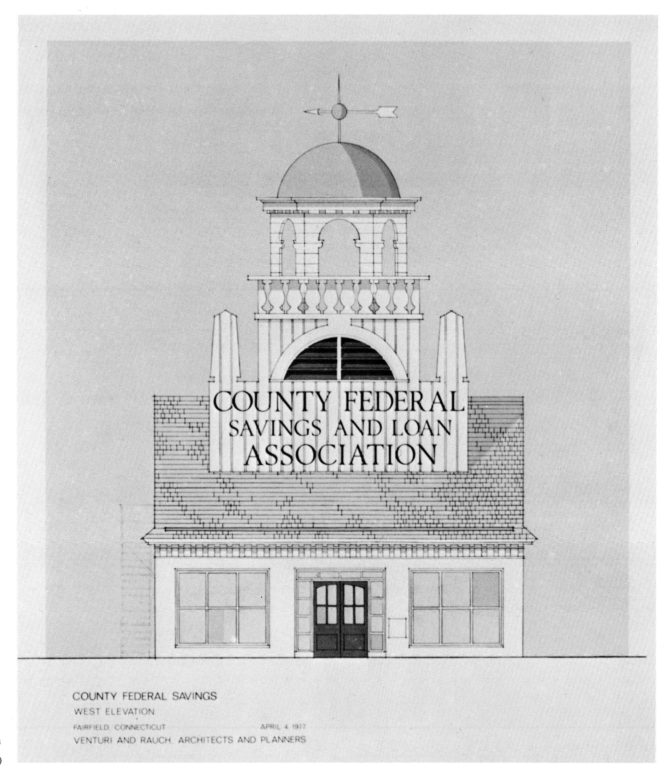

COUNTY FEDERAL SAVINGS
WEST ELEVATION
FAIRFIELD, CONNECTICUT   APRIL 4, 1977
VENTURI AND RAUCH, ARCHITECTS AND PLANNERS

First project with
dome (drawing:
Stanford Hughes)

44   BEST Products Catalog Showroom

Showroom for Household Goods and Furniture in Oxford
Valley, Pennsylvania (1977)
In charge: Robert Venturi
Project Manager: David Vaughan
with Denise Scott Brown, Stanford Hughes, Steven Izenour,
Virginia Jacobs, Robert Renfro

This catalog showroom is located in an area of vast parking
lots and numerous crossroads surrounding a major shopping
mall. Its purpose is to display mail-order household goods
and furniture of the BEST Products Company. The aim was
to create a distinctive identity for a standard steel-frame
structure by giving it a decorative exterior design.

Large abstract red and white flowers were chosen for their
obvious appeal to the viewer, while the random
"wallpaper" effect of the overall pattern in relation to the
panel module and the edges of the building reinforced the
two-dimensional graphic scale of the pattern.[1]

A local reporter described it as "the ugliest shower curtain in
Bucks County."

1   Venturi and Rauch, project description.

Literature
Buildings for Best Products (New York:
The Museum of Modern Art, 1979),
pp. 12, 14, 15. (Catalogue.)

G. McNally, "Best Launches Flower
Showroom Near Philadelphia," *Catalog
Showroom Business*, December 1979,
pp. 47–48.

a+u 12 (1981): 14–17.

View from parking lot

Facade study

View from parking lot

45 ISI Corporation Headquarters

Headquarters of the Institute of Scientific Information,
Philadelphia (1978)
In charge: Robert Venturi; John Rauch
Project Manager: David Vaughan
with Stanford Hughes, Missy Maxwell, Jeffrey D. Ryan,
James H. Timberlake, Amy Weinstein

The client desired a building "that everyone would
recognize as a lively and distinctive contribution to the
community and to the information industry."

The carefully established program mandated a flat square
building, thin strip windows, and the location of core
elements along one side of the building for future
expansion. Thus it left little leeway for architectural
improvisation. The architects state:

> Our design distinguishes the building from its surround-
> ings by imposing on the facade a geometric pattern of
> colored brick and porcelain panels. The tight, rigorously
> coded pattern of the overall facade is relieved by the
> juxtaposition of large abstracted flower forms marking the
> main entrance to the building.[1]

The axial symmetry of the brick pattern and the off-center
location of the building entrance establish, once again, the
Palladio-Aalto dichotomy in the firm's work.

Building seen in context

1 Venturi and Rauch, project description.

Literature

PA, December 1978, p. 36.

J. Quinn, "Computer Chic Enters the
Building Scene Courtesy of Venturi and
Rauch," *PM*, January 1979, pp. 91,
152–53.

G. E. Thomas, A Punchcard with its
Own Music," *The Bulletin*, August 26,
1979, p. D 9.

AA, October 1979, pp. 74–75.

G. E. Thomas, "Enter, Grand—Consider the Door," *The Bulletin*,
November 4, 1979.

E. Garfield, "New Year, New Building,"
Current Comments, January 7, 1980,
pp. 5–8.

E. Constantine, "The Sophisticated
Shed", *Arch. Rec.*, May 1980,
pp. 97–100.

P. Viladas, "Economy that Works,"
Interiors, November 1980, p. 71.

GA Document 1 (1981): 82–83.

Arch. Rec., February 1981, pp. 108–11.

R. T. Sachs, "Large Success From a
Small Budget," *Administrative Management*, March 1981, pp. 26–29, 68.

A. Busch, "The Decorated Surface,"
Metropolis, December 1981, pp. 14–17.

a+u 12 (1981): 56–59.

Vision, August 1983, p. 3.

G. Hargreaves, "Post Modernism Looks
Beyond Itself," *Landscape Architecture*,
July–August 1983, pp. 60–65.

Facade study

View of entrance facade

General view

46   BASCO Showroom

Reconstruction of the "Oxford Valley Mall" in Bristol
Township, Pennsylvania (1979)
In charge: Steven Izenour
with John Chase, Robert Venturi

In an earlier precedent for a smaller BASCO showroom (in
1978 in Concord, Delaware, Project Manager: Robert
Renfro), the architects had already limited their recom-
mendations to a face-lift of the store facade. The company's
logo was placed on the renovated front and sides of the store
where it would be readily legible from a passing car (pl.
below, right).

The BASCO showroom in Bristol Township prompted the
architects to ask:

> What do you do with a building that is 16 feet high and
> 1,100 feet long, with only two doors and no windows? In
> this project for a catalog department store chain, we were
> asked to "beautify" this building, a decrepit, abandoned
> 1950's shopping mall....
>
> The vast space of the parking lot coupled with the
> unrelieved banality of the architecture suggested a design
> of bold communication rather than one of subtle
> expression. Using a fresh manipulation of scale and color,
> we developed the store's logo into evenly spaced, steel
> framed, aluminum sheathed letters, 34 feet high by four
> feet deep and used the building as a contrasting
> "backdrop." These five monumental letters leap out to
> connect the driver to the store. The letters B-A-S-C-O
> have become the architecture of the roadside landscape
> and as a result, a well-known landmark that has served the
> company well.[1]

Interior view ▲   ▼ BASCO hall in Concord, Delaware (1978)

1   Venturi and Rauch, project description.

Literature

T. Hine, "Basco Gives the High Sign,"
The Philadelphia Enquirer, November
6, 1978, p. 1 B.

a+u 12 (1981): 100–101.

A letter, 34 ft. high

47 Khulafa Street Residential and Commercial Building

Project for a residential and commercial building in the center of Baghdad, Iraq (1981)
In collaboration with Ammann & Whitney, Inc., Engineers; Technical Studies Bureau, Architects
In charge: Robert Venturi; John Rauch
Project Manager: David Vaughan
with John Chase, Steven Izenour, Reyhan Larimer, Tim Lisle, James H. Timberlake

The site for this nine-story, six-hundred-foot-long building is envisaged in the heart of Baghdad. On the ground floor and mezzanine, it contains commercial retail space. The other four floors are occupied by offices, above which are three floors of apartments, a small meeting facility, and a day-care center for residents of the building.

The decorative detail of the commercial and residential floors evoke traditional Iraqi ornamentation, whereas the office floors symbolize an "office building." As the architects explain,

The design approach is to adapt the now universal form of the high rise slab, as developed by Le Corbusier, so that its front facade directs space along the avenue in a way which is traditionally urban and so that the *brise-soleil* is a layered element explicitly decorative as well as functional.[1]

1 VRSB, project description.

Literature
Architettura nei paesi islamici (Biennale di Venezia), Venice, 1982, p. 201.

P. Viladas, "Venturi, Rauch and Scott Brown," *PA*, October 1984, pp. 88–93.

"Khulafa Street," *Quaderns*, 162 (1984): 130.

Model view

Facade study

48 "Greenlands" Mixed Use Development

Project for office buildings, a shopping center, and a hotel in Princeton, New Jersey (1985)
In charge: Robert Venturi; John Rauch
Project Manager: John Chase
with Denise Scott Brown, Eric Aukee, Faith Baum, David Fox, Fran Read

The client, the Cavendish Development Company, is currently planning a small shopping center and a first-class hotel on a highway leading to Princeton, New Jersey. The company wanted designs that would meet stringent budget constraints yet relate to both the traditional Gothic architecture of the university and the gracious pedestrian-oriented scale of the campus. Development in phase I consists of two low-rise office buildings.

Perspective view (drawing: Richard C. Meyer)

Model view

49 Jacksonville Office Building

Commercial center with office towers for Jacksonville, Florida (1985)
In charge: Robert Venturi; John Rauch
Project Managers: David Marohn, John Chase
with Denise Scott Brown, Steven Izenour, Robert Marker, Richard Mohler, Willis Pember, Layng Pew, Ivan Saleff

Planned for downtown Jacksonville, the project consists of three office towers connected by an exterior arcaded promenade serving as the focus of the entire project. Shops, restaurants, and clubs open onto it as well. The promenade also gives access to the Jacksonville marketplace, a shopping center currently being developed on the bank of the St. John's River.

237

Jacksonville Office Building, view along the arcade towards waterfront (drawing: Richard Mohler)

Model view with "Jacksonville Marketplace" in the foreground

4 Houses

While it is true that concentrating on individual houses is socially irresponsible and technologically irrelevant, given the continuing housing crisis and the circumstances of practice for the individual architect, the little house should not be scorned. It is still the first job for most architects.[1]

That the little house should not be scorned has been—and continues to be—especially true for VRSB, particularly since the free-standing, single-family house has been the central focus of North American architecture in general from Columbus's days onwards. In the United States, thanks to apparently almost unlimited reserves of land, to the low

a Space and image in the suburbs. From *Learning from Levittown* (1976) (drawing: Robert Miller)

239

b   Manchester-by-the-Sea, Massachusetts: Black House (Kragsyde) (architects: Peabody and Stearn, 1882)

price of crude oil (at least until a few years ago), and to certain probably undeniable advantages of the automobile over public transportation, the sprawling suburb still epitomizes the American way of life. It is the unchallenged symbol of upward social mobility.

Laboratory Experiments

Single-family houses document Robert Venturi's personal Odyssey as an architect better than any other architectural genre. The same had also been true, of course, of Frank Lloyd Wright, Rudolph Schindler, and Richard Neutra earlier in this century. For all these architects, Vincent Scully's observation rings true: "Like lyric poetry, single-family houses most openly mirror the character and feelings of their architects."[2] It is not so important to decide whether these projects should be seen as laboratory experiments whose main purpose is to verify the theories these architects have on the interdependence of form, function, history, and representation or whether these theories are extrapolations of their practical experience as designers. Both viewpoints are correct.

Stylistically, these houses defy summary description, for the principles of Venturian house design and its "transformations of the American vernacular"[3] imply that each project relates to the architectural culture characteristic of the region, while at the same time expressing the architect's more general formal and symbolic preoccupations. The styles range from the skewed geometries of the beach house

 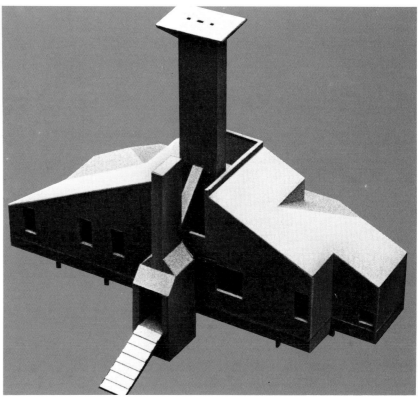

c   Robert Venturi: Beach House, model views (project, 1959)

project (1959; pl. c) to the ironic eclecticism of the Absecon House (1977; pl. d), in which the Colonial iconography of the ordinary American home is transformed into a precarious aesthetic order of interdependent functional and decorative elements. In another instance, Mount Vernon is paraphrased the Venturian way: via Levittown.[4]

From the Classical to the Picturesque Ideal and Back Again

In order to grasp the essential quality of these houses, one must compare them to the work of Charles Moore or Robert Stern, as Vincent Scully has done. The late nineteenth-century American country manor, for which Scully coined the term "Shingle Style,"[5] had a liberating effect on all these architects. The way in which they assimilated the work of Norman Shaw, H. H. Richardson, or McKim, Mead, and White, for example, allows one to distinguish their artistic identities. Venturi represents the "classical" pole within the "New Shingle Style"; Moore and Stern, the picturesque. "Where Venturi forcefully unifies the whole by means of the single symbolic and spatial gesture, Moore's reaction is to multiply, complicate, and confuse it."[6]

Thanks to the severity of its "forcefully unified" image and to its simplicity as an elemental statement of the home (as Kahn described it and as a child would draw it), the Vanna Venturi House in Chestnut Hill (1961; see pp. 244–48) has come to play a role in postmodern architecture that is comparable to that played by Le Corbusier's Villa Savoye in the International Style. Yet in the history of styles, the formal precedents for Venturi's "classical" *dimostrazioni* and some of the models for them are more often Mannerist buildings than neoclassical ones, as suggested by the enigmatic street facade of the Vanna Venturi House. This

241

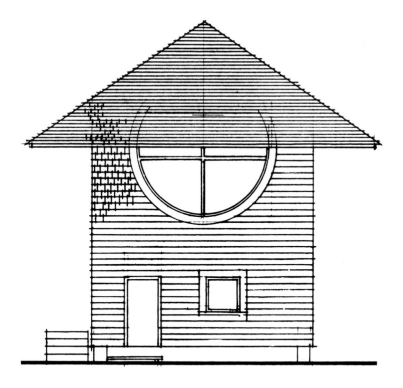

building conforms "to a Mannerist tradition" within the classical aesthetic, as Venturi has put it.[7] In more recent houses, the tensions of his earlier works tend to be resolved in more relaxed and more literally eclectic compositions. While more explicitly "classical" in its details than the Vanna Venturi House, the house in Tuckers Town, Bermuda, even reads, from some angles, as an informal grouping of pavilions in the landscape. Perhaps through the mediation of George Howe, it reintroduces the picturesque ideal.

1 RV and DSB, "Some Houses of Ill-Repute," *Perspecta* 13–14 (1971): 258–67, and LLV, 1st edition.

2 V. Scully, *The Shingle Style Today, or the Historian's Revenge* (New York: Braziller, 1974), p. 2.

3 R. Haag-Bletter, "Transformations of the American Vernacular: The Work of Venturi, Rauch & Scott Brown," in *Venturi, Rauch and Scott Brown: A Generation of Architecture,* exhibition catalogue (Urbana-Champaign: Krannert Art Museum, 1984), pp. 2–19.

4 See RV, "Il Proprio Vocabulario. Four Houses," *Gran Bazaar"* (February 1982): 152–57; reprinted in *AVC*, pp. 101–03.

5 *The Shingle Style and the Stick Style: Architectural Theory and Design from Downing to the Origins of Wright* (New Haven-London: Yale University Press, 1955).

6 Scully, *Shingle Style Today,* p. 29.

7 RV, "Diversity, Relevance, and Representation in Historicism, or *Plus ça change . . . Plus a Plea for Pattern all over Architecture with a Postscript on my Mother's House," *Arch. Rev.,* June 1982, pp. 114–19; reprinted in *AVC*, pp. 108–19.

d   Robert Venturi: Dream House (1974) and House in Absecon, New Jersey (project, 1977)

e Robert Venturi: "A garden
party of styles." Eclectic house
facades (1977)

243

50   Vanna Venturi House

Residence for Robert Venturi's mother in Chestnut Hill, Pennsylvania (1961)
Venturi and Short, Architects
In charge: Robert Venturi
with Arthur Jones

Robert Venturi's book, *Complexity and Contradiction in Architecture*, first published in 1966 but written almost five years earlier, coincided with the design of this house. It is therefore no coincidence that in Venturi's own words this building

> ... recognizes complexities and contradictions: it is both, complex and simple, open and closed, big and little; some of its elements are good on one level and bad on another; its order accommodates the generic elements of the house in general and the circumstantial elements of a house in particular.[1]

Plans and elevations are built on a rigid axial, even Palladian, symmetry, which becomes monumental in the street facade but looser at the extremities and rear of the house, in keeping with the domestic program. The architect stresses that

> The house is big as well as little, by which I mean that it is a little house with big scale.... Outside, the manifestations of big scale are the main elements, which are big and few in number and central or symmetrical in position, as well as the simplicity and consistency of the form and silhouette of the whole.... The main reason for the large scale is to counterbalance the complexity. Complexity in combination with scale in small buildings means busyness. Like the other organized complexities here, the big scale in the small building achieves tension rather than nervousness....[2]

In addition to the immediacy of its unique formal and functional qualities, the house is rich in references to historic architecture. The monumental street facade alludes to Michelangelo's Porta Pia in Rome and the back wall of the Nymphaeum at Palladio and Alessandro Vittoria's Villa Babaro at Maser. On the other hand, the broken pediment recalls the "duality" of the facade of Luigi Moretti's apartment house on the Via Parioli in Rome. Among its American precedents are McKim, Mead, and White's Low

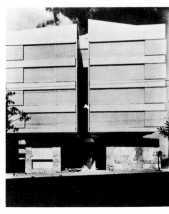

Rome: Porta Pia (architect: Michelangelo, 1561–1565)

Rome: Apartment building Via Parioli (architect: L. Moretti, *ca.* 1952)

Maser: Villa Barbaro, nymphaeum (architect: Alessandro Vittoria, 16th century)

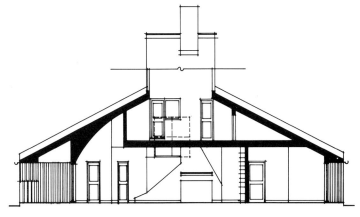

Section

244

Entrance facade

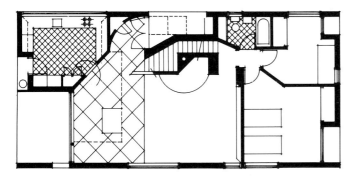

First floor plan

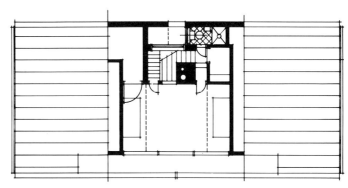

Upper floor plan

Living room

House and Frank Furness's "nowhere stair"[3] in the library
at the University of Pennsylvania (1888–1891). Most of these
buildings are illustrated in *Complexity and Contradiction*.

1 *CCA*, pp. 118–21.
2 *Ibid.*
3 *Ibid.*

 Upper floor studio with "stair to nowhere"

Rear facade ▲ ▼

Site plan

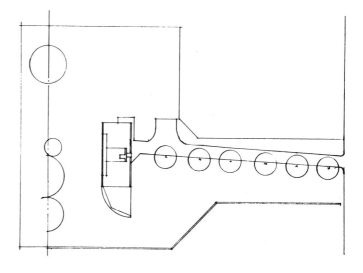

247

Vanna Venturi House, rear facade

Literature

M. Osborn (with R. Giurgola), "A Personal Kind of House," *The Philadelphia Evening Bulletin*, October 15, 1965, p. 55.

J. D. van Trump, "The House Made With Hands: Recent Houses Designed by Pennsylvania Architects," *Charrette. Pennsylvania Journal of Architecture*, November 1965, pp. 10-15.

Perspecta 9-10 (1965): 38-44.

"Venturi House-'Mannerist," *Arch. Rev.*, February 1966, p. 49.

"Are Young Architects Designing Prototypes of Your Future Models?" *American Builder*, October 1966, pp. 60-71.

AA, January 1967, pp. 26.

Y. Futagawa (ed.) *Venturi and Rauch: Vanna Venturi House* (etc.); *Global Architecture*, 39 (Tokyo: A. D. A. Edita, 1976), pp. 9-17.

E. Kaye, "New Kind of Ugly", *Philadelphia Enquirer Magazine*, September 12, 1976, pp. 30-31.

H. Klotz, "Rückblick auf 'My Mother's House,'" in *Jahrbuch für Architektur 1980/81*, ed. H. Klotz (Brunswick-Wiesbaden: Vieweg, 1980), pp. 90-94.

C. Jencks, *Current Architecture* (London: Academy), 1982, pp. 113-15, 200-1.

Revision der Moderne, pp. 325-30.

RV, "Diversity, Relevance and Representation in Historicism, or Plus ça Change ... plus a Plea For Pattern all over Architecture with a Postscript on My Mother's House," *Arch. Rec.*, June 1982, pp. 113-19; reprinted in *AVC*, pp. 116-19.

L. Ensor Stockman, "Originals," *Builder*, August 1984, pp. 82-95.

Rear facade

51   Lieb House

Beach in Loveladies, New Jersey (1967)
In charge: Robert Venturi; John Rauch
Project Manager: Gerod Clark

The Lieb House is, first of all, nothing but an ordinary shed clad in wood-grained asbestos shingles, the conventional building material of beach houses on Long Beach Island. It incorporates large elements, such as the staircase, which starts outdoors and gradually decreases from the width of the house at the base to three feet on the second floor.

The architects say:

Its unconventional elements are explicitly extraordinary when they do occur, as in the big round window that looks like a 1930s radio loudspeaker. It is a little house with big scale, different from the houses around it but also like them. It tries not to make the plaster Madonna in the bird bath next door look silly, and it stands up to, rather than ignores, the environment of utility poles.[1]

1   *LLV*, p. 162.

Literature
PA, April 1970, pp. 106–9.

R. Reif, "A Family Who Built a 'Real Dumb House' in a 'Banal Environment'," *NYT*, August 17, 1970, p. 22 L.

RV and DSB, "Some Houses of Ill-Repute," *Perspecta* 13–14 (1971): 258–67.

Entrance

First floor plan   Upper floor plan   Facade study

General view in context

52 Wike House

Residence in Devon, Pennsylvania (1968)
In charge: Robert Venturi

In their houses of the late 1960s, the architects seemed to mesh themes of the turn-of-the-century English country house with others derived from Le Corbusier's villas. As they put it,

> The program for this family with three small children and a live-in children's nurse was Lutyens-like in scope: a central hall for entertaining, one and one-half stories high, shallowly vaulted and spanning the long way, with a window facing the central exterior stairwell.[1]

The project is doubtless one of the most detailed and extensive house designs completed by the firm before 1970. The house's curved facade is reminiscent of a Vanbrugh manor, while the back recalls the formal language of early Gropius. The bay window is a traditional element of English and American houses that was highly refined by Lutyens. Not by chance, the staircase situated along the center axis reminds one of the ramp in Le Corbusier's Villa Savoye, though it also alludes to the obstacle course between the front door and the ceremonial rooms in some of Lutyens's houses. Behind the severe "public" main facade and the symmetrical reception spaces, the visitor discovers a much looser and more functional arrangement of rooms. Here again, the solution is reminiscent of the Villa Savoye with its rigid perimeter geometries and functional interior organization (see pl. p. 39).

1 *LLV*, pp. 167–68.

Literature

RV and DSB, "Some Houses of Ill-Repute," *Perspecta* 13–14 (1971): 259–67, reprinted in *AVC*, pp. 38–44.

S. von Moos and M. Weinberg-Staber, *Venturi und Rauch. Architektur im Alltag Amerikas* (exhibition catalogue), Zurich 1979, pp. 73, 102–3.

M. T. Munoz, "Sobre el Realismo en Arquitectura," *Arquitecturos*, March 1983, pp. 15–18.

RV, "Learning the Right Lessons from the Beaux-Arts," *AD* 1, (1979): 23–31, reprinted in *AVC*, pp. 70–95.

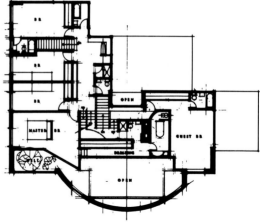

Top floor plan

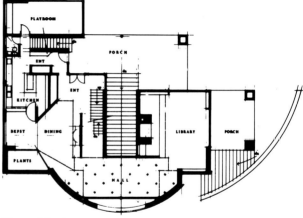

Piano nobile plan

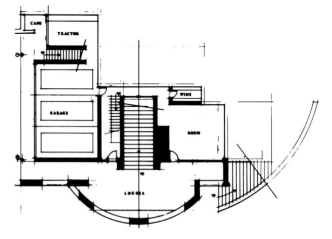

First floor plan

Model views

253

Model view

53   D'Agostino House

Project for a country house in Clinton, New York (1968; not excecuted)
In charge: Robert Venturi; John Rauch
Project Manager: W. G. Clark

In this generously-scaled house, the ground floor is raised half a story in order to make the most of the splendid view. The stepped gable of the main facade evokes images of Holland. The design of the driveway entrance had special importance: because of the cold winters, the client wanted to be able to leave the car and enter the house under shelter. The architects' note:

Instead of entering through a shabby garage and the back door of a kitchen, one enters the house through a magnificent garage (white and black glazed brick) and from there reaches the *piano nobile* over a splendid flight of stairs, like the approach of a Neapolitan villa of the eighteenth century.[1]

1   *LLV*, pp. 165–66.

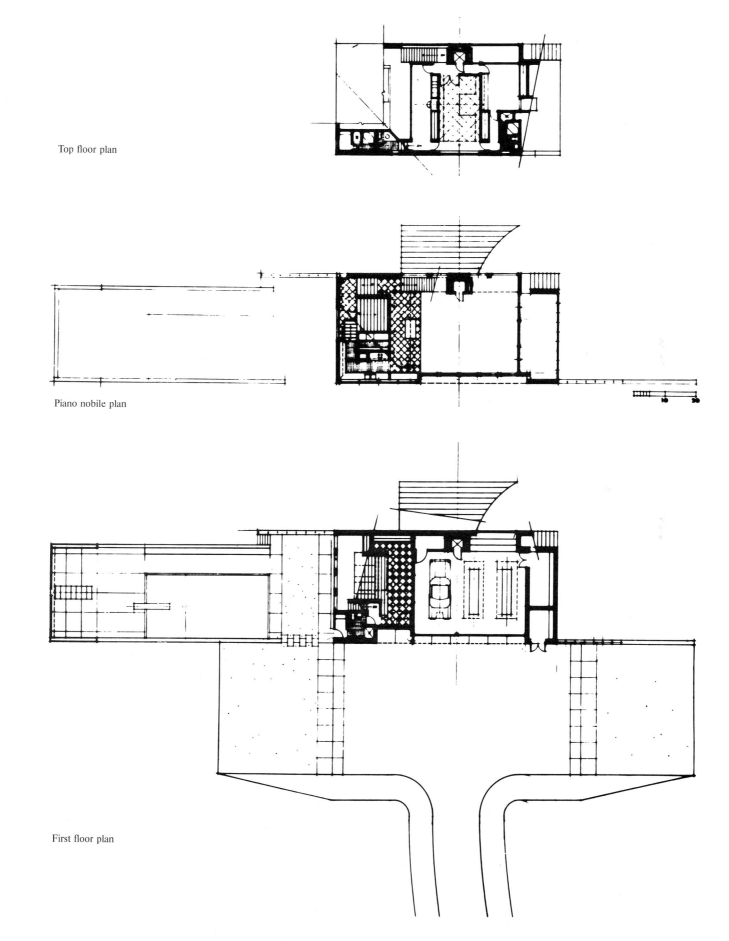

Top floor plan

Piano nobile plan

First floor plan

54 Trubek and Wislocki Houses

Summer houses on Nantucket Island, Massachusetts (1970)
In charge: Robert Venturi; John Rauch
Project Manager: Terry Vaughan

Portions of Nantucket Island are almost an open-air museum of eighteenth- and nineteenth-century America in a well-preserved New England landscape. New building must conform to strict codes based upon the traditional New England saltbox. Shingling and pitched roofs are prescribed.

For the architects, this restriction was a challenge. Although there was no question of simply reproducing a traditional type, they used the nineteenth-century Wanwimmet fisherman's cottage as a framework for articulating the complex functional relationships within the houses.

Linking vernacular traditions with the more complex requirements of suburban life-styles had been the preoccupation of late nineteenth-century architects. The "Shingle Style" country houses of McKim, Mead, and White; Henry Hobson Richardson; Peabody and Stearns, etc., as well as Frank Lloyd Wright's early houses, all embody an idealized recollection of the early American paradise.[1] The two small houses on Nantucket owe as much to this tradition as to the local vernacular. In their siting they refer to the two temples of Selinunte (Temple E and Temple F), which stand at an angle to each other, facing the sea.

The axially symmetrical entrance facade of the larger house is dominated by an arched window in an almost classical manner. Within its limited space and rigid perimeter, the facade registers a variety of functions. The southwest corner is cut obliquely to follow the form of the stairs. On the western facade, an oversized window affords a view into the interlocking spaces of the interior (see pl. p. 258).

In discussing the two houses, the architects refer to the larger one as "complex and contradictory" and the smaller one as "ugly and ordinary."

1 V. Scully, *The Shingle Style and the Stick Style*, (New Haven-London: Yale University Press, 1955, 1971).

Short Hills, New Jersey: Casino (architects: McKim, Mead, and White, 1882–1883)

York Harbor, Maine: "Redcote" (architect: William H. Dabney, Jr., 1882)

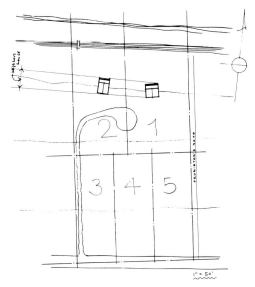

Site plan

General view

Wislocki House: plans

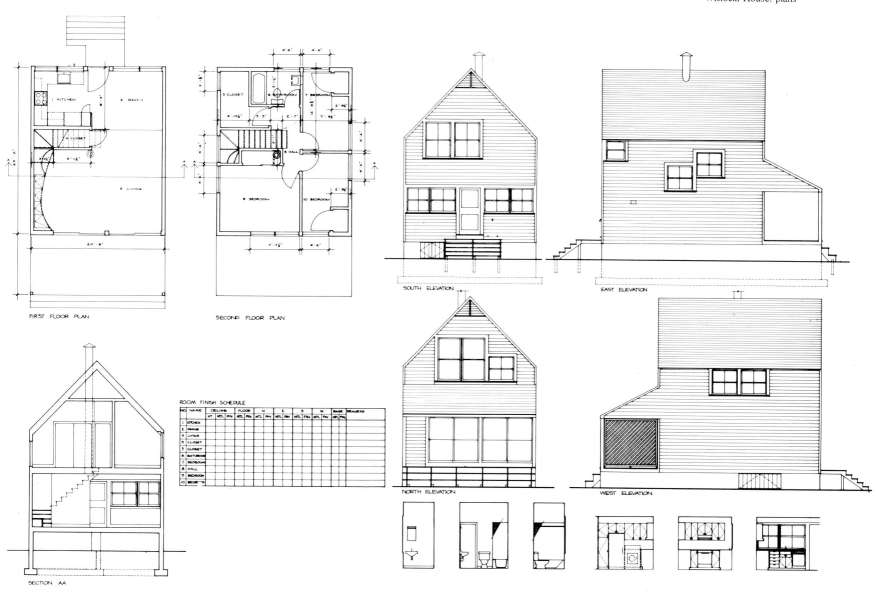

FIRST FLOOR PLAN

SECOND FLOOR PLAN

SOUTH ELEVATION

EAST ELEVATION

SECTION AA

NORTH ELEVATION

WEST ELEVATION

ROOM FINISH SCHEDULE

Literature

RV, DSB, "Some Houses of Ill-Repute," *Perspecta* 13–14 (1971): pp. 259–67.

LLV, pp. 169–71.

AA, January 1972, pp. 92–93.

Second Home, Spring-Summer 1974, pp. 68–71.

V. Scully, *The Shingle Style Today* (New York: Braziller, 1974), pp. 34 and *passim*.

P. Goldberger, "Siblings by the Seaside," *NYT Magazine*, May 21, 1978, p. 73.

H. Klotz, "Zurück zur Fassade," in *Gestaltung einer neuen Umwelt. Kritische Essays zur Architektur der Gegenwart* (Lucerne–Frankfurt a. M.: C. J. Bucher, 1978), pp. 95–102.

P. Goldberger, "Nantucket Gropes for Architectural Future," *NYT*, August 20, 1979.

Trubek House: view from stairs towards the living room

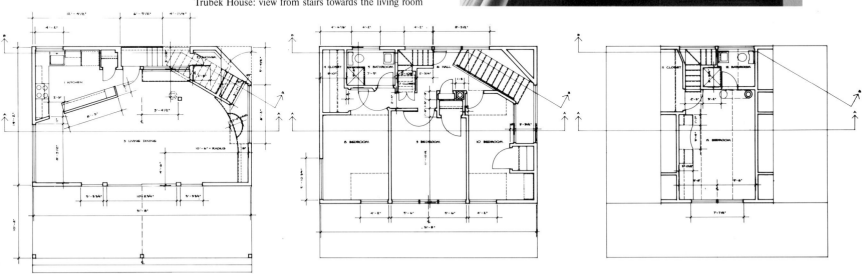

FIRST FLOOR PLAN

SECOND FLOOR PLAN

THIRD FLOOR PLAN

Trubek House: plans

Trubek House (left) and Wislocki House (right)

Trubek House: elevation and sections

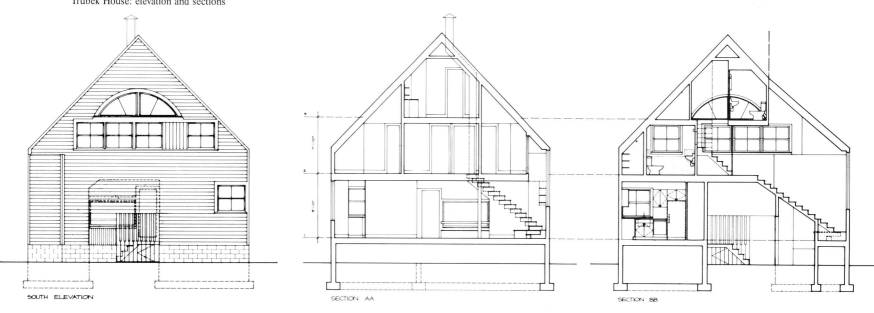

SOUTH ELEVATION

SECTION AA

SECTION BB

259

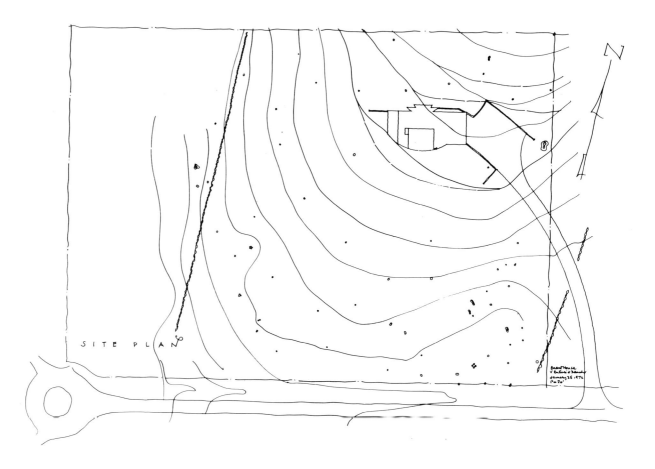

Site plan

55   House in Connecticut

House in Greenwich, Connecticut (1970)
In charge: Robert Venturi; John Rauch
Project Managers: Gerod Clark, Arthur Jones
with Denise Scott Brown, W.G. Clark, James Greifendorf,
Paul Hirshorn, Anthony Pellecchia

In this meticulously designed building, the architects further developed themes that had been initially formulated in the unrealized Wike House (see pp. 252f.). Here again, the symmetrical and curved main facade is at odds with the Aaltoesque circulation system and some of the spaces.

The house is situated on a gentle slope. The patterned facade of green glazed brick (see p. 43) recalls the owners' Art Déco art and furniture collection or, perhaps, the aging modernity of doctors' offices in American TV movies of the 1950s. The axial "Palladian" window that is not an entrance lights the kitchen, the home maker's center of gravity in an American suburban house.

The main entrance is from the sunken driveway and car garage. One reaches the bright living room via a wide staircase inside the house. In the central gallery room, paintings (primarily American Pop Art) and Art Déco furniture are displayed. On its north side is a proscenium-like dining niche. A loose sequence of rooms—library, kitchen, and a playroom—faces south. On the upper floors are the bedrooms.

In 1978 the architects planned a substantial extension to this house. Unlike the original building, with its difficult combination of Aalto and Déco, the addition follows the more classical precedent of an English manor house built about 1800.

General view

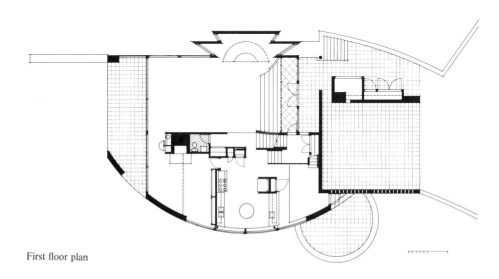

First floor plan

First floor play area

View from living room towards the entrance and stairway leading to upper floor

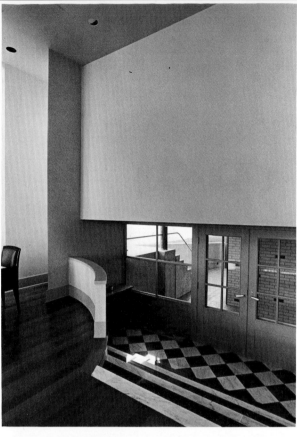

Literature

LLV, pp. 172–73.

P. Goldberger, "Tract House, Celebrated," *NYT Magazine*, September 14, 1975, pp. 68–69.

Y. Futagawa (ed.), *Venturi and Rauch: Vanna Venturi House* (etc.) *Global Architecture*, 39 (Tokyo: A. D. A. Edita, 1976), pp. 18–31.

C. Robinson, "Brant Conflict," *Arch. Rev.*, June 1976, pp. 360–64.

D. Morton, "Venturi and Rauch, Brant House, Greenwich, Conn.," *PA*, August 1976, pp. 50–53.

C. Vogel, "Architecture: Robert Venturi," *Architectural Digest*, October 1980, pp. 88–95.

a+u 12 (1981): 114–21.

Y. Futagawa (ed.), *Modern Houses, Global Architecture Book* vol. 3 (Tokyo: A. D. A. Edita, 1981).

C. Jencks, *Current Architecture* (London: Academy, 1982), pp. 114–15.

Revision der Moderne, pp. 334–35.

RV, "Il Proprio Vocabolario. Four Houses," *Gran Bazaar*, Jan.-Feb. 1982, pp. 152–57; reprinted in *AVC*, pp. 96–103.

Living room: view towards the entrance (top) and veranda (below)

East facade with garages

Model views with planned addition (1978, not built)

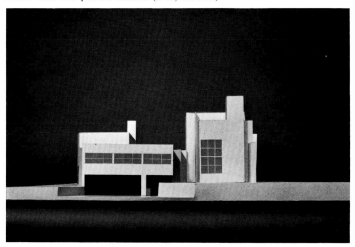

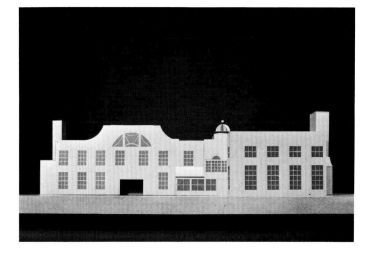

56   House in Westchester County

Residence in Westchester County, New York (1974)
In charge: Robert Venturi
Project Manager: Douglas Southworth

The house stands in a small wood. The sections seem to show a gabled roof but in reality, the roof is a steep pyramid that projects far over the facade on all sides of the house. The high living room is located in the middle of the house; a gallerylike library under the pyramid looks down into the living room.

The windows of the main facade, all of different sizes, are dominated by a big bull's eye that breaks boldly through the interior spaces and into the roof volume to light the library.

Facade

Literature

Y. Futagawa (ed.), *Venturi and Rauch: Vanna Venturi House* (etc.), *Global Architecture* (Tokyo: A. D. A. Edita, 1976), pp. 32–40.

J. M. Dixon, "Country Manners," *PA* 10 (1977): 64–66.

C. Jencks, *The Language of Post-Modern Architecture*, (London, 1977), pp. 70–71.

a+u 1 (1978): 32–36.

P. Goldberger, "Architecture: Venturi and Rauch," *Architectural Digest*, Jan.–Feb. 1978, pp. 100–7.

P. Goldberger, "Ten Buildings with a Style of Their Own," *Portfolio*, June–July 1979, pp. 32–39.

AD (May–June 1980): 30–32.

a+u 12 (1981): 70–75.

Y. Futagawa (ed.), *Modern Houses. Global Architecture Books*, vol. 3 (Tokyo: A. D. A. Edita, 1981), pp. 122–23.

J. Muntanola, *Poetica y arquitectura* (Barcelona: Editorial Anagrama, 1981), pp. 80–89.

D. Mackay, "Carl Tucker House," *The Modern House*, (Barcelona: Editorial Gustavo Gili, 1984), pp. 154–57.

Moderne und Postmoderne, pp. 171–72.

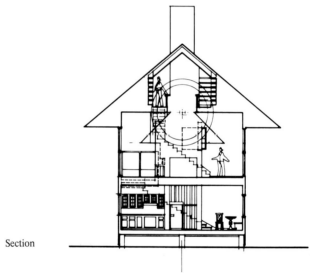
Section

Entrance

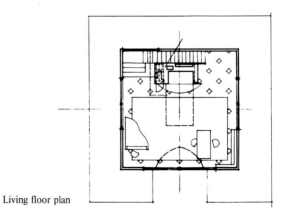
Living floor plan

Living room with "oculus"

57 House in Tuckers Town

Summer residence in Tuckers Town, Bermuda (1975)
In collaboration with Onions, Bouchard, and McCulloch, Architects
In charge: Robert Venturi; John Rauch
Project Manager: John Chase

This summer residence located in Bermuda on a sea bluff follows strict regulations regarding style and materials. The architects tried to accommodate these regulations and yet to achieve a free grouping of spaces.

The program fell into three loosely linked parts. Of the two flanking wings, one provides communal rooms, the others contain the kitchen, breakfast room, and servants' quarters. The one in the middle is built around a central staircase and contains several living rooms and bedrooms. From the entrance hall, one view straight out through the porch meets the horizon; another follows the line of the stairs downward and continues out to the shore. The result is a refined spatial relationship to the spectacular landscape,

similar to that of the staircase in the High Hollow country house in Chestnut Hill, Pennsylvania, by George Howe (1914–1916).[1]

The facades facing the entrance court are relatively closed; those facing the sea are open and colonnaded.

1 See Robert A. M. Stern and George Howe, *Toward a Modern American Architecture*, (New Haven and London: Yale University Press, 1975), figs. 3–9.

Literature

AA 197: 54–57.

AD (May–June 1980): 33–34.

C. Jencks (ed.), *Post-Modern Classicism—The New Synthesis: AD-Profile* (London, 1980), pp. 337.

C. Vogel, "Architecture: Robert Venturi," *Arch. Digest*, October 1980, pp. 88–95.

R. L. Miller, "Designs for Living," *TWA Ambassador*, April 1981, pp. 39–41.

C. K. Gandee, "Record Houses 1981—Private House, Bermuda," *Arch. Rec.*, May 1981, pp. 57–61.

M. Morris, "Beached in Bermuda," *Diversion*, December 1981, pp. 219–22.

P. Goldberger, "Collecting On A Grand Scale," *NYT Magazine*, Part 2, 1981, pp. 49–105 and *passim*.

a+u 12 (1981): 122–29.

C. Jencks, "Venturi, Rauch and Scott Brown," *AD* (January–February 1982): 68–71.

AD (January–February 1982): 14–102, especially pp. 68–71.

RV, "Il Proprio Vocabolario," *Gran Bazaar*, February 1982, pp. 152–57.

C. Jencks, *Current Architecture* (London, 1982), pp. 115–16.

Revision der Moderne, pp. 334–35, 338.

Site plan

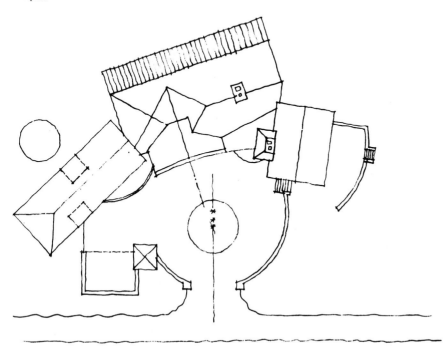

Chestnut Hill, Pennsylvania: Country home High Hollow, entrance hall with view towards the garden (architect: George Howe, 1914–1916)

Entrance

Bedroom

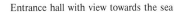

Entrance hall with view towards the sea

Entrance hall with view towards the bedroom area

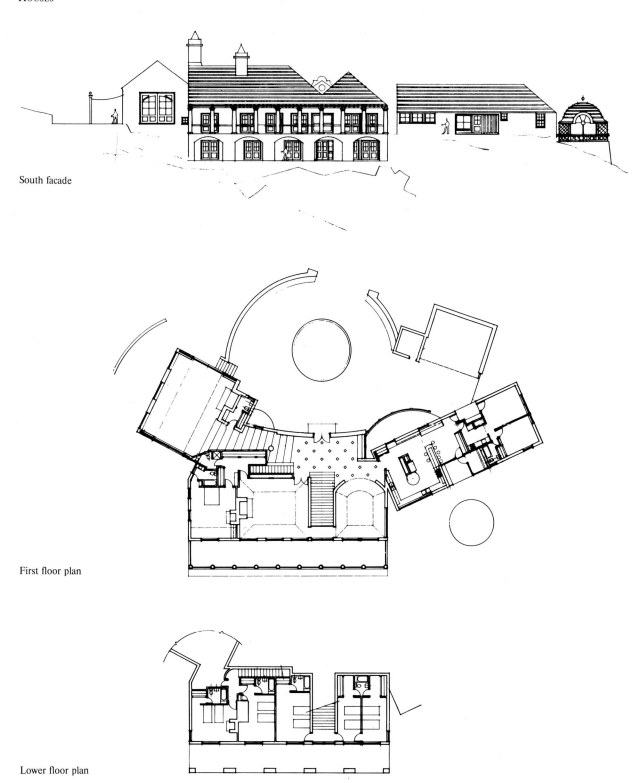

South facade

First floor plan

Lower floor plan

West view

58   House in Vail

Vacation House in Vail, Colorado (1975)
In charge: Robert Venturi; John Rauch
In collaboration with William J. Ruoff, Architect
Project Manager: Robert Renfro
with Elizabeth Plater-Zyberk, Douglas Southworth

This ski lodge, a variation on both the witch's house in Hansel and Gretel and on the severity of a Polish synagogue or a Scandinavian "Stabkirche,"[1] is situated in one of the most beautiful ski areas in the United States. It was planned for a family with two children but also had to accommodate many weekend guests. The ground floor contains storage rooms, the laundry room, and a sauna; the floor above has bedrooms; and on the third floor there is a kitchen, dining and living rooms, as well as guest rooms.

The fourth floor is comparable to a monumental attic story with arched dormers and a chimney. Although the house is relatively small, these elements give it a large scale.

The extremely luxurious interior decoration brings together elements of the arts-and-crafts tradition with the richly decorative style of country houses by Henry Hobson Richardson.

1   Oral communication by DSB

Literature

Architectural Monographs 1 (1977): 95–102.

D. Gebhard and D. Nevins, *200 Years of American Architectural Drawing*, New York (Architectural League and American Federation of Arts, 1977), p. 290.

D. Morton, "Mission accomplished," *PA* 10 (1977): 60–63.

a+u 1 (1978): 21–30.

RV, *Global Architecture Houses*, vol. 3, December 1977, pp. 160–67.

a+u 1 (1978): 21–30.

"Forceful Gesture on a Wooded Hillside," *AIA Journal*, May 1978, pp. 102–5.

L. Kallmeyer, "Funktionalismus und Widerspruch," *Problemfeld Architektur*, March 1979, pp. 113–22.

"Gute Nachbarn," *Der Spiegel*, March 23, 1980, pp. 248–54.

J. Coote, "Eight For the Eighties," *Texas Architect*, July–August 1980, pp. 67–78.

P. Camesano, "Post Modern Architecture—Is It for You?" *Building Manual*, Winter 1980, pp. 54–55, 166–67.

J. Rubin and C. Rubin, *Mission Furniture* (San Francisco, California: Chronicle Books, 1980), p. 29, front and back covers.

AA, February 1981, pp. 46–48.

P. Camesano, "Handcrafted Houses," *Building Manual*, Summer 1981, pp. 94–98.

a+u 12 (1981): 94–97.

P. Goldberger, "Collecting on a Grand Scale," *NYT Magazine*, Part 2, 1981, pp. 49–105, and *passim*.

Revision der Moderne, pp. 334–37.

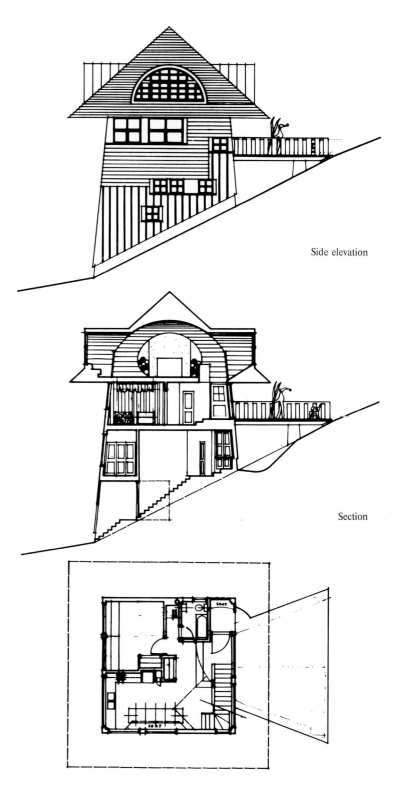

Side elevation

Section

Entrance floor plan

General view

59 Coxe-Hayden Studio Houses

Summer house with studio on Block Island near Rhode Island (1979)
In charge: Robert Venturi; John Rauch
Project Manager: Frederic Schwartz

The site lies next to a saltwater pond on Block Island. The larger of the two buildings contains living, dining, and bedrooms, as well as a writing studio in the attic; the smaller building has a garage-workshop below with two guest rooms and a bath above.

Concerning the design, the architects state:

The stylistic source is the countrified Classic Revival bungalow typical of many 19th century buildings on Block Island. Unlike the New England salt box tradition of small windows, asymmetrical gables, and small scale details, this style had a "Temple" front with symmetrical entrance, a simple profile and over-scaled overhangs, windows, batterboards and a trim.[1]

1 VRSB, project description.

Literature

Charles K. Gandee, "The Coxe Studio, Block Island, R. I.," *Arch. Rec.*, May 1982, pp. 54–55.

S. Stephens, "The Historicist Vision: The Shingle Genre," *Skyline*, July 1982, pp. 18–19.

P. Goldberger, "Architecture That Is Bred to the Sea," *NYT*, August 22, 1982, pp. 62–64.

"La doppia riflessione," *Gran Bazaar*, November 1982, pp. 150–55, 200.

T. Hine, "Awards Reflect a Rare Period of Pluralism," *The Philadelphia Inquirer*, May 8, 1983, p. 14H.

S. Grant Lewin, "An Old Tradition Reborn," *House Beautiful*, May 1983, pp. 112–17.

"In Architecture, Too, Anything Goes," *U. S. News & World Report*, August 1, 1983, p. 58.

Facade towards the lake

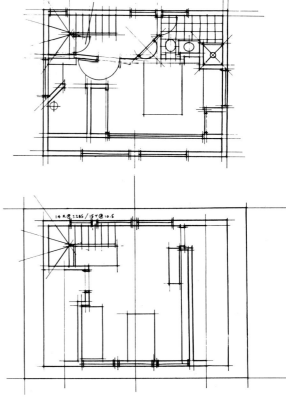

Plans

General view with guesthouse

Living room

Bedroom

60   House in Northern Delaware

Residence in Northern Delaware (1978)
In charge: Robert Venturi
Project Manager: John Chase

The building's overall form is derived from the area's traditional eighteenth-century country houses, which, with their ample scale and solid proportions, are almost Palladian in character. Yet, while it is in some respects formal and even monumental, it provides for the easy and unpretentious living style that the clients envisioned.

The program in itself was unusual, as the architects wrote:

The wife is a musician—a performer who required a music room containing an organ, two pianos, and a harpsichord that must also be appropriate for small gatherings. Another interest of the family is birdwatching so the big windows facing the woods especially in the breakfast area were important. The husband needed a study in a remote part of the house, and a suite of rooms was required for the son....

The music room is a high space with a latticed groin vault with Carpenter-Gothic proportions. This room also dominates the front and rear elevations of the house by its central location, but its big pediments, front and back, do not intrude on the silhouette of the whole of the house. Over the front pediment is an ornamental screen. Reminiscent of a Baroque lunette in Salzburg.[1]

West view

East view with "blind" in front of music room

1   VRSB, project description

Literature

AA, December 1978, pp. 96–9.

PA, January 1980, pp. 104–5.

R. Pain, "Venturi and Rauch, House in Delaware: Vernacular Layering. A Thematic Analysis," *International Architect* 2 (1982): 7–18.

P. Portoghesi, "Com'è vera quest'illusione," *Europeo*, June 22, 1983, p. 103.

Global Architecture Houses, February 17, 1985, pp. 48–59.

V. Scully, "Architecture: Venturi, Rauch and Scott Brown," *Architectural Digest*, March 1985, pp. 184–91, 236, 243.

M. J. Crosby, "Friendly House, Full of Surprises," *Architecture*, May 1985, pp. 226–33.

General view

Site plan

Section

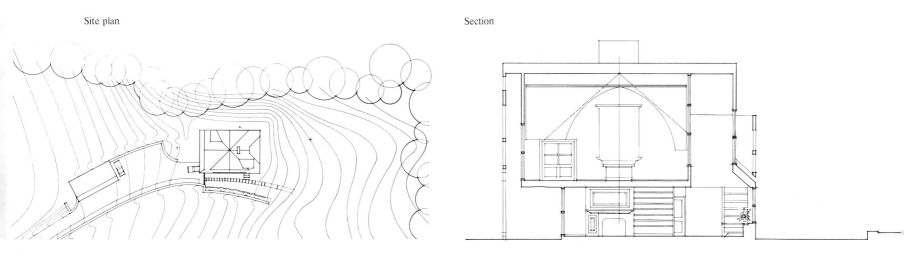

House in Northern Delaware,
music room

5   Housing

In countries like Holland, Germany, or the Soviet Union, the history of modern architecture between the two world wars unfolded largely within the context of public housing financed in part by cooperatives or the state itself. The United States, too, experienced a housing shortage at that time, but, as in France, neither the labor unions nor the government was prepared to undertake or coordinate such projects. Housing, though often federally subsidized, generally remained a matter for the private sector.

Even under the New Deal, the opportunities for organizations such as labor unions to become actively involved in public housing were limited. The astounding Mackley Houses in Philadelphia (1933–1935; pl. a), conceived by Kastner and Stonorov as a prototype of a modern American housing development for workers, were an exception to the rule.[1]

Urban Renewal

After World War II the situation changed, at least superficially. Partly because of pressure brought to bear by the federal government and its housing policies, the maxims of the "functional city" proclaimed by the CIAM, especially in the Athens Charter (1933), were belatedly accepted by the planning agencies of the large cities in the Northeast and Midwest (see p. 79). However, for the inhabitants of areas affected by urban redevelopment, "urban renewal" usually meant "urban removal." Under American capitalism social utopian thought and social idealism seemed to have turned into a menace for those for whom the quality of life needed to be improved most urgently: the urban poor.[2]

a   Philadelphia: Mackley Houses (architects: Kastner and Stonorov, 1933–1935)

279

Learning from Levittown

The thesis project by Denise Scott Brown and Brian Smith (1954), submitted to the Architectural Association, still contained a kind of megastructure composed of long rows of U-shaped housing units in a scheme reminiscent of Ludwig Hilberseimer (pl. b). Even before moving to the United States (1958), Scott Brown became interested in social housing, urban sociology, and the social, economic, and cultural background of the American "melting pot," which seemed completely impervious to all-encompassing urban utopias.[3] *Learning from Levittown*—the title itself recalls Herbert Gans's well-known book, *The Levittowners* (1966)—was one result of these studies. The call to learn to live with the often unfortunate results of urban renewal, to humanize rather than to ignore them, was another.[4]

It is not surprising, therefore, that the apartment buildings and housing planned and built by VRSB since 1962 have no utopian pretensions. Not only are their underlying programs conventional (student dormitories, a home for senior citizens, and a public housing project; see pp. 287, 282–86, 293 f.), their entirely unheroic nature—their "ordinariness"—is raised to an aesthetic, as demonstrated by the 1961 Guild House and, more recently, by housing built in Philadelphia's Chinatown in 1982 (pl. p. 293) that wonderfully succeeds in recapturing some of the simple dignity of anonymous eighteenth-century town houses.

1 P. Santostefano, *Le Mackley Houses di Kastner e Stonorov a Philadelphia* (Rome: Officina, 1982).

2 See pp. 77–82.

3 DSB, "A Worm's Eye View of Recent Architectural History," *Arch. Rec.,* February 1984, pp. 69–81.

4 DSB and RV, "CO-OP City: Learning to Like It," *PA*, February 1970, pp. 64–73.

HOUSING A 2500 PEOPLE

MAERDY

RHONDDA FACH

ARCHITECTURAL ASSOCIATION
SCHOOL OF ARCHITECTURE
FIFTH YEAR 1953–54

b Denise Scott Brown and Brian Smith: Housing for a Welsh mining town. Thesis project at the Architectural Association in London (1954)

LEVITTOWN

Common functional alterations made to Levittown houses are conversions of garages and attics to living spaces. Most other alterations are decorative and consist of the addition of masonry or siding facades or the applique of house and yard ornaments bought in stores. The fact that residents' alterations in general reinforce the styling of the house as acquired suggests that many Levittowners are basically happy with their houses despite what the critics say.

COLONIAL
'Twin Oaks' area

JUBILEE
'Kenwood' area

LEVITTOWNER
'Stonybrook' area

RANCHER
'Red Cedar' area

COUNTRY CLUBBER
'Forsythia Gate' area

On the twentieth anniversary of Levittown, Pa., a booklet was published by the Chamber of Commerce. One of the first residents was interviewed: "It was a never-to-be-forgotten experience. The advertisements were impressive and enticing. For only $100 down payment we could buy our own home in a fully planned community, with every modern convenience. The cost per month was less than that of the average city row house. They had much to offer the city dweller. The models were completely modern, with radiant heat, electric stoves, automatic washers, tiled baths with showers, carports or garages. Some even had refrigerators. The grounds were to be landscaped and would include fruit trees. The streets were to be tree-lined. The houses were far enough apart to suit the homeowner and yet close enough for companionship with neighbors. No wonder the sample homes were crowded. In the Falls Township sections, there were at first only two basic models available, the Levittowner and the Rancher. Later the Jubilee was added. A salesman advised us just which sections were available, and we then made application for the style we wanted in a specific section. After the application was accepted, notice was sent to us making an appointment to select the house of our choice. At the appointed time we were shown the plan of the section plots. This section plan, on paper, showed the entire section including the style house which was to be built on each lot. As for the land itself, in some instances the sections were still woods, or farmland. Sometimes it was possible in the Jubilee sections to see the actual plot, and so be able to choose more intelligently. But we were expected to decide and we did, from a paper plan and within minutes, where we would perhaps spend the rest of our lives. We know of one case where four couples chose their future homes in less than ten minutes, on paper too."

c A page from *Learning from Levittown*

61   Guild House

Home for senior citizens on Spring Garden Street,
Philadelphia (1961)
In collaboration with Cope and Lippincott, Architects
In charge: Robert Venturi
Project Manager: Gerod Clark
with Frank Kawasaki

The client, a Quaker community led by Francis Bosworth,
required a residence with ninety-one apartments of varying
size and a community room for its elderly members. The
building code limited the height to six stories. It was
important to relate the residence to the area, with which the
tenants would be familiar. In their design the architects also
tried to avoid overwhelming the modest housing to the
north.

Most of the apartments face Spring Garden Street to the
south, an orientation that enables the residents to participate
visually in the street life. The design also distinguishes
between the "ceremonial" front entry facade and the less
formal rear facade, which relates more to the neighboring
apartment houses.

The architects cite the small budget in explaining their
use of a conventional structure. Certain elements, however,
seem to subvert the ordinary character of the architecture.
Square double hung windows for example, recall the formal
language of public housing; they are, therefore, "ordinary."
At the same time some of these windows are "normal," some
unusually large, depending on their relation to the street.
A massive, polished granite column in the middle of the
entry portal contrasts with the white ceramic tile cladding.
This element and the out-scaled "Guild House" sign affixed
to the first-floor balcony clearly mark the entrance.

Originally, the middle of the entrance facade was topped
by a golden replica of a TV antenna, a friendly, if
embarrassingly literal, symbol of elderly people's leisure
activity and an ironic variation on the decoration of
classical pediments (see pp. 57 f.). The top floor contains the
social room, indicated by a large lunette window.

Thanks in part to extensive treatment in the Venturis'
books, this building has become emblematic of an
architectural philosophy that tries both to embrace the
conventions of the classical tradition and to be "ugly and
ordinary" (see pp. 62 f.).

Facade studies (version 3, built)

Frontal view

Literature

Perspecta 9–10 (1965): 45.

CCA, pp. 114–17.

PA, May 1967, pp. 133–37.

Lotus 4 (1967–68): 98–105.

V. Scully, *American Architecture and Urbanism* (New York: Praeger, 1969) (1977 ed.), p. 236.

New Directions, pp. 56–57.

LLV, pp. 65–73.

S. Cohen, "Physical Context/Cultural Context: Including It All," *Oppositions* 2 (January 1974): 2–39.

M. Filler, "Learning from Venturi," *Art in America*. April 1980, pp. 95–101.

T. Wolfe, *From Bauhaus to Our House* (New York: Farrar, Straus & Giroux, 1981), pp. 103–15.

Moderne und Postmoderne, pp. 152–56.

Revision der Moderne, pp. 322–24.

S. von Moos, "Rund um die Fernseh-antenne des Guild House. Anmerkungen zum Thema Architektur, Zeichensprache und Massenkultur," in Thomas Bolt and others (eds.), *Grenzbereiche der Architektur* (Basle, Boston, and Stuttgart: Birkhäuser, 1985), pp. 221–41.

(For additional references see above, "Anatomy of a Decorated Shed", pp. 28–31, 71; notes 36–46.)

Frontal view

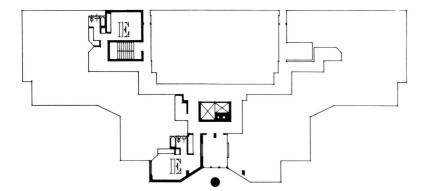

First floor plan

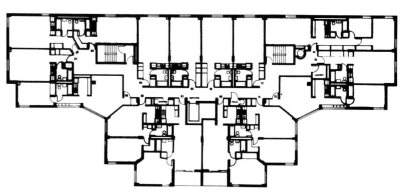

Typical floor plan

Common room
View towards Spring Garden Street

Wall decoration next to the entrance

Side facade, detail

62   Hun School Dormitory

Student dormitory in Princeton, New Jersey (1962)
Venturi and Short, Architects
In charge: Robert Venturi
with Mark Gurin, Arthur Jones, John Rauch

The program called for student housing with the necessary joint facilities like kitchens, showers, and clubrooms. Instead of using the heroic, original, or expressive language of American campus buildings popular at that time, the architects chose intentionally "ordinary" architecture consistent with the rather unspectacular nature of the commission and derived from Scandinavian or English "New Empiricism."

Literature
werk-archithese 7–8 (1977): 15.

General view

West elevation

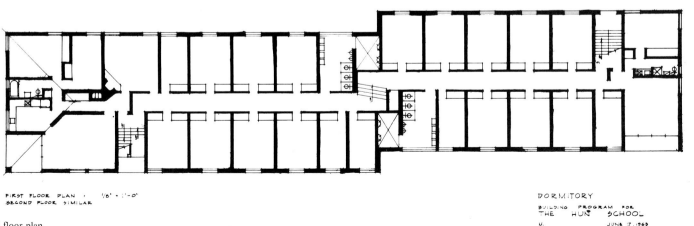

First floor plan

Model view

63 Brighton Beach Housing Competition

Competition for housing in Brooklyn, New York (1967)
In charge: Robert Venturi
Project Manager: Gerod Clark
with Denise Scott Brown, Frank Kawasaki

As with their Guild House project, the architects found that an "ugly and ordinary" formal language would be more appropriate here than a "heroic and original" one. In its details, the project keeps to the conventions of the International Style; the nature of the plans, the differentiated set-back of the facades, and the silhouettes of the roofs recall Aalto.

As two excerpts from the jury's comments show, the renunciation of the decorated modern architecture of that time provoked lively discussion. Philip Johnson, a member of the jury, wrote later:

> To the majority, of which I was one, [the Venturi and Rauch-Kawasaki submission] seemed a pair of very ugly buildings. We felt … that the buildings looked like the most ordinary apartment construction built all over Queens and Brooklyn since the Depression, that the placing of the blocks was ordinary and dull.[1]

By contrast, Donlyn Lyndon wrote:

> 1. The [Venturi and Rauch-Kawasaki] scheme has a modesty that is appropriate to the scale and location of the project.
>
> 2. The scheme does not detract from or demean the surrounding neighborhood.
>
> 3. In our view it offers real benefits for the people who might occupy it rather than polemic satisfaction to those who consider it.
>
> 4. The method of building is intrinsically so simple that it could be built well, not meanly. We think this would contribute to the personal dignity of its occupants.
>
> 5. We think that it in no way represents "more of the same," but is instead a thoughtful use of existing possibilities.[2]

1 *LLV*, pp. 134–37.
2 *Ibid.*

Literature

M. Osborn, "Dilemma in a Time of Change," *The Philadelphia Evening Bulletin*, April 26, 1968.

Record of Submissions and Awards,

Competition for Middle Income Housing at Brighton Beach, HDA, City of New York, Brooklyn 1968 (Comments of the Jury).

New Directions, pp. 8–10.

S. Cohen, "Physical Context/Cultural Context: Including It All," *Oppositions* 2 (January 1974): 2–39.

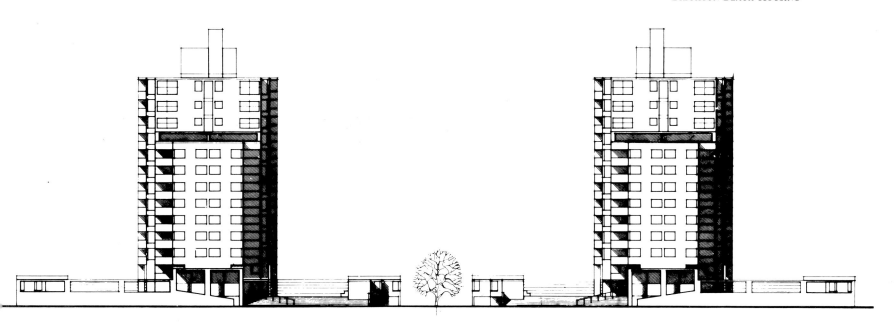

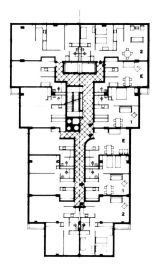

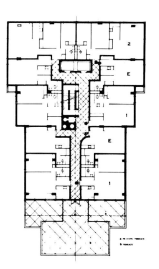

Elevations and typical plans

64   Wissahickon Avenue Houses

Proposal for a group of single-family houses near Philadelphia (1972)
In charge: Robert Venturi

As recently as 1972, the charming 1908 Philadelphia Art-Nouveau house in which Robert Venturi and his family now live, was still standing in its original estate. The project proposed the placement of residence pavilions along the tree-lined driveway. The pavilions recall small gatehouses of the Regency period. Ironically, however, a developer subdivided the land and built typical commercial ranch houses without reference to the architects' proposal.

Literature

A. Sky and M. Stone, *Unbuilt America*
(New   York: McGraw-Hill,   1976),
pp. 272–75.

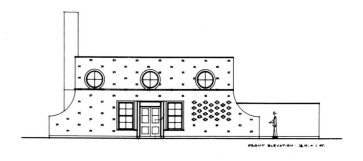

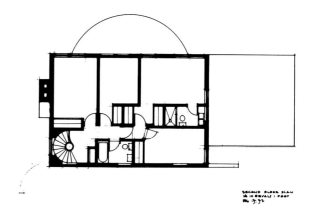

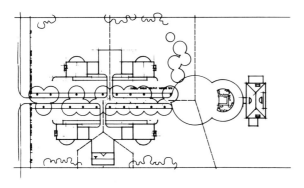

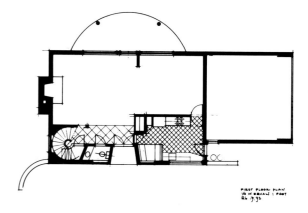

Site plan

Elevation and plans

290

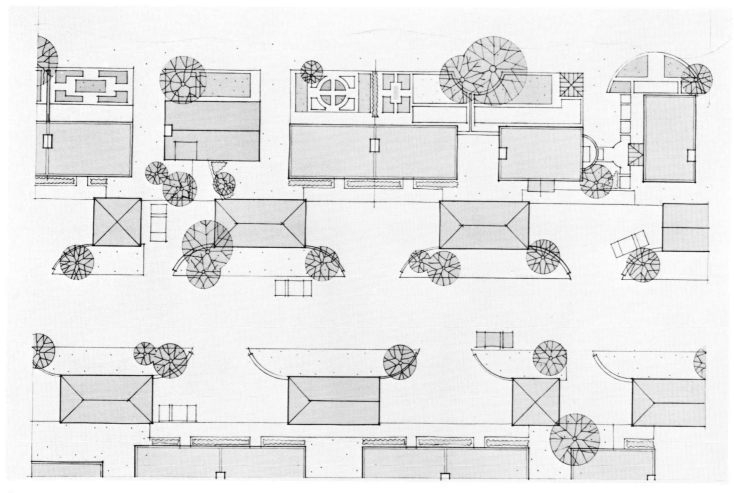

Site plan, detail

65   IAS Land Development Project

Project of Houses for the Institute for Advanced Studies, Princeton, New Jersey (1978)
In charge: Robert Venturi; John Rauch
Project Manager: James H. Timberlake
with Steven Izenour, James Allen Schmidt

The development program called for a total of 1,000 units consisting of single-family detached and semidetached houses. A key concern of the preliminary design shown here was to preserve as far as possible the integrity of the beautiful rural landscape. The houses evoke earlier buildings of the Regency and Greek-Revival style characteristic of the Princeton area.

It is an architecture of white walls, flat roofs, bays, and sash windows. Although it is rural, it is not rustic. Its character is one of unified diversity.[1]

1   Venturi and Rauch, project description.

Literature

J. Scholl, "Princeton Hires Firm to Guide Growth," *Trenton Times*, November 17, 1978, p. B1.

The Princeton Packet, November 29, 1978, p. 4A.

a+u 12 (1981): 12–13.

66 Park Regency Condominiums

Apartment building in Houston, Texas (1980)
In charge: Robert Venturi; John Rauch
Project Managers: Arthur Jones, James Bradberry
with Ronald McCoy, Christine Matheu

The complex is situated in Houston's Galleria area. The program called for a high-density complex of eighty apartment units and parking facilities for 110 cars. The name "Park Regency" recalls Regent's Park in London. The facades, with their large scale and repetitive decorative details, quote elements of nineteenth-century architecture, especially Georgian and Regency. In contrast to the outer facades, the inner courtyards have a more intimate character.

Literature

"Park Regency Cites Architect," *The Houston Post*, August 29-30, 1981, pp. 1DD, 5DD.

The Houston Post, September 5-6, 1981, p. 7DD.

"Park Regency Chosen for Exhibit," *The Houston Post*, October 3-4, 1981, p. 11DD.

P. Papdemetriou, "Go West John Nash," *PA*, February 1982, p. 22.

L. Germany, "The Comeback of the Column," *Texas Monthly*, August 1982, pp. 152, 154-58.

J. Kaliski, "Diagrams of Ritual and Experience: Learning from The Park Regency," *Site*, Spring 1983, pp. 8-13.

Plan and elevation

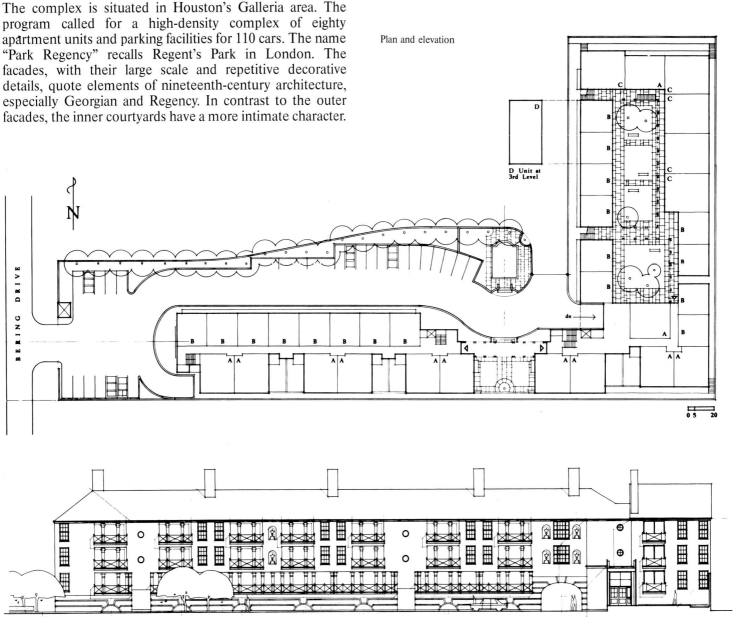

67 Chinatown Housing

Public housing in downtown Philadelphia (1982)
In charge: Robert Venturi; John Rauch
Project Manager: Arthur Jones
with James Bradberry, David Brisbin, Robert Desilets, David Marohn, Christopher Smith

Financed by the Philadelphia Redevelopment Authority, the project consists of twenty-five dwelling units—thirteen row houses (sold at market rates) and twelve duplex units, some of which are federally funded. The character of the architecture is modeled on Philadelphia prototypes. The duplexes, which are facing the street, feature flat roofs and have gardens and balconies on the rear sides, the latter with details derived from Georgian Chippendale patterns. The overall design of the project features generous windows for bright interior spaces and enhances the safety of offstreet pedestrian circulation.

View of twin houses

Literature

T. Hine, "The Rowhouse: A Home of Many Facets," *The Philadelphia Inquirer*, pt. H, July 29, 1979, pp. 1–2.

T. Hine, "Hard Bargain—Chinatown Getting New Homes, but, oh, the Price," *The Philadelphia Inquirer,* April 24, 1980, p. 3B.

Chinatown Housing, passageway between twin houses

6 Interior Designs and Exhibitions

Commenting on their former apartment in I.M. Pei's Society Hill Towers in Philadelphia, Denise Scott Brown stated in an interview:

> We had an austere, modern, concrete setting, and we played dark wood against it—Colonial, Chippendale, Queen Anne, even Victorian things. And then against that we put very stark Pop Art posters.... It was probably too simple a vocabulary for us.[1]

The house in which the architects have lived in Germantown, Philadelphia, since 1971 (built in 1908 by a German architect) offers opportunities for far more adventurous hybridizations. Art Nouveau architectural details, furniture of nearly every style, ceramic vases, *objets trouvés*, modern paintings, and graphics (ranging from William Nicholson to Roy Lichtenstein) are juxtaposed, with the wall stencil's large geometric and floral patterns and inscriptions providing a unifying background for this concert of styles.

In 1976, the year of the American Bicentennial, Venturi and Rauch designed commorative exhibitions in Philadelphia, Washington, D.C., and New York (pp. 304–307). More recently, there are plans for major renovations of the neoclassical Museum of Fine Arts in Philadelphia and the complete renovation of the magnificent library of the University of Pennsylvania by Frank Furness (1888–1891), one of the major works of the Victorian architecture that epitomizes the First Philadelphia School. These projects continue the VRSB theme of working within a given situation and enhancing it, if necessary, through adornment and decoration. A similar attitude prevails in both their urban and their interior design: What the facade of the bank and the billboard can be to Main Street, the mantelpiece and the Lichtenstein poster can be to the living room.

1 M. Filler, "Personal Patterns," *House and Garden*, January 1984, p. 92.

a   Atlantic City, New Jersey: Palley's Jewellers, shop design (1977)

b   Philadelphia: Venturi residence, view into dining room

68   James B. Duke House

Interior renovation of the Institute of Fine Arts, New York (1958)
In collaboration with Cope and Lippincott, Architects
In charge: Robert Venturi
Project Manager: John Rauch

It is symptomatic that Venturi's first major commission was for the interior renovation of a Fine Arts Institute. The mansion in question was built in 1912 and is located on upper Fifth Avenue. "It is a copy of the Hôtel Labottière in Bordeaux on the outside, but it is blown up in scale and expanded in size—a Louis XIV scale in a Louis XVI building. Its Edwardian-Louis XVI details are exceptionally fine inside and out."[1]

The house was designed by Horace Trumbauer; its interiors are by Alavoine. In the 1950s it was donated to New York University for use as a graduate school for the History of Art. Erwin Panofsky and Richard Krautheimer taught here, and Krautheimer had a hand in selecting Venturi for the job.

Rather than simply renovating the existing interior, the architects strove to contrast old and new elements. Wall panels, moldings, and other features were scrupulously retained; here and there, new elements were introduced sparingly, being considered as furniture rather than as architecture. The junction between old and new was detailed to maintain the separation and identity of each. By virtue of its juxtaposition with its classical interior, the furniture and equipment—steeltube chairs and steelframe racks—took on a surprising dimension. This installation was recently removed to make way for a more extensive renovation.

1   *CC4*, p. 107.

Literature

"From Repainting to Redesign," *Arch. Forum*, January 1960, pp. 122–30.

"NYU – Duke House," *Interiors*, March 1960, pp. 120–25.

Architecture Plus, March–April 1974, p. 80.

werk-archithese 7–8 (1977): 10–11.

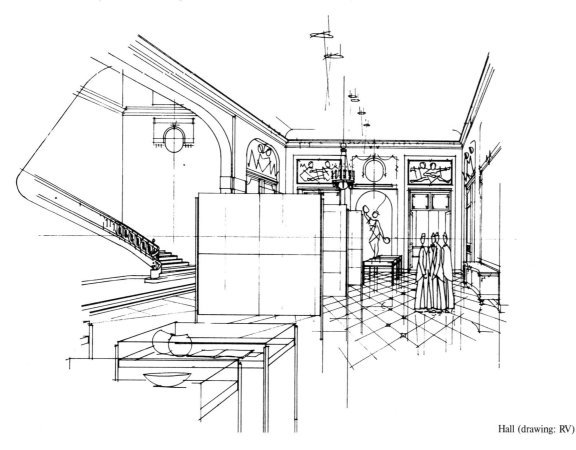

Hall (drawing: RV)

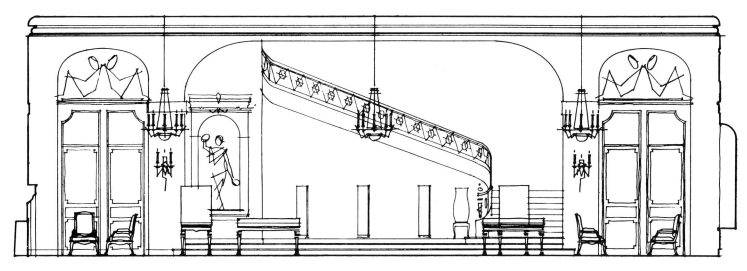

Hall (drawing: RV)

Horace Trumbauer's building

Typical seminar room after remodeling

Typical seminar room before remodeling

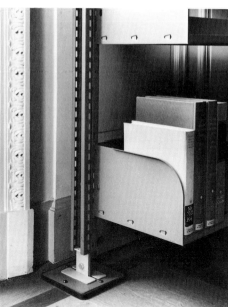

James B. Duke House, details with lamps and bookshelves

69   Grand's Restaurant

Renovation of a student restaurant in West Philadelphia (1961)
In charge: Robert Venturi
Project Manager: John Rauch

The renovation was based entirely upon the dualities inherent in the program. Two facilities, kitchen and restaurant, were involved, with a single ground floor extending across the entire width of two houses. The color scheme underlines this duality: one half of the facade is blue; the other, yellow. The kitchen can be seen from the restaurant through "windows" cut into the fire wall. The indoor graphics enhancing the public scale of the room (the first "supergraphics" in postmodern architecture) were inspired by the painter Jasper Johns, who had introduced stenciled letters into Pop Art painting shortly before (see pp. 52f.). The signboard on the facade represents a cup. It was removed during another renovation in 1978 but was used in a somewhat modified form above the portal of New York's Whitney Museum of American Art as the symbol of the 1985 exhibition entitled "High Styles" (see p. 316).

Literature

CCA, pp. 112–13.

"High Style for a Campus Eatery," PA, December 1963, pp. 132–36.

P. McLaughlin, "One-upmanship," Philadelphia Magazine, February 1986, pp. 171–73.

The Philadelphia Magazine—Interview with RV—subsequent reply by Harry Grand.

General view

Ground floor axonometric projection (Gerod Clark and RV)

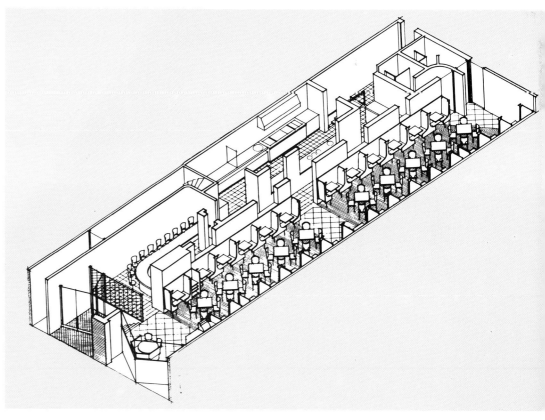

Grand's Restaurant, interior

70   St. Francis de Sales Church

Renovation of a Catholic church in Philadelphia (1968)
In charge: Robert Venturi; John Rauch
Project Manager: John Anderson
with Denise Scott Brown, Gerod Clark

The liturgical reform within the Catholic church mandated changes in the "furnishing" of choirs. One of the alterations made in the Parish of St. Francis de Sales was that the altar was moved from the choir's back wall toward the nave.

It was important to the architects to leave the existing neo-Byzantine architecture more or less intact. They tried to enhance the radiance of the yellow-white ceramic and cosmati ornamentation by choosing bright and smooth materials. The new altar, the pulpit, and the chair are made of opaque plexiglas about half an inch thick. The entire choir was lit by a curved, white neon tube.

Unfortunately, the light was removed at the behest of some members of the congregation, who argued that it was a symbol of commercial architecture. The architects, however, emphasized that they did not intend to profane the sacred, but to sanctify the profane.

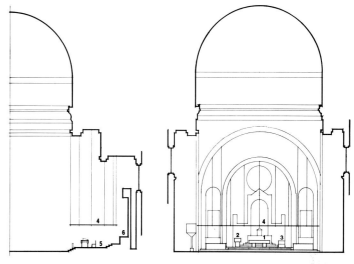

Sections

Literature

LLV, pp. 174–75.

"Saint Francis de Sales Church," *Liturgical Arts*, August 1970, pp. 124–26.

C. Ray Smith, "Electric Demolition, A

Milestone in Church Art: St. Francis de Sales, Philadelphia," *PA*, September 1970, pp. 92–95.

AD, June 1972, p. 379.

41st Eucharistic Congress (ed.), *Exhibition of Liturgical Arts*, 1976, pp. 63–64, fig. p. 274.

Details

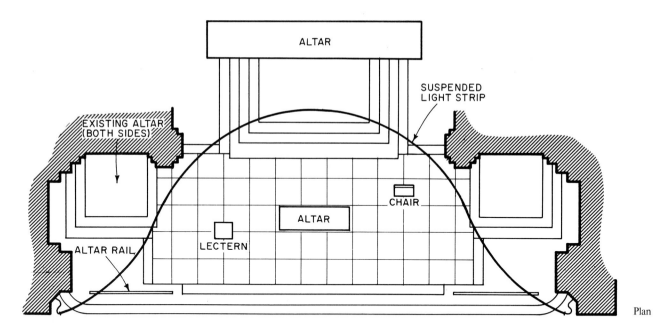

Plan

View of choir with neon tube

71 Bicentennial Exhibition

The exhibition "strip," detail (drawing: Steven Izenour)

Site plan

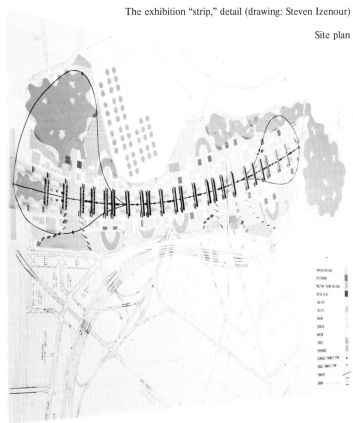

Design proposal for a world exhibition celebrating the American Bicentennial (1976), Philadelphia (1972)
In charge: Robert Venturi
Project Manager: Steven Izenour
with Denise Scott Brown, W. G. Clark, David Vaughan, Terry Vaughan

The central idea and spatial axis of this exhibition is the "street" as the arena for a great variety of activity. "We use large and small spaces, large entrance ways, water areas, occasional piazzas, and especially important signs.... These signs function both emblematically as an identity-image... and traditionally as the symbolic value of an available existing technology, our Crystal Palace or Eiffel Tower.... In McLuhan terms the messages on the signs will provide interest and will take on importance as the message-media will, we believe, become a main forum for people-to-people communications."[1]

1   *a+u* 11 (1974): 56.

Literature

N. Love, "The Deflatable Fair," *Philadelphia Magazine*, April 1969, pp. 137–40.

DSB and RV, "The Bicentennial Commemoration 1976," *Arch. Forum*, October 1969, pp. 66–69.
RV and DSB, "Bicentenaire de l'indépendance américaine," *AA*, November 1973, pp. 63–69.

72 "Signs of Life: Symbols in the American City"

Exhibition in the Renwick Gallery, Washington, D.C. (1976)
In collaboration with Dian Boone, Interior Designer; Steven Shore, Photographer; John Baeder, Painter
In charge: Denise Scott Brown, Steven Izenour, Robert Venturi
Project Managers: Janet Colesberry, Missy Maxwell with Paul Hirshorn, Elizabeth Izenour, Stephen Kieran, Daniel Rauch, Dan Scully, Douglas Southworth, James H. Timberlake

Following the appearance of *Learning from Las Vegas* (1972), R. Venturi, D. Scott Brown, and S. Izenour had planned the publication of their second Yale research project under the title "Learning from Levittown" (see pp. 49, 84, 85, 281). This book was never completed, but the research material became the basis for a 1976 exhibition in Washington, D.C.

For the Bicentennial exhibition at the Renwick Gallery, the Smithsonian Institute commissioned the architects to arrange a large exhibition on the symbolism and the aesthetics of everyday American culture. The focus was on suburban life-styles and the symbolic decoration on and in middle-class homes. Occupying three halls of the Renwick Gallery, the exhibition included authentic samples of commercial signs and billboards as well as architectural and sociocultural analyses of domestic and commercial sym-

bolism. The interiors of typical American living rooms were documented in lavish replicas.

Although conceived as a museum of American everyday life, the exhibition turned out to be a unique *Gesamtkunstwerk* of America's visual reality from suburb to city and a precursor of the Venturis' move from popular culture to history.

Literature

Signs of Life, Symbols in the American City (exhibition catalogue) (Washington, D. C.: Aperture, 1976).

W. von Eckhardt, "Signs of an Urban Vernacular," *WP*, February 28, 1976, pp. 1, 3C.

B. Forgey, "Keeping the City's Insight," *The Washington Star*, February 29, 1976, pp. 1, 24C.

M. Orth and L. Howard. "Schlock is Beautiful," *Newsweek*, March 8, 1976, p. 56.

"Symbols," *The New Yorker*, March 15, 1976, pp. 27–29.

A. L. Huxtable, "The Pop Word of the Strip and the Sprawl," *NYT*, March 21, 1976, p. 28D.

R. Rosenblatt, "The Pure Soldier," *The New Republic*, March 27, 1976, p. 32.

B. Shore, "'Symbols of American City' a Monument to Bad Taste?" *St. Louis Missouri Globe Democrat*, April 8, 1976.

P. Richard, "Rooms With a View on Life," *WP*, April 13, 1976, pp. 1B–2B.

B. Marvel, "On Reading the American Cityscape," *National Observer*, April 19, 1976.

B. Stein, "The Art Forms of Everyday Life," *The Wall Street Journal*, April 22, 1976.

B. Haddad Ryan, "Gaudy Reality of American Landscape Shines in Renwick Show," *Denver Post*, May 9, 1976.

S. Stephens, "Signs and Symbols as Show Stoppers," *PA*, May 1976, p. 37.

J. Geddes, "Is Your House Crawling With Urban Symbolism?" *Forecast*, May 1976, pp. 40–41.

S. von Moos, "Americana, zwei Ausstellungen in Washington," *Neue Zürcher Zeitung*, no. 165, July 17–18, 1976.

B. Russel, "Real Life: It's Beautiful," *House and Garden*, August 1976, pp. 79–80.

Section through "strip" room (drawing: Steven Izenour)

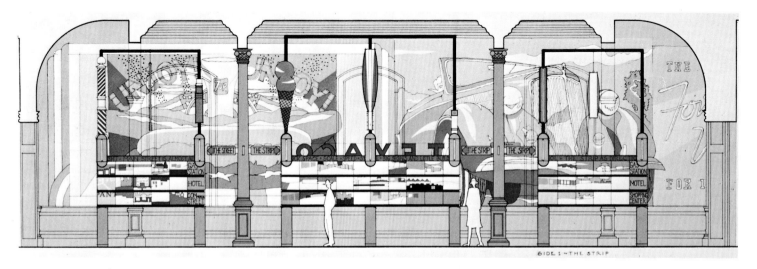

"City Room"

"Strip Room"

Typical ethnic row house, perspective study of the exhibition's installation
(drawing: Missy Maxwell)

"Williamsburg"

306

Interior of a typical suburban row house

DSB, "A House is More than a Home," (with Steven Izenour, Diane Boone, Missy Maxwell, Robert Venturi, Elizabeth Izenour, and Janet Schueren), August 1976, pp. 62–67.

DSB, "House Language" (with Elizabeth Izenour, Missy Maxwell, and Janet Schueren), *American Home*, August 1976.

P. Goldberger, "How to Love the Strip: Symbols In The American City," *Art News*, September 1976, pp. 50, 54.

J. Quinn, "Learning From Our Living Room," *PM*, October 1976, pp. 160–63, 165–68, 170, 172, 175.

"Signs of Life," *Signs of the Times*, November 1976, pp. 38–39.

"Signs of Life: Symbols in The American City—le Paysage urbain américain," *Créations et Recherches Esthétiques Européennes*, November 1976, pp. 46–49.

A. Wallach, "Levittown, You're Really OK," *Newsday's Magazine For Long Island*, November 14, 1976, pp. 8–11, 32–33; "America: An Exhibition by Venturi and Rauch," *Domus*, December 1976, pp. 46–47.

C. Jencks, *The Language of Post-Modern Architecture* (London: Academy Editions, 1976), p. 70.

DSB, "The Symbolic Architecture of the American Suburb," *Suburban Alternatives: 11 American Projects.* (The American Architectural Exhibition for the 1976 Venice Biennale.)

S. von Moos, "Zweierlei Realismus," *werk-archithese* 7–8 (1977): 58–62.

M. Fox and E. K. Carpenter, *Print Casebooks 2, Second Annual Edition: The Best in Exhibition Design* (Washington, D. C.: R. C. Publications, 1977), pp. 5, 6, 56–59.

Interior of a "tasteful" upper middle-class house

73 Two Hundred Years of American Sculpture

Installation for an exhibition of American Sculpture in the Whitney Museum of American Art, New York (1976)
In charge: Robert Venturi
Project Managers: Tony Atkin, Steven Izenour

To celebrate the American Bicentennial, the architects were commissioned to install a comprehensive exhibition of American sculpture since 1776 in the Whitney Museum of American Art (architect: Marcel Breuer; opened in 1966) on New York's Madison Avenue. Mounted above the museum's main entrance was a two-dimensional reproduction of one of the show's most important exhibits: Hiram Power's neoclassical sculpture of a *Greek Slave* (1847), a homage by the young American democracy to the Greek struggle for liberation.

Inside, the architects used decoration and color in keeping with stages in the history of American sculpture. Thus, the space had a theatrical atmosphere in stark contrast to the modern stereotype of immaculate white museum walls. The intention was to avoid creating an environment in which the glare of a spotlight isolates a work of art from its historical context. As expected, Venturi's concept for the exhibition was sharply criticized in some quarters.

Installation, detail

Entrance of the Whitney Museum of American Art, with decorated portal

Literature

200 Years of American Sculpture (exhibition catalogue) (New York: Whitney Museum of American Art, 1976).

H. Kramer, "A Monumental Muddle of American Sculpture," *NYT*, March 28, 1976, pp. 1, 34D.

T. B. Hess, "White Slave Traffic," *New York*, April 5, 1976, pp. 63–64.

R. Hughes, "Overdressing for the Occasion," *Time*, April 5, 1976, pp. 42–47.

"Off the Skyline and Into the Museum," *Newsday*, April 14, 1976, pp. 4A–5A.

M. Hoelterhoff, "A Little of Everything at the Whitney," *The Wall Street Journal*, June 9, 1976.

M. Fox, E. K. Carpenter, *Print Case-books 2, Second Annual Edition: The Best in Exhibition Design.* (Washington, D. C.: R. C. Publications), 1977, pp. 5, 6, 76–79.

74   INA Capital Management

Design of a floor of offices in Philadelphia (1976)
In charge: Robert Venturi; John Rauch
Project Manager: Jeffrey Ryan
with John Chase, Peter Clement, Janet Colesberry

At first glance the interior design seems to be conventional.
But diverse styles of furniture, fabrics, and art are combined
to form a collage of corresponding, harmonious, yet often
heterogeneous elements.

Interior

Literature

AA, June 1978, pp. 38–42.

P. Viladas, "Rich With Eclecticism," *Interiors*, November 1979, pp. 76–77.

a+u 12 (1981): 52–55.

R. Yee (ed.), "Where INA/CIGNA Investment Goes Public," *Corporate Design*, November–December 1982, pp. 52–57.

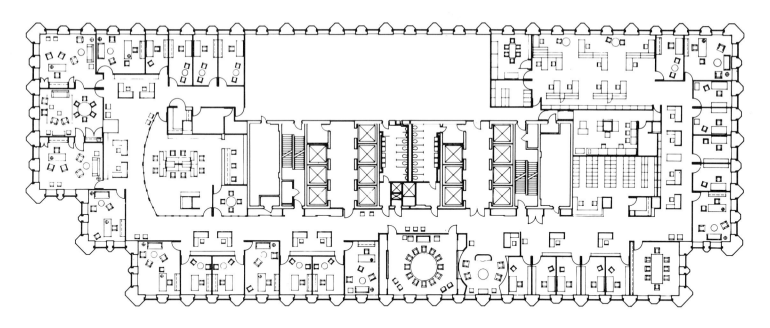

Plan

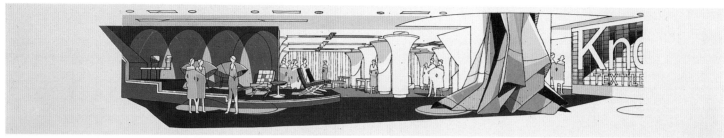

Entrance with cascade (drawing: Stanford Hughes)

Typical detail of exhibition space

Entrance

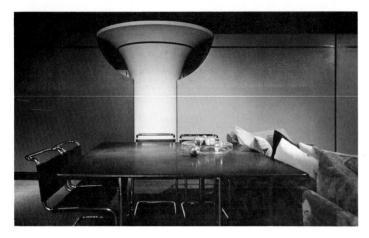

75   Knoll Showroom

Design of a showroom for Knoll International, New York (1981)
In charge: Robert Venturi; John Rauch
Project Managers: Stanford Hughes and John Chase
with Mark Hewitt, Steven Izenour, David Marohn, James H. Timberlake

The distinctive architectural identity of traditional department store interiors often depends on the ornamentation of structural and functional elements such as columns and elevators. These architectural effects can seldom be achieved today because of high costs. Moreover, the market demands more flexible, and perhaps more theatrical, arrangements.

In the Knoll Showroom, which covers two floors of an office building, the architects tried to combine both the permanent (architectural) and the transitory (ornamental) methods of decorating a store. A cascading fabric connects both floors and dominates the showroom entrance where changing exhibitions are held. Behind is a daylit, more restrained area for viewing Knoll's furniture collection.

Literature

S. Slesin, "Two New Furniture Showrooms: Venturi and Saladino," *NYT*, December 13, 1979, pp. C1, C10.

A. MacNair, "Venturi and the Classic Modern Tradition," *Skyline*, March 1980, pp. 4–5.

E. Lee Cohen, "Complexity and Contradiction," *Interior Design*, March 1980, pp. 226–31.

A. Friedman, "Postmodernism," *Interior Design*, March 1980, pp. 232–35.

C. K. Hoyt, "Interiors: Knoll Center by Robert Venturi," *Arch. Rec.*, March 1980, pp. 97–102.

"The New York Showroom", *PA*, July 1980, pp. 74–76.

"Centre d'exposition Knoll," *AA*, September 1980, pp. XV, 56–57.

P. Viladas, "Life After Mies," *Interiors*, January 1981, p. 64.

B. Galletta, "Knoll International, New York," *L'Industria delle Costruzioni*, January 1981, pp. 70–72.

a+u 12 (1981): 18–21.

M. Filler, "History Reinvented: Adam and his Heirs," *Art in America*, Summer 1982, pp. 87–97.

B. D. Schwartz, "Knoll International: The Revolution Revived," *Town and Country*, March 1984, pp. 223–34.

76 Princeton University Interior Adaptations

Renovation of several colleges at Princeton University, Princeton, New Jersey (1980)
In collaboration with: Dian Boone, Interior Designer
In charge: Robert Venturi; John Rauch
Project Managers: Ian Adamson, John Chase, Stephen Kieran
with Dan McCoubrey, Robert Marker

The renovation of several colleges at Princeton University is part of a comprehensive planning study that the university assigned to Robert Venturi, a former graduate, and his office in 1980 (see pp. 163 f.). These renovations became necessary when Princeton decided to introduce the college system for freshman and sophomore students. The changes involved the conversion of former dormitories into five separate, residential colleges. A key factor in design development was to create environments that would encourage informal and spontaneous interaction among students, advisors, and faculty.

Two of the new colleges—Rockefeller and Mathey—were housed in some of the best examples of the Collegiate Gothic style in America. The alterations here were kept to a minimum. The modification of a previously unused attic floor to accommodate dormitories (Blair Hall: see pl. p. 312) involved design of new interior elements.

What is now Malcolm S. Forbes Jr. College was originally the Princeton Inn, a hotel built in the 1920s. Again, the transformation involved refinishing and refurnishing the charming architecture that already existed. Surface alterations and additions—a new yellow table, white-and-silver-patterned wallpaper (see pl. 313), a wooden bench, and chandeliers—were made to create a positive sense of tension.

Literature

Campaign Bulletin, Princeton University, April 1982, pp. 4–5.

American School & University, November 1984, pp. 16–18.

Rockefeller College, interior

Forbes College, interior

Blair Hall
Blair Hall

Mathey College
Rockefeller College, basement

312

Forbes College, hall

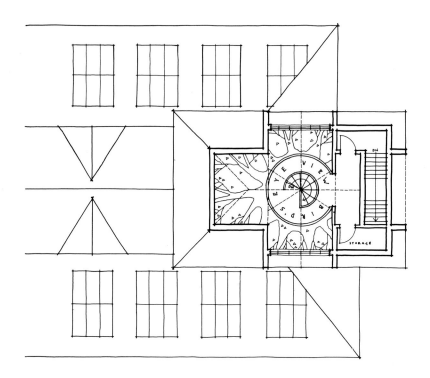

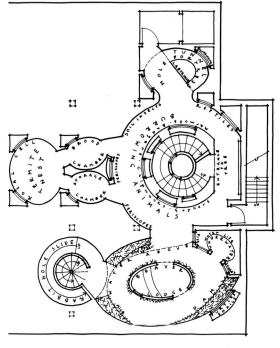

Plans

77   George D. Widener Memorial Tree House for the Children's Zoo

Conversion of a late nineteenth-century building into an exhibit for a Children's Zoo in the Philadelphia Zoo (1980)
In collaboration with: Dennis Aufiery, painting; Christopher Speeth, sound design; Sculpture Workshop
In charge: Steven Izenour
Project Managers: Dan McCoubrey, Christine Matheu, Lou Rodolico, with Frances Hundt, Louisa McIlwaine, Robert Venturi

The program called for the creation of an unusual type of natural science museum to promote children's understanding of and sympathy with nature and animals.

Together with Dr. Mary Scott Cebul, in charge of interpretive zoo planning, the architects decided to use the former Antilope House—an architecturally distinguished Victorian building—as an innovative pedagogical "learning environment." Instead of presenting children with isolated facts, they tried to immerse them in a fantasy physical context, in which visitors have the illusion of walking among dinosaurs, frogs, bees, butterflies, and ants in their respective environments. The architects emphasized that

the exhibits are intimately associated with the architecture of the building, with structures and contexts placed to complement and be complemented by the building's many spatial characteristics. The visitors' experience of the wonderful old architecture becomes integral to the exhilarating experience of the exhibits themselves.[1]

The project is a *Gesamtkunstwerk*, for it is also an elaboration of studies made by Robert Venturi for a Science Museum in Charlotte, Pennsylvania (1977), a variation on the theme of the nineteenth-century diorama and panorama, and a tribute to Walt Disney.

1   VRSB, project description

Literature

Arch. Rec., December 1981, p. 41.

P. Viladas, "Venturi, Rauch & Scott Brown," *PA*, October 1984, pp. 88–93.

T. Hine, "The Zoo's New Answer to the Call of the Wild," *The Philadelphia Inquirer*, April 10, 1985, pp. 1D, 6D.

T. Hine, "Zoo's New Tree House Wins the Laurels of Local Architects," *The Philadelphia Inquirer*, June 21, 1985, p. 3E.

D. K. Dietsch, "George D. Widener Memorial Tree House for the Children's Zoo, Philadelphia," *Arch. Rec.*, September 1985, pp. 120–25.

"Museum of Life," *Building*, April 4, 1986, pp. 38–40.

Interior

78 "High Styles" Exhibition Design

Installation for an exhibition of twentieth-century American interior design in the Whitney Museum of American Art, New York (1985)
In charge: Robert Venturi
Project Managers: Christine Matheu, Steven Izenour
with James Kolker, Willis Pember, Layng Pew, Fran Read

This project was curated by seven experts on the history of twentieth-century American furniture. The difficulty in presenting furniture and decorative objects dating from 1900 to 1985 stemmed from the extraordinarily wide variety of styles involved. It was necessary to provide a context that unified the diverse material and facilitated an understanding of the design qualities and the stylistic properties of the individual pieces.

Literature

High Styles: Twentieth Century American Design (exhibition catalogue) (New York, 1985).

C. Vogel, "Celebrating American Design," *NYT Magazine*, September 15, 1985, pp. 44–46, 48, 50, 70, 73.

S. Slesin, "Tracing the Paths of the 20th Century American Design," *NYT*, September 19, 1985, pp. C1, 6.

P. Goldberger, "When American Design Grew Up," *NYT*, September 20, 1985, pp. C1, 25.

Entrance section

Section

7 Decorative Arts

Studies of the legs of Rococo furniture, an interior view of the hall of mirrors at Amalienburg, Gaudí's dressing table in the Casa Güell in Barcelona, Aalto's bentwood furniture, and other specimens of European interior design are reminders that decorative arts were one of Robert Venturi's preferred experimental preoccupations in architecture even before 1966, when these examples were cited in *Complexity and Contradiction in Architecture*.[1] In fact, dating furniture and fashion styles has been among his hobby since childhood, and he has been actively designing furniture since 1972. Yet, while the scale and details of Venturi's houses always seem to relate to furniture and objects, it is only after 1978 that the firm began to have these designs executed.

In blending these different pursuits, the Venturis are not motivated by any utopia of "total design" in the sense of Art Nouveau or of De Stijl movement. Their aim is, rather, that of taking the art of mixing scales, juxtaposing traditional symbolism with modern industrial processes, and extending it from architecture into decorative arts, in which complexity and contradiction in both function and style have always been inevitable. In that sense, the Venturis' furniture and tableware point to rediscovered traditional modes of cooperation between architect and production—as with Van de Velde and Aalto—and recall historical styles—as with the Alessi George II traditional teapot and the Knoll Chippendale furniture.

1 *CCA*, pp. 64, 77, 79, 97, 102, and *passim*.

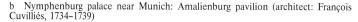

b Nymphenburg palace near Munich: Amalienburg pavilion (architect: François Cuvilliés, 1734–1739)

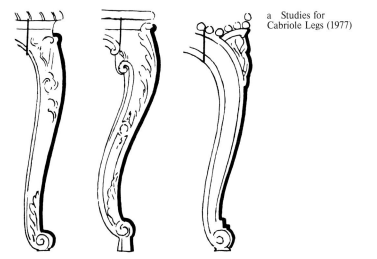

a Studies for Cabriole Legs (1977)

Table

Chair, preliminary study

79 Knoll Furniture

Bentwood chairs, table, and sofa for Knoll International (1979)
In charge: Robert Venturi
Project Manager: Maurice Weintraub
with Denise Scott Brown, Erica Gees, Paul Muller, John Rauch

The intention behind this assortment of nine chairs, three tables, and a sofa is to create usable furniture rather than sculptures that look like furniture. Furthermore, the pieces refute "the Modern notion of unity and clarity" in favor of "the Postmodern notion of diversity and ambiguity."

Moreover, Venturi says: "This furniture breaks the boundary between traditional and Modern design by adapting a series of historical styles to industrial processes."

What he means is the technique of molding and laminating plywood for chairs, a material that was often employed by Aalto. Unlike Aalto, but still quite in keeping with traditional styles, Venturi stresses the back of the chair in its function as an ornament and a signal. He offers nine different stylistic varieties ranging from Queen Anne to Chippendale, richly perforated and, if desired, decoratively patterned.

Literature

M. Kimmelman, "Sitting Pretty," *Horizon*, September 1982, pp. 16-24.

RV, DSB, "Process and Symbol in the Design of Furniture for Knoll, Venturi Collection," (New York: Knoll International, 1983).

B. D. Schwartz, "Knoll International: The Revolution Revived," *Town and Country*, March 1984, pp. 223-34.

T. Hine, "His Chairs Aren't Just Furniture," *The Philadelphia Inquirer*, May 2, 1984, pp. 1D, 3D.

P. Goldberger, "Venturis Wilfully Excentric Furniture," *NYT*, May 3, 1984, p. C12.

A. Truppin, "Neocon Preview: Two Way Stretch," *Interiors*, May 1984, pp. 228, 258.

J. Weinraub, "Breaking Boundaries: Robert Venturi's Unorthodox Designs," *WP*, May 24, 1984, Home Section, pp. 1, 22-23, 30, 32.

S. Holt, "From A Single Root," *Industrial Design*, May-June 1984, pp. 28-37.

J. Giovannini, "By Venturi: Something Borrowed, Something New," *NYT*, June 7, 1984, p. C10.

C. K. Gandee, "Profiles in History," *Arch. Rec.*, June 1984, pp. 166-70.

M. Thorne, "My Tailor Is Rich," *Quaderns*, 163 (1984): 122-25.

P. Viladas, "Remembrance of Chairs Past," *PA*, June 1984, p. 24.

M. Walsh, "Venturi's New Chairs Are Tongue In Chic," *Chicago Sun-Times*, June 13, 1984, p. 47.

M. Hamm, "Architect's Furniture Designs are Fat, Flat, Fun," *Houston Chronicle*, June 21, 1984, section 6, pp. 1, 2.

M. Filler, "Past With a Future," *House and Garden*, July 1984, pp. 46-50.

B. Plumb, "Living One-of-a-Kind," *Vogue*, August 1984, pp. 256-58.

L. McDevitt, "Special Report: Neocon 16 Review," *Designer's West*, August 1984, pp. 46, 48.

"Design eclettico," *Domus*, September 1984, pp. 74-75.

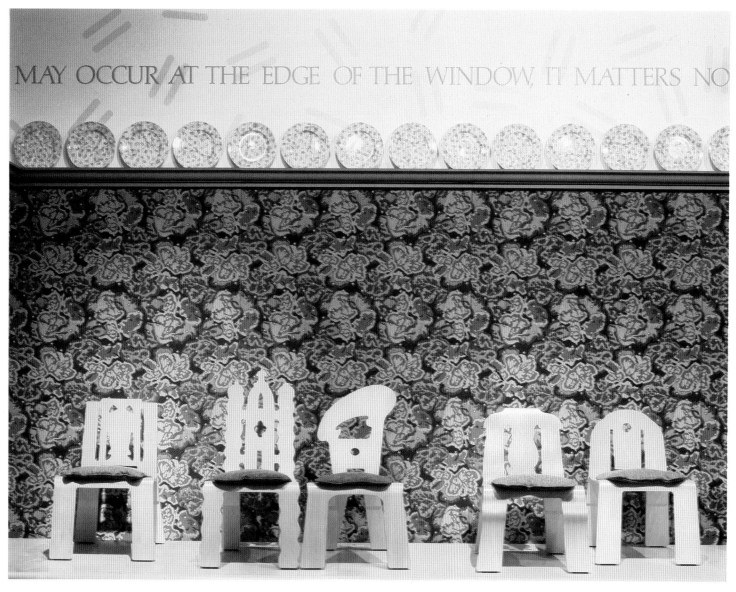

Exhibition 1985

P. Vanni, "Robert Venturi: Il gioco delle ombre cinesi," *Casa Vogue*, September 1984, pp. 336–39.

A. Truppin, "Jury on Venturi," *Interiors*, September 1984, pp. 154–55.

T. Ohashi, "Empathy and Estrangement", *Space Design*, October 1984, pp. 54–55.

M. Ogawa, "Second Glance Chair," *Space Design*, October 1984, p. 60.

P. Phillips, "Robert Venturi," *Art Forum*, November 1984, pp. 97–98.

M. Weinberg-Staber, "Lernen von Venturi," *du*, January 1985, pp. 64–65.

Tea service

80 Alessi Tea Service

Tea service for Alessi (1984)
In charge: Robert Venturi
Project Managers: James Bradberry, Maurice Weintraub
with Denise Scott Brown

The Alessi silver tea service comprises a coffeepot, teapot, creamer, sugar bowl, and tray. Each piece presents itself as an end-product of the centuries long evolution of its species. Pot, creamer, bowl, and tray are also reminiscent of different historical styles abstracted and symbolized through various patterns that embellish the silver surfaces and call to mind additional examples from the history of architecture and the decorative arts. Despite the many associations evoked by its programmatic eclecticism and deliberately complex and ambiguous form, the set evokes a sense of inviting serenity.

Literature

Arch. Rec., February 1982, p. 35.

J. Giovannini, "Design Notebook: Tea Services with the Touch of an Architect," *NYT*, November 17, 1983.

Officina Alessi: *Tea and Coffee Piazza.*

11 Servizi da te e caffè disegnati da Michael Graves (etc.), (Grusinallo: Alessi, 1983), pp. 31, 70–73.

B. Adams, "Architects at Tea," *House and Garden*, May 1984, pp. 52–60.

"Architects Product Designs," *Avenue*, April 1984, pp. 141–45.

Elevation study (drawing: Maurice Weintraub)

81 A Bureau in William and Mary Style

Bureau for the Triennale di Milano (1985)
In charge: Robert Venturi

Literature

Carlo Guenzi (ed.), *Le affinità elettive. Ventuno progettisti ricercano le proprie affinità* (Milan: Triennale di Milano), pp. 153–59.

Three plates

82 Swid Powell Table Line

Chinaware and crystal glasses (1984)
In charge: Robert Venturi
Project Manager: Erica Gees
with Maurice Weintraub

In addition to plates available in two sizes in the "grandmother" and "notebook" patterns, the line includes coffee cups and drinking glasses. The ornamentation, which both establishes the decorative character of this markedly "ordinary" dishware and alludes to everyday durable goods made of other materials such as textiles and paper, is expressly set in relief.

Recently, candelabra and a tea service in the form of an "Italian village" were also executed for the same firm.

Literature

N. Miller, "Grandmother Never Looked So Good," *Metropolis,* June 1984, pp. 24–28, 39.

M. Slavin, "Out on the Table," *Interiors,* August 1984, pp. 152–55.

C. Vogel, "Home Design: Design Trends 1985," *NYT* Magazine, August 26, 1984, pp. 44–50.

M. Filler, "The Architectural Tabletop," *House & Garden,* October 1984, pp. 96, 98, 104.

B. Loderer, "Der 'Louis toujours' von morgen," *Tages-Anzeiger* (Zurich), December 11, 1985, p. 25.

"Italian Village"

83 "Italian Village"

A tea and coffee service in porcelain (1984)
In charge: Robert Venturi
Project Manager: Erica Gees
with Maurice Weintraub

This "Italian Village" may be the Venturis' answer to Paul Davidoff, the social planner who once asserted at the height of the Civil Rights Movement that architects who said that they could design the environment from the teaspoon to the region must have delusions of grandeur.[1] The Venturis would always have agreed. But if it is true that a whole region should not be designed like an architectural project, there is no reason why a creamer cannot evoke the form of Palazzo Strozzi or a teapot that of the Pantheon!

It should be noted, however, that even if these objects look like buildings, they are not designed like buildings, but rather according to the rules dictated by their own function and traditional typology.

1 Oral communication from DSB.

323

Acknowledgments

Many of the buildings and projects described in this book were documented in an exhibition I organized at the Zurich Museum of Arts and Crafts in 1979. I am grateful to both Margit Weinberg-Staber, then curator at Zurich's Kunstgewerbemuseum, Dr. Hansjörg Budliger, its director, who allowed the use of many pictures from the catalogue that had been prepared for that occasion, and to Silvio Schmed. They were responsible for the success of the exhibition, of which this book is a kind of amplified reflection. It is impossible to list all the people who helped me with this book, often unknowingly. Eduard F. Sekler (Harvard University) made it possible for me to teach four-and-a-half years at his university. François Burckhart and Heinrich Klotz brought me together with Robert Venturi and Denise Scott Brown at the International Design Center (IDZ) in Berlin in 1974. Among the students of architecture and art history at the Technical University of Delft and the University of Zurich who are to thank for ideas and help, I want to mention Peter Couwenbergh, Hans Frei, Ute Lehrer, and Patricia Nussbaum. I am also indebted to the following colleagues in Europe and in the United States: Hubert Damisch, David Dunster, Heinrich Klotz, Peter Krückmann, Helga von Kuegelgen, Barbara Miller Lane, Thomas A. S. van Leeuwen, Mary McLeod, Fritz Neumeyer, Jürgen Paul, Werner Sewing, Jeannot Simmen, Martin Steinmann, and Ed Taverne.

This book would certainly never have appeared in its present form had it not been for the intellectual stimulation and the technical support of the Center for Advanced Study in Berlin, where I was a fellow with Tilmann Buddensieg, Vittorio Magnago Lampugnani, and Kenneth Frampton during the academic year of 1985/86. Their interest, agreement, and disagreement did much to further my work. I am especially grateful to Julius Posener, Thomas Hughes, Agatha Hughes, and, last but not least, Irène von Moos for their many useful comments on the manuscript. I thank Teresa Köbele of the *Wissenschaftskolleg* in Berlin for her careful work on the text's four successive German versions and my translator, David Antal, for more than just professional work on the English version. Lynette Widder, Thomas Müller, and Stefan von Senger und Etterlin have my sincere appreciation for their assistance in preparing English drafts for parts of the book and in tracking down bibliographical information. The Otto and Martha Fischbeck Foundation helped finance the translation. In Fribourg, the staff of Office du Livre deserve thanks for understanding the exigencies of what was probably a "difficult" book (and author).

To leave the compilation of one's own work to an architectural historian living on another continent is not the obvious decision to take for a leading architectural office. I am therefore especially grateful to Robert Venturi, John Rauch, Steven Izenour, Steven Estock, and David Dashiell for their active cooperation across the Atlantic. Yet it was Denise Scott Brown who has devoted more energy to this book than anyone else in the office. Although I assume full responsibility for the shortcomings of the text and the opinions expressed therein, I owe her more than is revealed by the selected bibliography at the end of this study.

Select Bibliography

compiled in collaboration with Ute Lehrer

A   General works

Cook, John W. and Klotz, Heinrich, *Conversations with Architects* (London: Lund Humphries, 1973).

Curtis, William, *Modern Architecture since 1900* (Oxford: Phaidon Press Limited, 1982).

Diamonstein, Barbaralee, *American Architecture Now* (New York: Rizzoli, vol. 1, 1980; vol. 2, 1985).

Drew, Philip, *The Third Generation: Changing Meaning in Architecture* (London: Praeger, 1972).

Frampton, Kenneth, "America 1960–1970. Notes on Urban Images and Theory," *Casabella* 389/390, XXV (1971): 24–38.

Handlin , David P., *American Architecture* (London – New York: Thames and Hudson, 1985).

Jencks, Charles, *Modern Movements in Architecture* (Harmondsworth: Penguin Books, 1973).

––, *The Language of Post-Modern Architecture* (London: Academy Editions, 1977).

–– (ed.), *Post-Modern Classicism* (London: Academy Editions, 1980).

––, *Current Architecture* (London: Academy Editions, 1982).

Klotz, Heinrich (ed.), *Die Revision der Moderne. Postmoderne Architektur 1960–1980* (Katalog Deutsches Architektur-museum, Frankfurt am Main) (Munich: Prestel, 1984).

Klotz, Heinrich, *Moderne und postmoderne Architektur der Gegenwart, 1960–1980* (Brunswick–Wiesbaden: Vieweg, 1984).

Lampugnani, Vittorio Magnago, *Architektur und Städtebau des 20. Jahrhunderts* (Stuttgart: Hatje, 1980).

McCoy, Esther, "Buildings in the United States," *Lotus,* vol. 4, 1967–8: 15–123.

Müller, Michael, *Architektur und Avantgarde* (Frankfurt am Main: Syndikat, 1984).

Portoghesi, Paolo, *Dopo l'architettura moderna* (Bari: Laterza, 1980).

Portoghesi, Paolo (*et al.*), *The Presence of the Past: First International Exhibition of Architecture – Venice Biennale 1980* (Venice: La Biennale di Venezia and London: Academy Editions, 1980).

Scully, Vincent, *American Architecture and Urbanism* (New York: Praeger, 1969).

––, *The Shingle Style Today. Or: The Historian's Revenge* (New York: Braziller, 1974).

Smith, C. Ray, *Supermannerism: New Attitudes in Post Modern Architecture* (New York: Dutton, 1977).

Stern, Robert A. M., *New Directions in American Architecture* (New York: Braziller, 1969).

Tafuri, Manfredo and Dal Co, Francesco, *Architettura contemporanea* (Milan: Electa Editrice, 1976).

Vogt, Adolf M., Strathaus, Ulrike Jehle-Schulte, and Reichlin, Bruno, *Architektur 1940–1980* (Frankfurt am Main – Vienna – Berlin: Propyläen, 1980).

Wolfe, Tom, *From Bauhaus to Our House* (New York: Farrar, Straus & Giroux, 1981).

B   Writings about Venturi, Rauch and Scott Brown

Chimacoff, Alan and Plattus, Alan, "Learning from Venturi," *Architectural Record*, September 1983: 86–97.

De Seta, Cesare, "Robert Venturi, dissacratore e provocatroe," *Casabella* 394 (October 1974): 2–5.

Filler, Martin, "Learning from Venturi," *Art in America,* April 1980: 95–101.

Goldberger, Paul, "Less is More – Mies van der Rohe. Less is a Bore – Robert Venturi," *The New York Times Magazine,* October 19, 1971: 24–37.

Haag-Bletter, Rosemarie, "Transformations of an American Vernacular," in *Venturi, Rauch and Scott Brown: A Generation of Architecture* (Exhibition Catalogue), (Krannert Art Museum and the University of Illinois at Urbana-Champaign), March 1984: 2–19.

Jencks, Charles (ed.), *Post-Modern Classicism* (London: Academy Editions, 1980): 5-19, 30-34.

Jencks, Charles, *Current Architecture* (London: Academy Editions, 1982): 113-15, 174, 200, 208, 324.

Jordy, William H., "Robert Venturi and the Decorated Shed," *The New Criterion,* May 1985: 58-68.

Klotz, Heinrich, *Moderne und postmoderne Architektur der Gegenwart 1960-1980* (Brunswick-Wiesbaden: Vieweg, 1984): 147-80.

Maxwell, Robert, "The Venturi Effect," *Venturi and Rauch: The Public Buildings. Architectural Monographs,* no. 1 (London: Academy Editions, 1977): 7-28.

Moos, Stanislaus von, "Las Vegas oder Die Renaissance des Futurismus," *Neue Zürcher Zeitung,* September 23, 1973, p. 53.

--, "Lachen um nicht zu weinen" (interview with Robert Venturi and Denise Scott Brown), *archithese* 13 (1975): 17-26.

--, "A Postscript on History, 'Architecture Parlante' and Populism," *a + u,* 12 (1981): 199-204.

--, "Robert Venturi," *Macmillan Encyclopedia of Architects* (New York-London: The Free Press, 1982), vol. 4: 305-8.

--, and Weinberg-Staber, Margrit, *Venturi and Rauch. Architektur im Alltag Amerikas* (exhibition catalogue) (Kunstgewerbemuseum der Stadt Zürich, Zurich, 1979).

Oliver, Richard and Allen, Gerald, "Robert Venturi, John Rauch and Denise Scott Brown," *Architectural Drawing: The Art and the Process* (New York: Whitney Library of Design, 1981): 142-47.

Pelli, Cesar (ed.), *Yale School of Architecture, Seminar Papers* (New Haven: Yale University, 1981): 187-241.

"Recent Works by Venturi and Rauch," a + u, January 1978: 2-80.

Sanmartín, A. (ed.), *Venturi, Rauch & Scott Brown: Works and Projects 1959-1985* (Barcelona: Gustavo Gili and London: Academy Editions, 1986)

Sarbib, Jean-Louis, "Complexité et contradiction d'une architecture pluraliste"; "Venturi et Rauch, urbanistes. Projets récents," *L'Architecture d'aujourd'hui,* June 1978: 2-6, 76-79.

Schmertz, Mildred F., "Learning from Denise: The Role in Architecture of DSB," *Architectural Record,* July 1982: 102-7.

Vogt, Adolf M., Strathaus, Ulrike Jehle-Schulte, and Reichlin, Bruno, *Architektur 1940-1980* (Frankfurt am Main - Vienna - Berlin: Propyläen, 1980): 80-84, 258-59.

Wolfe, Tom, *From Bauhaus to Our House* (New York: Farrar, Straus & Giroux, 1981).

C Special Issues of Periodicals

a + u, November 1974.
werk-archithese, 7-8 (1977).
L'Architecture d'aujourd'hui, June 1978.
a + u, December 1981.
Quaderns 162 (1984).

D Writings by Robert Venturi

"The Campidoglio: A Case Study," *Architectural Review,* May 1953: 333-34.

"A Justification for a Pop Architecture," *Arts and Architecture,* April 1965.

Complexity and Contradiction in Architecture (New York: Museum of Modern Art, 1966; second edition, 1977).

"Three Projects: Architecture and Landscape, Architecture and Sculpture, Architecture and City Planning," *Perspecta* 11 (1967): 103-6.

"A Bill-Ding Board Involving Movies, Relics and Space," *Architectural Forum,* April 1968: 74-76.

"Complexity and Contradiction in the Work of Furness," *Pennsylvania Academy of the Fine Arts Newsletter,* Spring 1976: 5.

"Alvar Aalto," *Arkkitehti,* July-August 1976: 66-67.

"A Definition of Architecture as Shelter with Decoration on It, and Another Plea for a Symbolism of the Ordinary in Architecture," *a + u,* January 1978: 3-14.

"Learning the Right Lessons from the Beaux Arts," *Architectural Design,* January 1979: 23-31.

"Il Proprio Vocabolario. Four Houses," *Gran Bazaar,* January-February 1982: 152-57.

"RIBA Discourse July 1981," Transactions 1, *RIBA Journal,* May 1982: 47-56.

"Diversity, Relevance and Representation in Historicism, or Plus ça Change... plus A Plea For Pattern all over Architecture with a Postscript on my Mother's House," *Architectural Record,* June 1982: 114-19.

"On Aalto," *Quaderns* 157 (April-May-June 1983): 55.

"Proposal for the Iraq State Mosque, Baghdad," *L'Architecture d'aujourd'hui,* September 1983: 28-35.

"A Bureau in William and Mary Style," in Carlo Guenzi (ed.), *Le Affinita' Elettive. Ventuno progettisti ricercano le proprie affinità* (Milan: Triennale di Milano, 1985): 153-58.

E Writings by Denise Scott Brown

"Form, Design and the City," *Journal of the American Institute of Architects,* November 1962.

"The Meaningful City," *Journal of the American Institute of Architects,* January 1965: 27–32.

"Planning the Expo," *Journal of the American Institute of Planners,* July 1967: 268–72.

"Planning the Powder Room," *Journal of the American Institute of Architects,* April 1967: 81–83.

"Teaching Architectural History," *Arts and Architecture,* May 1967: 30.

"Team 10, Perspecta 10, and the Present State of Architectural Theory," *Journal of the American Institute of Planners,* January 1967: 42–50.

"The Bicentennial's Fantasy Stage," *The Philadelphia Evening Bulletin,* March 8, 1968.

"Mapping the City: Symbols and Systems," *Landscape,* Spring 1968: 22–25.

"Urban Structuring," *Architectural Design,* January 1968: 7.

"Learning from Pop," and "Reply to Frampton," *Casabella* 389–390 (May/June 1971): 14–46.

"On Architectural Formalism and Social Concern: A Discourse for Social Planners and Radical Chic Architects," *Oppositions* 5, Summer 1976: 99–112.

"Signs of Life: Symbols in the American City" (with Stephen Izenour), *Aperture* (New York), no. 77 (1976): 49–65.

"Forum: The Beaux Arts Exhibition," *Oppositions,* Spring 1977: 165–66.

"On Formal Analysis as Design Research," *Journal of Architectural Education,* vol. XXXII, no. 4, May 1979: 8–11.

"Learning the Wrong Lessons from the Beaux-Arts," *Architectural Design Profile* 17 (1979): 30–32.

"Architectural Taste in a Pluralistic Society," *The Harvard Architecture Review,* 1 (Spring 1980): 41–51.

"Between Three Stools: A Personal View of Urban Design Practice and Pedagogy," *Education for Urban Design,* (Institute for Urban Design, Purchase, N.Y., 1982): 132–72.

"Drawing for the Déco District," *archithese,* March 1982: 17–21.

"A Worm's Eye View of Recent Architectural History," *Architectural Record,* February 1984: 69–81.

"Zeichnen für den Deco-Distrikt," *Center* 1 (1985): 44–63.

F Writings by Robert Venturi and Denise Scott Brown

"A Significance for A & P Parking Lots, or Learning from Las Vegas," *Architectural Forum,* March 1968: 36–43.

"Learning from Lutyens," *Journal of the Royal Institute of British Architects,* August 1969: 353–54.

"Mass Communications on the People Freeway, Piranesi is Too Easy," *Perspecta* 12 (1969): 49–56.

"Some Houses of Ill-Repute: a Discourse with Apologia on Recent Houses of Venturi and Rauch," *Perspecta* 13/14 (1971): 259–67.

"Ugly and Ordinary Architecture, or the Decorated Shed," Part I, *Architectural Forum,* November 1971: 64–67; Part II, December 1971: 48–53.

Learning from Las Vegas (with Stephen Izenour) (Cambridge, Mass.: MIT Press, 1972; 2nd edition, 1977).

"Functionalism, Yes, But...," *a + u,* November 1974: 33–34.

"Interview, Robert Venturi and Denise Scott Brown," *The Harvard Architecture Review,* 1 (Spring 1980): 228–39.

A View from the Campidoglio: Selected Essays, 1953–1984 (New York: Harper & Row, 1984).

G Writings by Denise Scott Brown and Robert Venturi

"On Ducks and Decoration," *Architecture Canada,* October 1968: 48.

"Co-op City: Learning to Like it," *Progressive Architecture,* February 1970: 64–73.

Aprendiendo de todas las cosas (Barcelona: Tusquets Editor, 1971).

Short Biographies

Robert Venturi

Robert Venturi was born in Philadelphia. He received the Bachelor of Arts and Master of Fine Arts degrees from Princeton University and, as the recipient of the Rome Prize in Architecture, was in residence at the American Academy in Rome from 1954 to 1956, returning there in 1966 as Architect-in-Residence. During his early career he worked for Louis Kahn and for Eero Saarinen, was a faculty member at the University of Pennsylvania and was named Charlotte Shepherd Davenport Professor of Architecture at Yale University. He has been a partner with John Rauch since 1964 and with Mr. Rauch and Denise Scott Brown since 1967. The firm Venturi, Rauch and Scott Brown, of which he is head and principal in charge of design, was awarded the American Institute of Architects' Firm of the Year Award in 1985. He has lectured and written widely, including three books: *Complexity and Contradiction in Architecture* (1966); *Learning from Las Vegas* (written with Denise Scott Brown and Steven Izenour, 1972); and *A View from the Campidoglio* (written with Denise Scott Brown, 1985).

John Rauch

John Rauch was born in Philadelphia. He received his Bachelor of Architecture degree from the University of Pennsylvania. From 1967 to 1969 he was a lecturer at the University of Pennsylvania and has served as chairman of several committees of the Philadelphia chapter of the American Institute of Architects, as President of the chapter, and on the AIA Documents Board. He has been a Trustee of the Foundation for Architecture. Since the firm's inception he has acted as principal in charge of management and construction; he is VRSB's chief policy strategist and a much-sought-after design critic.

Denise Scott Brown

Denise Scott Brown was born in Zambia. She received an Architectural Association (London) diploma and Master's degrees in City Planning and Architecture from the University of Pennsylvania. Ms. Scott Brown has taught at the University of Pennsylvania, the University of California at Berkeley, UCLA, and Yale. She has written and lectured extensively. She is the firm's principal in charge of urban planning and urban design, participates in the firm's architectural projects, and is a close collaborator with Robert Venturi in design, writing, and the development of architectural theory.

List of Works and Projects (1958-1985)

Venturi and Short

1958

James B. Duke House, New York University (Institute of Fine Arts), New York, N. Y.
Interior renovation

1959

H. Justice Williams, Twin houses, Philadelphia, Pennsylvania
Renovation

Gwynnedd Friends Meeting, Gwynnedd, Pennsylvania
Housing for the elderly, project

Altschul House, Religious Center, New York, N. Y.
Renovation

Language Laboratory, New York University, New York, N. Y.
Renovation project

Beach House
Project

1960

Mills House
Alteration and extension project

F.D.R. Memorial Park, Washington, D. C.
Competition project

1961

Dudley Miller House, Easthampton, N. Y.
Project

Dunn House, Jarrettown, Pennsylvania
Renovation

Friends Neighborhood Guild (Guild House), Philadelphia, Pennsylvania
Housing for the elderly

North Penn Visiting Nurses' Association Headquarters, Ambler, Pennsylvania
Visiting nurses' headquarters and clinic

Grand's Restaurant, Philadelphia, Pennsylvania
Conversion and renovation (demolished)

Vanna Venturi House, Chestnut Hill, Pennsylvania

1962

Zinser House, Woodbury, Connecticut (John Rauch: designer)

Millard Meiss House, Princeton, New Jersey
Project

Language Laboratory, New York University, New York, N. Y.
Second renovation project

Hester Apartment, New York, N. Y
Penthouse alteration and extension, project

Hun School Dormitory, Princeton, New Jersey
Student housing

Hun School Gymnasium, Princeton, New Jersey
Project

1963

City Hall, Philadelphia. Fire Control Center
Interior renovation project

Haas House, Ambler, Pennsylvania
Alteration and garage

1964

T. T. Flemings House, Rydal, Pennsylvania
Alteration, project

Venturi and Rauch

Poplar St. Park, Wilmington, Delaware (George Patton, landscape architect)
Park building project

Fairmount Park Fountain Competition, Philadelphia, Pennsylvania
Competition project

Berkeley Museum and Art Gallery Competition, Berkeley, California
Competition project

1965

"The Footlighters" Playhouse, Chester County, Pennsylvania
Project

Haas Greenhouse, Ambler, Pennsylvania
Second project

North Canton Town Center, Ohio
Planning study

1966

Copley Square Competition, Boston, Massachusetts
Competition project

Varga-Brigio Medical Office Building, Bridgeton, New Jersey
Medical Office Building

Mills House, Princeton, New Jersey
Extension. Pool house project

Princeton Memorial Park, Princeton, New Jersey
Park buildings. Project

YMCA and Library Building, North Canton, Ohio
Project

Fire Station 4, Columbus, Indiana

County Federal Savings and Loan Association, Fairfield, Connecticut
Renovation project

Frug House, Princeton, New Jersey
Garden Pavilion projects A and B

329

1967

National Football Hall of Fame Competition, Rutgers University, New Brunswick, New Jersey
Competition project

Lieb House, Loveladies, New Jersey
Vacation house

Dixwell Fire Station, New Haven, Connecticut

Transportation Square Office Building, Washington, D. C.
Competition project

Kron Residence, Philadelphia, Pennsylvania
Renovation project

"Work of Venturi and Rauch," Art Alliance, Philadelphia, Pennsylvania
Exhibition design

Brighton Beach Housing Competition, N. Y.
Competition project

1968

G. L. Hersey House, Hyannisport, Massachusetts
Project

Humanities Building, State University of New York, Purchase, N. Y.

D'Agostino House, Clinton, N. Y.
Project

The Philadelphia Crosstown Community, South Street, Philadelphia, Pennsylvania
Planning study

St. Francis de Sales Church, Philadelphia, Pennsylvania
Church renovation

Wike House, Devon, Pennsylvania
Project A and B

1969

Washington Square West, Philadelphia, Pennsylvania
Housing project

Yale Mathematics Building Competition, New Haven, Connecticut
Competition project

Thousand Oaks Civic Center, Thousand Oaks, California
Competition project

1970

Times Square, New York, N. Y
Development project

Southeastern Pennsylvania Transportation Authority (SEPTA) – Development Scope of Services, Philadelphia, Pennsylvania
Project

Urban Design Study (UDS) for New Rochelle, N. Y.
Urban design study

California City Planning, California
Study and urban design project

Social Sciences Building, State University of New York, Purchase, N.Y.

Carol W. Newman Library (Virginia Polytechnic Institute), Blacksburg, Virginia
Extension
(Execution: Vosbeck, Kendrick, and Redinger)

"Venturi and Rauch," Whitney Museum of Art, New York, N. Y.
Exhibition design

Trubek and Wislocki Houses, Nantucket, Massachusetts
Summer residences

House in Greenwich, Connecticut

1971

Hartford Stage Company, Hartford, Connecticut
Theater building

1972

Philadelphia Housing Development Corporation (PHDC), Philadelphia, Pennsylvania
Housing project

Bicentennial Exhibition for 1976, Philadelphia, Pennsylvania
Master Plan I and II for proposed international exhibition

Wissahickon Avenue Houses, Philadelphia, Pennsylvania
Project

Franklin Court, Philadelphia, Pennsylvania

Cusack House, Sea Isle City, New Jersey
Renovation and extension project

Bushnell Memorial Hall, Hartford, Connecticut
Renovation

Fairmount Manor, Philadelphia, Pennsylvania
Project

Lieb House, Philadelphia, Pennsylvania
Extension and renovation project

National Heritage Visitors' Center, Thunder Bay, Ontario, Canada

1973

Saga Bay Development Corporation, Dade County, Florida
Sign project

Allen Memorial Art Museum, Oberlin College, Oberlin, Ohio
Extension and renovation

East River Park, New York, N. Y.
Urban design project

University of Pennsylvania Signage
Competition entry

Haas Carriage Shed, Ambler, Pennsylvania

1974

Penn State Faculty Club, University Park, Pennsylvania

NAVFAC Community Center, Philadelphia, Pennsylvania

House in Westchester County, N. Y.

Lieb Pool House, Penn Valley, Pennsylvania
Project, scheme A and B

Morris Arboretum, Education Center, Philadelphia, Pennsylvania
Project

Galveston Development Project, Galveston, Texas
Planning study

1975

City Edges Planning Study, Philadelphia, Pennsylvania
Planning and urban design study

House in Vail, Colorado

House in Tuckers Town, Bermuda

Wolf Residence, Philadelphia, Pennsylvania
Restoration and addition

"Three Centuries of American Art," Philadelphia Museum of Art, Philadelphia, Pennsylvania
Exhibition design

1976

"Signs of Life: Symbols in the American City," Smithsonian Institution, Washington, D. C.
Exhibition design

"Two Hundred Years of American Sculpture," Whitney Museum of American Art, New York, N. Y.
Exhibition design

House in Greenwich, Connecticut
Extension project, scheme A

Biennale, Venice, Italy
Exhibition of the firm's work

Scranton Murals, Scranton, Pennsylvania
Project for murals

INA Capital Management, Philadelphia, Pennsylvania
Interior design

Salem Signs, Salem, Massachusetts
Project for signage

BASCO Store, Concord, Delaware.

"Arisbe," Milford, Pennsylvania
Project for historic house museum exhibit

1977

Haas House, Ambler, Pennsylvania
Interior renovation

Marlborough-Blenheim Hotel and Casino, Atlantic City, New Jersey
Renovation and addition, project A and B

Palley's Jewellers, Atlantic City, New Jersey
Shop renovation

Old City, Philadelphia, Pennsylvania
Planning study

County Federal Savings and Loan Association, Westport, Connecticut
Renovation project

St. Christopher's Hospital, Philadelphia, Pennsylvania
Planning study

Western Plaza, Washington, D. C.
Urban design

Pennsylvania Avenue Development Corporation, Washington, D. C.
Project for urban design

BEST Products Catalog Showroom, Oxford Valley, Pennsylvania

Jim Thorpe Opera House, Jim Thorpe, Pennsylvania

Mauch Chunk Historic District Study, Jim Thorpe, Pennsylvania
Historic revitalization study of a small mining town

Science Museum, Charlotte, North Carolina
Preliminary design

Goldstein House, Long Island, N. Y.
Project

Eclectic Houses
Facade studies

1978

Nichol's Alley Jazz Club, Houston, Texas
Project

Institute for Scientific Information Office (ISI) Corporation Headquarters, Philadelphia, Pennsylvania

St. Christopher's Hospital, Philadelphia, Pennsylvania
Planning study, phase II

Westway Urban Design Project, New York, N. Y.
Planning and urban design study

House in Northern Delaware

Settlement Music School, Philadelphia, Pennsylvania
Renovation and extension

Washington Avenue Revitalization Plan, Miami Beach, Florida
Planning study

Hartwell Lake Regional Visitors' Center, Hartwell Lake, Georgia
Competition project

Moore School Computer Museum, Philadelphia, Pennsylvania
Preliminary design

House in Greenwich, Connecticut
Second extension project

Princeton Urban Design, Princeton, New Jersey
Planning study

Institute for Advanced Studies (IAS), Land Development Project, Princeton, New Jersey
Development project

1979

Jenkintown, Pennsylvania
Urban design study

Energy expo '82, Knoxville, Tennessee
Competition project

House in Pittsburgh, Pennsylvania

BASCO Showroom, "Oxford Valley," Bristol Township, Philadelphia

Chinatown Housing, Philadelphia, Pennsylvania
Public housing

Canberra Parliament House Competition, Canberra, Australia
Competition project

Knoll Furniture
Furniture design

Coxe-Hayden Studio Houses, Block Island nr. Rhode Island

Museum of Arts and Crafts, Frankfurt am Main, Germany
Competition project

The Shore Mall, Atlantic City, New Jersey
Project for revitalization

Reading Art Center, Reading, Pennsylvania
Competition project

Venturi, Rauch and Scott Brown

1980

Philadelphia Museum of Art, Philadelphia, Pennsylvania
Interior restoration, master plan

Hennepin Avenue Redevelopment, Minneapolis, Minnesota

Prototypical Store for Dansk International
Competition project

Metropolitan Tower, Philadelphia, Pennsylvania
Interior transformation of former YMCA

Gordon Wu Hall, Princeton University, Princeton, New Jersey
Dining hall and social facilities, Butler College

George D. Widener Memorial Tree House for the Children's Zoo, Philadelphia, Pennsylvania

Penn's Light, Philadelphia, Pennsylvania
Urban design project

Social Ecology Building for University of California at Irvine, Irvine, California
Programming study and project

International Fair Hall, Frankfurt am Main, Germany
Competition project

Wheelabrator Frye Corporate Headquarters, Hampton, New Hampshire
Project for addition

Houston Hall, University of Pennsylvania, Philadelphia, Pennsylvania
Restoration and renovation

Park Regency Condominiums, Houston, Texas

1981

Knoll Showrom, New York, N. Y.
Showroom and office design

Blair Hall, Princeton University, Princeton, New Jersey
Interior alterations

House on Long Island

Western Plaza, Washington, D. C.
Additions to original design

"Contemporary American Realism since 1960," Pennsylvania Academy of Fine Arts, Philadelphia, Pennsylvania
Exhibition design

Shippensburg State College, Shippensburg, Pennsylvania
Project

Khulafa Street Residential and Commercial Building, Baghdad, Iraq

Hubbard House, Nantucket Island, Massachusetts

Preliminary design

1982

Welcome Park, Philadelphia, Pennsylvania

Primate Center, Philadelphia Zoo, Philadelphia, Pennsylvania

Philadelphia Museum of Art, West Foyer
Interior renovation study

Reading Civic Center, Reading, Pennsylvania
Preliminary design

Best Showroom
Signing study

State Mosque of Iraq Competition, Baghdad, Iraq
Competition project

Chinatown Housing, Philadelphia, Pennsylvania
Project for housing

1983

Lewis Thomas Laboratory for Molecular Biology, Princeton University, Princeton, New Jersey

Laguna Gloria Art Museum, Austin, Texas

Central Austin
Development study for the Watson-Casey Company

Graduate School of Management and Organized Research Building, University of California, Irvine, California
Project

Republic Square District Master Plan, Austin, Texas
Master plan

Malcom S. Forbes Junior College, Princeton University, Princeton, New Jersey
Interior transformation and renovation

Winterthur Housing, Winterthur, Delaware
Project for housing

Kalpakjian House, Glen Cove, N. Y.

1984

Swarthmore Student Center
Restoration of Commons building

ARC Goodman
Furniture design

Center City Development Plan, Memphis, Tennessee
Planning study

Rome, Italy
Project for outdoor exhibition

Alessi Biblioteca, Omegna, Italy
Project for corporate library

Alessi Tea Service

Princeton, New Jersey
Suburban park development

Institute for Advanced Studies Housing, Princeton University, Princeton, New Jersey
Preliminary design

Izenour House, Stony Creek, Connecticut

Times Square Plaza Design, New York, N. Y.
Urban design

Swid-Powell
Glassware design

"Italiah Village"
Porcelain service design

1985

"High Styles," Whitney Museum of American Art, New York, N. Y.
Exhibition design

Ponte dell' Accademia, Venice
Project

Westway, New York, N. Y., Ventilation Building
Project

Munari Jewelry
Jewelry design

Furness Library, University of Pennsylvania, Philadelphia, Pennsylvania

House in North Carolina
Project

Office Tower
Project

Sunshine Foundation, Orlando, Florida
Project for housing

The National Gallery, London, England
Competition project

Marconi Plaza Monument, Philadelphia, Pennsylvania
Project

"Greenlands" Mixed Use Development, Princeton, New Jersey
Project

Jacksonville Office Building Project, Jacksonville, Florida
Project

Index

Photo Credits

The author and publishers are grateful to all those who provided the material for the illustrations reproduced in this volume. Special thanks are due to the VRSB Office in Philadelphia for supplying most of the illustrations. The numbers refer to the pages; a. = above, b. = below, l. = left, r. = right, m. = middle.

Tom Bernard   140b., 184b.r., 185, 203, 205, 206a., 206b.l., 206b.r., 207, 230b., 231, 269 (4), 271, 275 (3), 293, 294, 316 (2); 188b., 228, 229b. (with S. Izenour)
Mark Cohn, Pennsauken, N. J.   106b., 107, 108, 109
Stephen Hill, Philadelphia   173a., 253 (4), 302b.
David Hirsch, Brooklyn, N. Y.   159 (4)
Leni Iselin   297 l.m., 297 r.b., 298 (3)
Rollin R. La France, Philadelphia   148a., 149a., 155a., 245a., 246a., 246b.l., 246b.r., 247a., 287a.
Norman McGrath, New York   153a.
Ellen Perry, Berkeley   25a., 285l.b., 285r.b.
George Pohl, Philadelphia   34r., 41a., 149b., 156a., 156m., 162a., 248, 285a.
Stan Ries, New York   165
Cervin Robinson, New York   50, 178a.l., 179, 261a., 263
Skomark Associates, Philadelphia   38r.b.
Paul Warchol, New York   295r.
Matt Wargo   2, 278, 315
William Watkins   286

The following illustrations were kindly supplied by:

Harry N. Abrams, Inc., New York   52b.
Alinari, Florence   244a.l.
Architectural Association, London   28r. (photo: F. R. Yerbury), 81, 280
Atlantis Verlag, Zurich   34l., 37l., 162b.r.
Bayerische Verwaltung der staatlichen Schlösser, Gärten und Seen, Munich   317r.
Country Life, London   39a.
George Cserna, New York   64b.
gta, Institut für Geschichte & Theorie der Architektur, ETH, Zurich   16l.
Micheline Hilber, Fribourg   322, 323
Historical Society of Pennsylvania, Philadelphia   29
G. Kleine-Tebbe, Bremen   32a.
Kunstgeschichtliches Seminar der Universität Zürich, Zurich   161a.
Kunsthaus, Zurich   51 (photo: Walter Dräyer)
Las Vegas News Bureau, Las Vegas   18

Dieter Leistner, Dortmund   69a.
Editions du Moniteur, Paris   61r.
S. von Moos, Zurich   54m., 164a.m., 164a.r., 247b.l.
Collection, The Museum of Modern Art, New York   106a.; 146 (photo: John Szarkowski)
National Collection of Fine Art, Washington, D.C.   306b., 307b. (photo: Margery Byers)
The National Gallery, London   19
Demetri Porphyrios, Athens   33l., 212a.
Christiane Riboulleau, Paris   40m.
Aldo Rossi, Milan   61l.
Edward Ruscha, Los Angeles   82–83
Ronald Sautebin, Fribourg   13, 30, 62b., 64a., 202a.l., 202a.r.
Whitney Museum of American Art, New York   47l., 308b. (photo: Geoffrey Clements)
Lawrence S. Williams, Upper Darby, PA   78, 300
Yale Art Library, New Haven, CT   28l., 240
Author's archives   45b., 180a.r., 256m.

The following illustrations were reproduced from writings by VRSB:

Complexity and Contradiction in Architecture, New York, 1966   13, 17, 54r., 244a.r.
Learning from Las Vegas, Cambridge, MA, 1972   18, 24a., 24b., 25b., 216
A View from the Campidoglio, New York, 1984   145

Additional material for illustrations was kindly provided by:

Archigram, London, 164   59r.
a+u, Tokyo, 1975   26
R. Banham, *New Brutalism in Architecture*, London, 1966   62a.
M. Girouard, *Robert Smythson and the Elizabethan Country House*, New Haven – London, 1983   202a.l., 202a.r.
Le Corbusier, *Œuvre complète*, Zurich, 1964 –   14r., 27r., 45a., 77
Pelican History of Art, Harmondsworth   45m., 158a.
A. Saint, *The Image of the Architect*, New Haven – London, 1983   58r.
P. Santostefano, *Le Mackley Houses di Kastner e Stonorov a Philadelphia*, Rome, 1982   279
V. Scully, *The Shingle Style and the Stick Style*, New Haven, 1955   256a.
R. Stern, *George Howe*, New Haven – London, 1975   268r.
Werk, Zurich, 1960   60

Setting: Typobauer Filmsatz GmbH, Ostfildern (Scharnhausen)
Photolithographs (color): Photolitho Bienna AG, Biel
Photolithographs (black and white): look graphic sa, Acacias-Geneva
Printing and binding: Dai Nippon Printing Co., Ltd., Tokyo
Editorial: Hubertus von Gemmingen
Layout: Stanislaus von Moos

Printed and bound in Japan

35⁰⁰ AI

#122939-ARCH